ATHEISM IS FALSE

Richard Dawkins
and
The *Improbability of God* Delusion

David Reuben Stone

www.atheismisfalse.com

Published July, 2007 by David Reuben Stone.

ISBN: 978-1-4303-1230-7

To those who seek truth.

CONTENTS

PREFACE

Atheism Is False is a journey…a quest for truth regarding the existence of God. This journey could not have been accomplished without faithful support and encouragement from my family and friends. I wish to thank them for their patience and understanding. In writing the book, I have benefited from the published works of many others, both theists and atheists. I am indebted to them for their efforts to understand and explain their views. Finally, I apologize for any errors in this book, and I hope that your feedback will help ensure that future editions will contain the modifications needed to correct them. For author contact details, please visit www.atheismisfalse.com.

David Reuben Stone
July 2007, 1st Edition

INTRODUCTION

The existence of God is an issue of fundamental significance. If it is reasonable to not believe that God exists, then shall we live our lives however we prefer? If there is a God, then are we accountable to God for our actions? The importance of determining whether God exists can not be underestimated. This subject clearly has practical implications for the manner in which we live our daily lives.

The purpose of this study is to participate in the project of answering these critical questions by presenting new arguments for the existence of God, and by refuting contemporary arguments for atheism. Chapter 1 is a presentation of the Argument From The Laws Of Physics (AFTLOP). This argument is originally developed by the author, David Reuben Stone, and is first published here. Chapter 2 is a presentation of my Fine-Tuning Argument for the existence of God, and is also first published here. In chapter 3 through chapter 6, the book "The Improbability of God" edited by Michael Martin and Ricki Monnier[1] is critically examined. Chapter 7 contains a critical response to the atheistic argument found in the book "The God Delusion" by Richard Dawkins.[2] Please be sure to obtain a copy of both books so that my critical analysis will be understood in light of the original context of the referenced texts. The atheistic arguments in these two books are refuted in detail, and theism is shown to be strongly confirmed by my theistic arguments.

The AFTLOP hinges on the claim that most (if not all) physical events are caused by a person, and since humans are not the cause of most physical events, it follows that God must exist, where God is defined as the personal cause of most physical events. This idea (and its defense) is my own, although I have discovered that it is not an entirely original concept. Claude Beaufort Moss has written: "Everything that happens is caused by the will of some person: either by man, or by some other created being (as an angel, or a devil), or by God. There is no such thing as an impersonal cause. When we say that one thing causes another, we mean, or we ought to mean, that we have observed that the latter always follows the former, and that we believe that God has made them in such a way that it always will follow it."[3] Although the AFTLOP does not precisely follow the reasoning quoted here, Moss keenly observed that all causation is personal, and this aspect of the nature of causation plays a key role in the AFTLOP.

The AFTLOP helps to provide an answer to the following fundamental questions: "From where do physical things come? Why doesn't the physical world just cease to exist?" The answer, somewhat oversimplified, is that physical things are caused by God to continue to exist in accordance with the laws of physics. The precise structure of the AFTLOP is more detailed and subtle, and many anticipated objections are addressed throughout its presentation.

It is worth considering, briefly, the implications of the AFTLOP. A common erroneous assumption is that since physical events explained by the laws of physics are in need of no further explanation in terms of divine activity, modern progress in science continues to close the gaps where theists thought "God of the gaps" explanations were still needed. To the contrary, the AFTLOP shows that continuing scientific discovery increasingly reveals the existence of the *very* powerful and knowledgeable God who is the sustaining cause of the continuing existence of physical entities which change in accordance with the laws of physics. The knowledge gaps closed by scientific progress do not eliminate the need for theistic explanations, but rather strengthen the case for God's existence and action. Since physical laws are evidence of God's regular causal activity in the world, theists need not be concerned by possible future discoveries of new physical laws that might close gaps that were allegedly evidence of miraculous divine action by virtue of being a gap. Rather, physical events described by laws of physics are God's regular pattern of causal activity, and physical events explained neither in terms of known physical laws nor in terms of human action may be understood as being probably God-caused events which are to be explained either in terms of presently unknown physical laws or as an exception to the regular physical event patterns physical laws can describe. The theistic inference, therefore, need not be grounded in the "knowledge gap" theology which Richard Dawkins so strongly opposes.[4]

Appeal by theists to divine action in the physical world does not frustrate the scientific enterprise by squelching motivation for further research. Regarding physical events not presently explained by any known law of physics, theists need not say, "God did it, so stop looking for a law of physics to describe it!" Instead, theists may say, "God did it, so let's seek a law of physics that describes it!" If a known law of physics describes a physical event, then that law provides an insight into the nature of God's creative intelligent power that caused the event. If no known law of physics describes a physical event, then we may search for a new law so that we might enjoy discovering more of God's creative nature expressed in the new law. Theists may encourage and contribute to ongoing scientific progress, therefore, knowing that such progress continues to confirm theism by revealing God's creative intelligence and power.

Atheists, however, must modify their worldview so as to account for the AFTLOP. It is difficult to imagine how this modification can reasonably proceed without the atheistic worldview evolving into a substantially altered worldview no longer properly identified as atheistic.

Chapter 2 contains a new defense of the theistic implications of anthropic coincidences widely popularized by proponents of fine-tuning teleological arguments. In writing this book, I did not even intend to develop this chapter, but my fine-tuning arguments here emerged from my contemplation of probabilistic considerations raised by critics of Hugh Ross. Specifically, I developed my fine-tuning arguments in response to the critical online article entitled "The Anthropic Principle Does Not Support Supernaturalism," by Michael Ikeda and Bill Jeffreys.[5] My fine-tuning arguments rush to the defense of the general line of argumentation presented by Ross,[6] and shore up that defense with a greater measure of philosophical rigor and technical precision.

Confirming the need for rejection of atheism is the failure of arguments for atheism, as detailed in chapter 3 through chapter 7. The response to atheistic arguments in these chapters is a very thorough, comprehensive, and devastating critique of many recent atheistic arguments presented by leading atheistic authors. The failure of atheistic philosophy, in conjunction with the strength of the AFTLOP and my fine-tuning arguments, shows that it is highly improbable that theism is highly improbable. Those who believe (perhaps even sincerely) that the existence of God is improbable, therefore, suffer from a delusion…the *improbability of God* delusion.

Authors (atheists *and* theists) often do not seek to publish in compliance with the high standard of providing comprehensive responses to objections raised by critics. Hopefully *Atheism Is False* will be found compliant with this standard, and hopefully future editions of atheism books will also be found compliant by virtue of responding, in detail, to the issues raised in *Atheism Is False*.

If ten well-informed theists, each representing distinct philosophical approaches and theological inclinations, addressed the arguments critiqued in *Atheism Is False*, then a diverse body of results would surely obtain. Readers should bear in mind, therefore, that the specific approach in this book depicts only one of a wide range of options available to the theist.

The following convention will be used to document quotes from other reference sources. References in the form (p. X) document page number X. A reference in the form (p. X-Y) documents pages X through Y. References in the form (p. X:Y) document the sentence appearing on line Y of page X. ("Line" refers to a horizontal line of text on a page, and does not refer to titles, subtitles, blank space, or text in headers/footers.) A reference in the form (p. X:Y-Z) documents the sentence(s) on page X that range from line Y to line Z. Finally, a reference in the form (p. W:X-Y:Z) documents the body of text that ranges from the sentence beginning on line X of page W to the sentence ending on line Z of page Y. This convention is adopted for the purpose of avoiding excessive direct quotations, and for the purpose of reducing the total length of *Atheism Is False*. Thus, identification of a specific quotation in *Atheism Is False* will generally require referencing a copy of the quoted source, unless the complete quote happens to be provided.

For the record, I am personally a conservative Evangelical Christian theist. However, theists of all stripes will likely find my natural theology compatible with (and supportive of) the components of their worldview which entail there exists a personal creator-sustainer-designer of the physical world.

This project would surely be benefited by including my responses to critical reviews. Future editions of this book will hopefully contain responses to any new objections critics may raise. All comments are welcome and strongly encouraged. Please visit www.atheismisfalse.com for author contact details.

Projects of such magnitude are challenging, time-consuming, and expensive! Any assistance readers might provide would be welcome and greatly appreciated. Again, for more information, please visit www.atheismisfalse.com.

NOTES

1. Martin, Michael and Monnier, Ricki, eds. (2006). *The Improbability of God.* Amherst, NY: Prometheus Books.

2. Dawkins, Richard (2006). *The God Delusion*. Boston: Houghton Mifflin Company.

3. Moss, Claude Beaufort (2005). *The Christian Faith: An Introduction to Dogmatic Theology*. Eugene, OR: Wipf & Stock Publishers, p. 6.

4. Dawkins (2006), pp. 125-134.

5. http://quasar.as.utexas.edu/anthropic.html. Reprinted in chapter 3 of part 2 of Martin, Michael and Monnier, Ricki, eds. (2006). *The Improbability of God*. Amherst, NY: Prometheus Books, pp. 150-166.

6. Ross, Hugh (2001). *The Creator and the Cosmos: How the Latest Scientific Discoveries of the Century Reveal God*. Colorado Springs, CO: Navpress, 3rd edition, pp. 175-199.

CHAPTER 1

The Argument From The Laws Of Physics

The Argument From The Laws Of Physics (AFTLOP) consists of an analysis of the nature of physical event causation. This analysis reveals that the laws of physics describe patterns of physical events caused by the free exercise of immense power by a person(s) with immense knowledge. The free exercise of power by a human person is insufficient as a cause of the physical event patterns described by the laws of physics. Therefore God exists, where God is defined as the person(s) whose free exercise of immense power with immense knowledge is the cause of the physical events described by the laws of physics. As the number of known laws of physics continues to rapidly increase with the progress made through scientific discovery, the evidence for the existence of God, consequently, continues to rapidly increase.

The AFTLOP begins with the following:

(1) The proposition "S is an event" is true, where S represents a statement of fact concerning all the features and processes associated with the Crab Nebula supernova first seen on Earth in the year 1054.

Concerning the term "event", let X be an event if and only if X is the meaning of a true proposition. A proposition is an element of meaning that can be expressed in the form of a sentence in a language. A proposition is true if and only if the meaning of the proposition describes the nature of reality (i.e., describes the way things are). For evidence of the Crab Nebula, see "The Crab Nebula and Related Supernova Remnants" edited by Minas C. Kafatos and Richard B. C. Henry.[1] So, (1) is simply the assertion that the Crab Nebula is an event. Technically speaking, it is a composite event which consists of a large number of features and processes. Nevertheless, the term "event" will suffice, as S may be construed as a single statement which comprises the conjunction of all propositions which describe the features and processes associated with the Crab Nebula. Thus, (1) is clearly true.

(2) S is a physical event.

Proposition (2) is the claim that the Crab Nebula is a physical event. X is a physical event if and only if X is an entity (or entities) consisting wholly of either a region (with nonzero volume) of space-time (i.e., a region of the three spatial dimensions and one temporal dimension with which humans are so familiar) or consisting wholly of matter/energy occupying a nonzero volume of that space-time. X is a nonphysical event if and only if X is not a physical event. Also, X is a nonphysical event if and only if X is an abstract entity. Thus, the terms "nonphysical events" and "abstract entities" are taken to be synonymous. Abstract entities are things that are not physical, such as numbers, properties, relations, procedures, mathematical/logical truths, ideas, etc. Given these definitions, S is a physical event and (2) is true.

(3) S is either a caused physical event or an uncaused physical event.

There are many ways to define the term "cause". Here, I define "cause" such that event A is the cause of event B if and only if A brings about or produces B. Thus, a cause is an event that brings about an effect. When A causes B, event A makes event B happen. Also, event A is uncaused if and only if there is no cause of event A. Other definitions of "cause" may be useful in other contexts, but are not relevant to the present discussion. So, (3) is clearly true.

(4) Uncaused physical events probably do not exist.

We may begin to establish (4) by examining the evidence that all physical events are probably caused. (It should first be noted that "the laws of physics" or "natural laws" are terms that refer to the description of regular patterns of physical events. These descriptions can often be expressed mathematically.) Now, since uncaused physical event sequences would probably be random and form no actual pattern (i.e., no natural law, no law of physics), physical events described by the laws of physics are probably caused events. The set of physical events known to be described by the laws of physics contains a very large number N of members. The value of N continues to rapidly increase as our scientific knowledge grows, while the set of physical events known to be uncaused is an empty set. These observations suggest that most physical events will eventually be explained in terms of the laws of physics. Given these considerations, most physical events are probably caused.

The line of reasoning above is grounded in the assumption that uncaused physical event sequences would probably be random and form no actual pattern. This assumption appears consistent with the nature of a universe U in which all physical events are causeless, random and purposeless. Note that U is not the universe in which we exist, since U consists only of random physical events, whereas the universe in which we exist consists of a multitude of nonrandom physical events described by physical laws. (A physical event E that occurs at time T is random for person J if and only if: (1) J knows E occurs at T, and (2) J does not know whether a law of physics determines E at T from a physical state that exists at a time prior to T). Since a universe devoid of physical causes is presumably more likely to be random than nonrandom, the nonrandom nature of physical events in our universe (evidenced by physical laws describing a vast range of physical phenomena) more strongly confirms the hypothesis that our universe is not devoid of physical causes.

Furthermore, to the extent that one grants the existence of purpose (intelligent design) within our universe, the hypothesis that our universe is devoid of physical causes is thus disconfirmed, since purpose (intelligent design) in the physical world implies the existence of a personal cause of the purposed physical events. Since a universe devoid of purpose is presumably more likely to be random than nonrandom, the nonrandom nature of physical events in our universe (evidenced by physical laws describing a vast range of physical phenomena) more strongly confirms the hypothesis that our universe is not devoid of physical causes. My fine-tuning arguments (see chapter 2) provide compelling evidence of divine design and, consequently, provide an additional means by which the hypothesis is disconfirmed that our universe is devoid of physical causes.

It is conceivable that hypothesis H1 is true, where H1 is the hypothesis that some categories of physical events in our universe are caused and other categories are uncaused. H1 is more complex than the hypothesis H2 that all physical events in our universe are uncaused. Also, H1 is more complex than the hypothesis H3 that all physical events in our universe are caused. So, absent a good reason to favor H1, it follows that H2 or H3 is preferable to H1. However, evidence E for the existence of caused physical events in our universe tips the balance in favor of H3. Arguments in favor of H1 or H2 are considered and refuted below. Since we have no good reason to override E and favor H1 or H2, it follows that H3 is to be favored.

All instances in which it is not unknown whether a physical event is caused or uncaused are instances in which the physical event is known to be caused. In other words, we have many examples of physical events known to be caused, and we have no evidence of uncaused physical events. This fact disconfirms H1 and is consistent with both H2 and H3.

However, H3 is simpler than H2, and H3 is to be preferred over H2, given considerations examined here.

A common belief in modern science is that physical events with no presently known physical cause probably have a physical cause that is presently unknown. This belief is grounded in the assumption that most (if not all) physical events are probably caused. Thus, (4) is a common assumption in modern science.

Additional evidence in support of (4) is expressed in the principle P, which states: from nothing nothing comes. In other words, P implies that (4) is true, since uncaused physical events come from nothing, and since P entails that physical events can not come from nothing. Indeed, in the absence of anything whatsoever, it may be difficult to imagine that it is reasonable to suppose that an uncaused physical event could spontaneously occur. Even given the existence of our universe, it may be difficult to imagine uncaused physical events coming from nothing. So, to the extent that one finds P plausible, this provides additional evidence in support of (4). (Arguments in favor of the existence of uncaused physical events are examined, and discarded, below).

Granted, it is conceivable that uncaused physical events could actually exist and form a pattern which could be described by a law of physics. If this were the case, then it would be wrong to infer that physical events described by laws of physics may be properly identified as being probably caused events by virtue of being described by laws of physics. In this case, the laws of physics could be descriptions of uncaused physical event patterns. However, we have no evidence that uncaused physical events probably form patterns described by any laws of physics. In fact, we have no evidence that uncaused physical events probably exist, period. I now continue to establish proposition (4) by exposing the absence of evidence that uncaused physical events probably exist.

The objection might be raised that one could argue for the existence of uncaused physical events as follows:

(i)   If multiple physical event patterns exist which are similar in some physical respect, then it is necessarily the case that laws L of physics are identifiable which describe the nature of those physical event patterns.

(ii) Multiple similar physical event patterns exist.

(iii) It is necessarily the case that L is identifiable.

(iv) All actually identified physical laws are members of L.

(v)   It is necessarily the case that all actually identified physical laws are identifiable.

(vi) If it is necessarily the case that X, then X is uncaused.

(vii) X is uncaused, where X represents "all actually identified physical laws are identifiable".

In response to this objection, observe that although an identifiable law of physics necessarily results from the existence of similar physical event patterns, the existence of such patterns is not also consequently necessary. Also, similar physical event patterns necessarily enable the formulation and identification of physical laws that describe those patterns, but there is no good reason to consequently suppose that those laws cause the described physical events. Therefore, physical laws are not fully explained by simply noting that it is logically necessary (and uncaused) that the existence of multiple physical event patterns entails the existence of identifiable physical laws. Rather, physical laws are fully explained when the cause of the law-described physical events is identified. Even if, at this stage in the argument, we are not yet sure whether law-described physical events are probably caused, it is, nevertheless, the case that (vii) does not even establish that uncaused physical events exist, since (vii) simply expresses a logically necessary truth that is consistent with (4). That is, identified physical laws are necessarily identifiable, and although this truth is uncaused, it is also consistent with all physical events being both described by physical laws and caused by an entity, where that entity is not the physical laws themselves.

The objection could be raised that it is possible that our known physical universe is only a small part of a vastly larger universe or multiverse (or meta-universe, super universe, megaverse, or universe of physical universes). It is also possible that the vast majority of physical events in our universe (or in any other physical universes which may exist) comprise sequences of random physical events which form no pattern, while we happen to find ourselves in a "rare" universe (or in a "rare" region of the universe) which consists of regular patterns of physical events that we may describe as "the laws of physics". We do not have evidence, however, that the laws of physics do not generally apply throughout the history of the entire universe. Also, we have no evidence of the existence of any physical universe other than the one in which we exist. Furthermore, the existence of a single universe in which the laws of physics describe patterns in sequences of caused physical events is a simpler (and, thus, preferable) explanation which is favored over the more excessively complex explanation that the laws of physics describe patterns in sequences of caused physical events in our relatively small region of a vastly larger, unknown, undetectable universe (or multiverse which consists of many universes) throughout which predominantly pattern-less sequences of physical events occur. Thus, we have no evidence that our universe (or our region of the universe) is an island of order and regularity within a vastly greater universe (or multiverse) predominantly characterized by pattern-less randomness and disorder.

It has been objected that the multiverse hypothesis is actually simpler than the hypothesis that only our universe exists.[2] One could conceivably construct a Theory of Everything that identifies the fundamental laws of physics according to which every universe that exists in a hypothesized multiverse evolves, where the statement of the Theory of Everything has less algorithmic complexity than that of the conjunction of that statement and the specific conditions that determine the particular universe we inhabit. (The term "algorithmic complexity" simply denotes a particular formal way of precisely representing the information content of a statement or hypothesis.) However, it is a faulty comparison which grounds the assumption that a hypothesized multiverse that evolves in accordance with such a Theory of Everything is simpler and ought to be favored over the anti-multiverse hypothesis that only our particular universe exists/evolves in accordance with that theory. Since a full explication of the anti-multiverse hypothesis has the algorithmic complexity needed to state the Theory of Everything and identify merely the conditions that determine our particular physical universe, whereas a full explication of the hypothesis that a multiverse actually exists has the algorithmic complexity needed to describe the Theory of Everything *and* identify all the conditions that determine the many allegedly existing actual physical universes, the anti-multiverse hypothesis is, thus, shown to be *much* simpler. Even if the multiverse hypothesis were somehow shown to be a better explanation than the anti-multiverse hypothesis, then this would establish that the multiverse evolves in accordance with the laws described by the Theory of Everything. We would still have no evidence that our universe is an island of order and regularity within a vastly greater multiverse predominantly characterized by pattern-less randomness and disorder. In fact, a basic assumption in science is that the laws of physics generally (if not always) apply throughout our universe, and the laws describing the evolution of universes by natural selection in the multiverse (assuming such a multiverse even exists) generally (if not always) apply throughout the multiverse. So, even if a multiverse exists, both the physical events in each universe of the multiverse, as well as the physical events described by the hypothesized evolution of universes, are described by physical laws and are, thus, probably caused events, since uncaused physical event sequences would probably be random and form no actual pattern. Even if the laws of physics were different in each universe of the multiverse, the physical events in each universe would be described by the physical laws of that particular universe and, thus, those physical events would probably be caused. These considerations provide further evidence that all physical events are probably caused.

Some quantum events apparently spontaneously occur in ways not presently known to be deterministically predictable. Consider, for example, the (often alleged to be uncaused) random physical event of the coming into (or going out of) existence of an electron. It should be noted that this event is not purely random (it occurs in accordance with the Heisenberg uncertainty principle) and, since uncaused physical event sequences would probably be random and form no actual pattern (i.e., no natural law, no law of physics), this physical event, being described by a law of physics, is, thus, probably a caused event. The objection may be raised that this event is not fully described by a known law of physics, but is simply constrained by the Heisenberg uncertainty principle, and, as such, is not known to be probably caused by virtue of being known to be fully described by a law of physics. Likewise, it may be objected that the probabilistic form of some laws of physics, such as those describing the decay of radioactive nuclei, does not fully describe the physical event patterns, but only describes a constraint on the physical event patterns and, thus, physical events described by probabilistic laws of physics are not known to be probably caused by virtue of being known to be fully described by a law of physics.

In response to these objections it should be noted that such allegedly random uncaused physical events are not evidence that uncaused physical events probably exist, but are evidence that we presently know no deterministic law of physics that describes such physical events. Present lack of knowledge of deterministic physical laws describing certain physical events does not entail those events are probably uncaused. For example, lack of knowledge of deterministic physical laws describing how life originated on Earth would not entail the nonexistence of any deterministic physical laws that could possibly describe the origin of life on Earth.[3] Indeed, the nonexistence of a deterministic physical law describing certain physical events would not entail those events are probably uncaused, regardless of whether the physical events are in the realm of quantum mechanics or classical mechanics. The claim "The nonexistence of a deterministic physical law describing physical event E entails E is uncaused" requires the unwarranted assumption that it is impossible for a person to cause physical events which do not form a pattern in which subsequent events in the pattern can be determined from prior events in the pattern. (An entity is a person if and only if the entity has beliefs, desires, and freely performs actions.) It is surely possible for a person to cause physical events which form no deterministic pattern, and, therefore, it should not be assumed, without warrant, that a person is not the cause of physical events which form no deterministic pattern. Since physical events which form no deterministic pattern could be caused by a person, it follows that such physical events could be caused. Thus, physical events that apparently spontaneously occur in ways not known to be deterministically predictable are not evidence that uncaused physical events probably exist. Likewise, physical events described by probabilistic laws of physics are not evidence that uncaused physical events probably exist.

Therefore, physicists such as Taner Edis are begging the question in favor of the existence of uncaused quantum events, when assuming that such events are not caused by a person to form no apparent deterministic pattern. Regardless of whether a deterministic pattern to quantum events is ever discovered, such physicists are wrong to suppose that the randomness of quantum physical events is evidence that "quantum physics is all about uncaused events."[4] The "no physical law, no causation"[5] inference is unfounded, and the assumptions remain unjustified that "uncaused events are the rule in our universe,"[6] and that causation applies "only to a macroscopic world emerging from a random substrate, where events just happen."[7]

Some scientists and philosophers appear to support the position that the emissions from a singularity are an instance of uncaused physical events. Their reasoning might be structured as follows:

(viii) A physical law can describe only patterns of physical events which occur in a region of space-time.

(ix) A singularity is not a physical event in a region of space-time.

(x) A physical law can not describe a singularity.

(xi) The singularity is a lawless state.

(xii) If the evolution of a lawless state forms an uncaused event sequence, then that evolution is unpredictable and patternless.

(xiii) The evolution of a singularity forms an uncaused event sequence.

(xiv) Therefore, the evolution of a singularity is unpredictable and patternless.

Reasoning along these lines appears to be what Stephen Hawking, Paul Davies, and Quentin Smith have in mind when arguing for the patternless unpredictability of singularity emissions.[8] In response, observe that (xii) assumes uncaused event sequences are patternless. This assumption, in turn, entails that physical event sequences that form a pattern are caused. Since all physical event sequences that form patterns may be described by laws of physics, it follows that all physical event sequences described by laws of physics are caused. As mentioned earlier, the set of physical events known to be described by the laws of physics contains a very large number N of members. The value of N continues to rapidly increase as our scientific knowledge grows, while the set of physical events known to be uncaused is an empty set. These observations suggest that most physical events will eventually be explained in terms of the laws of physics. Given these considerations, most physical events are probably caused, confirming (4).

Thus, we have shown that a line of reasoning that some might use to support the claim that uncaused events (e.g., singularities or singularity emissions) exist actually rests on an assumption (xii) that may be used to confirm (4). Now that line of reasoning will be shown unsound. It is unsound not because (xii) is false, but for the following reasons. First, (xi) does not follow from (x), since it is possible that nonphysical laws could exist which describe singularities. If it is possible that a singularity (an allegedly nonphysical entity) can exist, then surely it is possible that nonphysical laws could exist that describe such nonphysical events. We need not arbitrarily assume that all laws (i.e., descriptions of regular event patterns) must be physical laws. Second, (xiii) remains unsupported. Even if the evolution of a singularity occurs lawlessly, it does not follow that the evolution of a singularity is uncaused. If an event E is unique in the sense that it does not form a pattern of events that can be described in more general terms, then no law exists which explains E. It does not follow, however, that E is uncaused, since it is possible that E is a unique caused event. So, (xiii) is seen to assume, without justification, the nonexistence of unique caused events. Therefore, (xiv) is not established, as it rests upon unjustified premises.

Uncaused nonphysical events exist. For example, the proposition "All trinomials are polynomials" is an uncaused nonphysical event. The concept expressed by "$i^2 = -1$, where $i = (-1)^{0.5}$" is also an example of an uncaused nonphysical event, i.e., an uncaused true proposition describing a nonphysical concept. (Recall that nonphysical concepts or ideas are examples of abstract entitites.) The existence of uncaused nonphysical events, however, is not evidence that uncaused physical events exist. Physical events and nonphysical events are two categories of events that are clearly distinguished in that abstract entities are evidently either not the kind of events a person can cause, or if particular abstract entities are caused, then those are caused by a person. Physical events clearly can be caused by a person, and there is no reason to suppose any physical event can not be caused by a person. This significant difference between physical and nonphysical events is such that the existence of properties of nonphysical events ought not be assumed to provide rational grounds for the belief that those properties also exist in the case of physical events. Specifically, the fact that uncaused nonphysical events exist ought not be viewed as rational grounds for the belief that uncaused physical events also exist. So, consideration of the nature of abstract entities does not provide a counterexample to proposition (4).

A physical event freely caused by the exercise of a person's power is probably not an example of an uncaused physical event. For when a person J freely causes a physical event E, J freely exercises J's power to cause E. Since J's action is free if and only if J's exercise of J's power to act is uncaused, the event "J freely exercises J's power to cause E" is uncaused. Event E, however, is not uncaused, as E is caused by J's free exercise of power. Also, since most physical events may eventually be explained in terms of deterministic laws of physics, and since it is self-evident that my free exercise of power is not determined by any law of physics, it follows that my free exercise of power is probably a nonphysical event. Since the experience of perceiving the self-evident nature of one's free exercise of power is probably a perception shared by persons in general, the event "J freely exercises J's power to cause E" is probably a nonphysical event in general. In fact, there is no evidence that a person's free exercise of power is a physical event, even though the exercise of that power may cause a physical event.

It may be objected, here, that when person J freely exercises J's power to cause physical event E, the occurrence of event E *is* J's free exercise of power, in which case a person's free exercise of power could *be* an uncaused physical event. However, this objection fails by entailing that when cause C causes effect E, C can be identical to E. There is no evidence that an effect can be its own cause.

The objection may also be raised that when person J freely exercises J's power to cause physical event E, *J's free exercise of power* is a wholly physical event that is distinct from E, and that causes E. However, this objection is not supported by evidence that each person's choices to freely exercise power to cause physical events are not merely correlated to, but are identical to, say, physical states of some kind in the brain. Even if such evidence will someday exist, this would establish that one's free exercise of power is probably an uncaused personal physical event. And if uncaused physical events could thus be known to exist in the form of an uncaused personal physical event that is the cause of other physical events, then the door could be opened to the possibility that event S (as defined earlier) is an uncaused personal physical event. However, this highly speculative possibility is a door through which no atheist would likely pass, given that if S is a person's free exercise of power, then the physical events of the universe, in general, could presumably also be the action of a super-powerful being.

The objection could be raised that an incompatibilist notion of freedom has been uncritically assumed, wherein person J freely causes event E if and only if the event "J causes E" is uncaused. An alternative compatibilist construal of freedom, it may be argued, should also be considered, wherein J freely causes E if and only if "J causes E" is a caused event. In response to this objection, note that it is the case that if free actions are caused, then free actions are not possibly an instance of an uncaused physical event. Given caused free action X, and given uncaused physical event Y, it necessarily follows that X is caused and Y is uncaused. Consequently, X can not be Y. A caused free action can not be an uncaused physical event. Compatibilism provides no counterexample to proposition (4).

Thus, probably, a physical event E freely caused by the exercise of a person's power is not an example of an uncaused physical event. Rather, it is a case in which an uncaused nonphysical event (i.e., the person's free exercise of power to cause E) causes E. Consideration of the nature of events caused by free agents, therefore, does not provide a counterexample to proposition (4).

It is conceivable that progress in physics may eventually lead to a super-deterministic Theory of Everything (TOE) that would subsume all known laws of physics (as well as *every* particular physical event) into a single fundamental physical law which would be the logically necessary consequence of, say, the geometrical nature of matter and energy in a region of space-time. This would entail that, given a physical universe with initial conditions, all subsequent physical events are necessary (and uncaused) physical events. It could be argued that such a TOE appears logically impossible, however, given Gödel's Incompleteness Theorems. However, even if such a TOE were somehow possible, we probably couldn't trust our beliefs (including our belief that the TOE is true), since our beliefs (which are probably correlated with certain physical brain processes) would not necessarily correspond to perception of truth, but could be occurring as the logically necessary determined consequence of the TOE regardless of whether the beliefs were true or false. And then, we couldn't trust our belief that we couldn't trust our beliefs, etc., leading to a vicious regress that would preclude knowledge. In particular, if we know the TOE is true, then we can not know the TOE is true. This self-refuting state of affairs implies that the TOE is not true. Since humans do possess knowledge, the TOE should be rejected. In addition, every person should not be trusted who physically claims to know the TOE is true, since, on the TOE, all physical claims (including mutually contradictory physical claims) are necessarily physically determined, and there is no reason to suppose any physical claim is more likely than its contradictory, since every such claim is simply a physically determined consequence of laws which do not guarantee that those making their claims have knowledge that their claims are true.

Also, on this TOE, any perception of being free to exercise power to cause physical events would be an illusion, contradicting our perception that it is self-evident that we have freedom to exercise power to cause physical events not determined by any law of physics. This contradiction disconfirms the TOE.

Additionally, on this TOE, human moral responsibility would be largely nonexistent, for no physical event would be caused by a human, but rather, all physical events would be logically necessary. Society's punishment of "bad" behavior is designed not merely to curb undesired effects of such behavior, but is also grounded in the conviction that the individual who performed the "bad" action could have (and should have) performed a "not bad" action instead. This contradiction of the general perception that humans are morally responsible for their physical behavior disconfirms the TOE.

Another objection to the claim that the TOE is evidence of uncaused physical events is the observation that physical changes in a universe that continues to exist in accordance with the TOE are a necessary feature of that continuously existing universe, yet the TOE does not entail that the continuing existence of the universe is, itself, necessary or uncaused. The assumption is unwarranted that, given a physical universe, it necessarily continues to exist. Also, the assumption is unwarranted that all logically possible universes described by the TOE continue to exist uncaused. It follows, then, that the TOE does not establish that the physical events described by the TOE are probably uncaused, since the TOE in no way rules out the possibility that the events it describes are the effects of a continuous sustaining cause of the existence of the universe (and multiverse, if it exists). Indeed, the TOE turns out not to be a theory of *everything*, after all, since it only explains how continuously existing physical entities physically necessarily change, yet it does not explain the continuous existence of those entities. The laws of physics describe changes in physical existents, but do not identify the cause of the existence of those existents. To simply assume that the TOE explains the cause of the existence of the changing physical entities it describes is to make an unwarranted assumption.

The objection may be raised that it is reasonable to believe that physical entities continue to exist uncaused and continue to change in accordance with the TOE so long as there is no reason to expect a change in the applicability of the TOE to continuously changing physical events. That is, if we have no reason to expect the laws of physics to change, then we should not be surprised that physical events continue to occur as they do, and the continuing existence of physical entities which change in accordance with the laws of physics may be considered uncaused and in need of no explanation.[9] This objection fails, however, for the fact that I do not expect the laws of physics to change neither renders the cause of the continuing existence of physical entities in need of no identification, nor identifies the cause. What calls for explanation is the cause of the continuing existence of physical entities which continue to change as described by the same unchanging laws of physics. The fact that the laws of physics are not expected to change does not eliminate the need to identify this sustaining cause as the explanation.

The objection may be raised that all possible physical universes described by the TOE necessarily continue to actually exist uncaused. Well, needless to say, this is merely a bald assertion. We have no reason to suppose this is true. Possible worlds are not necessarily actual worlds. It is possible that some mathematically possible physical universes are not actual. So, this objection is unfounded.

Thus, given the considerations above, the TOE seems likely nonexistent, and even if the TOE does exist, then it establishes not that the physical events it describes are probably uncaused, but only that if physical entities continuously exist, then it is necessary that those entities physically change as determined by the TOE. The TOE in no way rules out the possibility that the events it describes are the effects of a continuous sustaining cause of the existence of the universe (or multiverse, if it exists), since the assumption is unwarranted that all logically possible universes described by the TOE exist uncaused, and since the assumption is unwarranted that given a physical universe, there is no cause of the continuing existence of that universe. Therefore, the TOE is not a counterexample to proposition (4).

It is possible that progress in physics may eventually lead to a Theory of Everything #2 (TOE$_2$) that would simply subsume all known laws of physics into a single fundamental physical law which describes the regular patterns of physical events in the universe, where the TOE$_2$ would either not be a necessary law, or, if the TOE$_2$ were necessary, then it would apply only to a subset of all physical events such that human knowledge, freedom, and moral responsibility are real. It would, thus, not be necessary that every physical event be described by the TOE$_2$, since the TOE$_2$ would describe only regular patterns of physical events, whereas not all physical events occur in regular patterns. In particular, a physical event E caused by the free exercise of a person's power would not be determined by the TOE$_2$, and this is consistent with the perception that it is self-evident that we have freedom to exercise power to cause physical events not determined by any law of physics, and this is also consistent with the perception that humans are morally responsible for their physical behavior. In addition, cases in which human knowledge allegedly exists would not necessarily be physically necessary and determined, but could be genuine cases in which human knowledge actually exists.

The TOE$_2$ would not entail that uncaused physical events exist, since the TOE$_2$ would either not be a necessary physical law, or, if TOE$_2$ were somehow a necessary physical law, then, as mentioned in discussion of the TOE, it would not follow that uncaused physical events probably exist. For just as in the case of the TOE, if the TOE$_2$ were a necessary physical law, then physical changes described by the TOE$_2$ in a universe that continues to exist in accordance with the TOE$_2$ would be a necessary feature of that continuously existing universe, yet the TOE$_2$ would not entail that the continuing existence of the entities whose physical changes are described by the TOE_2 is, itself, necessary or uncaused. The assumption is unwarranted that, given the existence of physical entities whose changes are described by the TOE_2, the physical entities necessarily continue to exist uncaused. The assumption is also unwarranted that all logically possible universes described by the TOE_2 exist uncaused. It follows, then, that even if the TOE_2 is a necessary physical law, the TOE_2 does not establish that the physical events it describes are probably uncaused, since the TOE_2 in no way rules out the possibility that the events it describes are the effects of a continuous sustaining cause of the existence of the physical entities which comprise the physical events described by the TOE_2. The TOE_2 only explains how continuously existing physical entities described by the TOE_2 necessarily (or contingently) physically change, yet it does not identify the cause of the continuous existence of those entities. Therefore, the TOE_2, if it exists, does not provide evidence for the existence of uncaused physical events, and is not a counterexample to proposition (4).

It is conceivable that a law L of physics (perhaps some version of a Theory of Everything) may be discovered which establishes that it is necessary that some physical events occur randomly and, thus, occur uncaused. In response to this possibility, it will first be noted that random events are not necessarily uncaused. A physical event E that occurs at time T is random for person J if and only if: (1) J knows E occurs at T, and (2) J does not know whether a law of physics determines E at T from a physical state that exists at a time prior to T. From this definition it follows that laws of physics possibly describe all necessarily random physical events that may exist. It also follows that all necessarily random physical events are possibly caused. The existence of necessarily random physical event E for person J, therefore, would not be evidence that an uncaused physical event exists, but would simply be evidence that it is necessary that J does not know whether a law of physics determines E. Since J's lack of knowledge of a physical law that determines E does not entail that E is uncaused, law L should be rejected, since L is grounded in the erroneous assumption that random events are necessarily uncaused.

Another reason for rejecting L is that if random events are essentially unnecessary, then this law would appear to entail a contradiction by asserting that it is necessary that random (unnecessary) physical events exist. A physical event can not be both necessary and unnecessary.

An additional reason for rejecting L is that it is difficult to imagine how a physical event could plausibly (or even possibly) be necessary, unless a necessarily existing person(s) K necessarily causes a physical event. So, if K does not exist, then it is unlikely that necessary physical events exist, and if K exists, then any existing necessary physical events would likely be caused by K. In either case, necessary uncaused physical events are unlikely, rendering the existence of L unlikely.

Even if a necessarily unnecessary physical event is logically possible, it is difficult to imagine how a physical event could plausibly (or even possibly) be necessarily unnecessary, unless a necessarily existing person(s) K necessarily causes a physical event to be unnecessary. So, if K does not exist, then it is unlikely that necessarily unnecessary physical events exist, and if K exists, then any existing necessarily unnecessary physical event would likely be caused by K. In either case, necessarily unnecessary uncaused physical events are unlikely, rendering the existence of L unlikely.

Thus, if a necessarily random event R exists, then it is probably caused by K, and, therefore, L probably does not exist, since L entails R is uncaused. Most importantly, L probably does not exist because it is based on the erroneous assumption that necessarily random physical events must be uncaused. Consideration of L, therefore, provides no counterexample to proposition (4).

It is conceivable that a law M of physics (perhaps some version of a Theory of Everything) may be discovered which establishes that it is necessary that some uncaused physical events exist. Necessary physical events, if they exist, are probably more likely to occur in a regular pattern than not, and thus are probably more likely to be described by a law of physics than not, and, consequently, are probably more likely to be caused than uncaused. So, for this reason, M is unlikely to exist.

Similar to the case in our earlier consideration of physical law L, another reason for rejecting M is that if uncaused physical events are essentially unnecessary, then M would appear to entail a contradiction by asserting that it is necessary that uncaused (unnecessary) physical events exist. A physical event can not be both necessary and unnecessary.

An additional reason for rejecting M is that it is difficult to imagine how a physical event could plausibly (or even possibly) be necessary, unless a necessarily existing person(s) K necessarily causes a physical event. So, if K does not exist, then it is unlikely that necessary physical events exist, and if K exists, then any existing necessary physical events would likely be caused by K. In either case, necessary uncaused physical events are unlikely, rendering the existence of M unlikely.

Even if a necessarily unnecessary physical event is logically possible, it is difficult to imagine how a physical event could plausibly (or even possibly) be necessarily unnecessary, unless a necessarily existing person(s) K necessarily causes a physical event to be unnecessary. So, if K does not exist, then it is unlikely that necessarily unnecessary physical events exist, and if K exists, then any existing necessarily unnecessary physical event would likely be caused by K. In either case, necessarily unnecessary uncaused physical events are unlikely, rendering the existence of M unlikely.

It is possible (though unlikely) that since the free exercise of a person's power to cause a physical event could, itself, be an uncaused physical event, it is, thus, possible that event S is the free exercise of a person's power, where S is a necessary uncaused physical event as described by M. This possibility is a door through which no atheist would likely pass, however, given that if S is a person's free exercise of power, then the physical events of the universe, in general, could presumably also be the action of a super-powerful being. This possibility is also dubious, given that it entails that a person's free exercise of power is a necessary uncaused physical event, whereas the existence of necessary free actions is implausible. This possibility is also unlikely, given the absence of evidence that the free exercise of any person's power is a physical event.

Another important consideration is that if beliefs and knowledge are correlated with physical events in the brain, then when person J claims to believe or know M exists, J's claim could be unjustified, since it is unlikely that uncaused physical brain events would generally produce true beliefs. In fact, if uncaused physical brain events frequently influence human cognitive processes and human behavior, then human cognitive processes would generally be unreliable and humans would, in general, not be responsible for performing moral actions. However, it is evident that human cognitive processes are generally reliable and humans are generally responsible for performing moral actions. Therefore, uncaused physical brain events probably don't frequently occur, rendering the existence of M less likely.

Thus, consideration of M shows that it probably does not exist and, therefore, is not a plausible counterexample to proposition (4). Furthermore, even if M exists, it does not necessarily follow that event S is uncaused. It is possible that some uncaused physical events necessarily occur, yet S is a caused physical event.

Another conceivable argument for the existence of uncaused physical events could be structured as follows:

(xv)   If some physical events were uncaused, then those events would probably form no regular pattern and, thus, could be described by no law of physics.

(xvi)   Some physical events can be described by no law of physics.

(xvii) Therefore some physical events are probably uncaused.

The above argument is a clear case of the fallacious form called *affirming the consequent*. Even if it is true that some physical events can be described by no law of physics, it may still be the case that such events are caused.

Therefore, I have shown that all physical events are probably caused. Also, I have shown that we have no evidence that uncaused physical events probably exist. These considerations reasonably establish that proposition (4) is probably true.

(5) S is probably a caused physical event.

Proposition (5) follows from (3) and (4). Since (3) and (4) have already been established, (5) is now also established.

(6) S is probably caused by a physical event or a nonphysical event.

Given proposition (5), either a physical event or a nonphysical event is the cause of event S. Proposition (6) is, therefore, true.

(7) S is probably not caused by a physical event.

There are a number of considerations which help to establish (7). First, we simply have no evidence that any physical event is caused by a physical event.

Second, the existence of the laws of physics is not evidence that physical events cause physical events. Rather, the laws of physics are evidence that physical events occur in patterns which can be described in general terms. The laws of physics can often be expressed mathematically, and are, by definition, descriptive. We have no evidence that the laws of physics somehow cause the physical event patterns they describe,[10] as the popular atheist David Mills even clearly acknowledges.[11]

Also, there is no good reason to suppose "each state of the universe is sufficiently caused by an earlier state", as atheist Quentin Smith has recently assumed.[12] In this article, Smith repeatedly assumes, without justification, that a physical event can cause a physical event. See, for example, "…the existence of each state is caused by earlier states…"[13]

Also, the universe's "parts exist because each of them is caused to exist by an earlier part."[14] And again, "Each state of the universe is caused by earlier parts and causes later parts."[15] Also, when explaining the origin of the basic laws of nature L, Smith assumes "Since each state's exemplification of L is caused by an earlier state, the obtaining of L is explained…..God cannot cause the laws to be instantiated by the states, since the earlier states have already performed this task, so to speak."[16] Smith is thus seen to have asserted that a physical event can cause a physical event, but he has offered no evidence in support of this contention.

Daniel Dennett also offers mere proof by assertion, assuming, without justification, that natural laws are "mindless, mechanistic processes" which can cause physical events.[17] And again, Dennett assumes, without proof, that a physical event can be caused "by something dogged and mindless."[18]

Niall Shanks blunders just the same, presuming that identification of physical laws describing physical phenomena justifies the inference to "the misleading appearance of intelligent design can be generated by the combined effects of chance and dumb mechanisms operating in accord with the dumb laws of nature."[19] Shanks is, in effect, claiming that "physical law L describes physical event pattern P" entails "P is the natural effect of an impersonal cause". This inference is especially in need of support, given that descriptions do not necessarily cause what is described, and given the contrary position favored by consideration of evidence adduced here in the AFTLOP. Sadly, Shanks provides no support.

Outspoken atheist Richard Dawkins likewise embraces this fundamental naturalistic fallacy by assuming, without justification, that his natural selection explanations are causal in the sense that they describe how a thing can *make* a thing, as his Daniel Dennett quotation[20] illustrates that he takes natural selection to be a counterexample to the claim that it must be the case that to *make* a lesser thing, a big fancy smart thing must do the *making*. Also, Dawkins claims that natural selection is causal in the sense that the effects of natural selection are "brought about"[21] through natural selection. In addition, Dawkins claims that natural selection is causal in the sense that it is "capable of *generating* complexity out of simplicity."[22] In response, unless Dawkins, Dennett, or someone else provides a reason for supposing that natural selection explanations are themselves causal (rather than merely descriptive), these claims may be properly viewed as merely begging the question. Dawkins would do well to accept the position advocated by atheist David Mills, which is that it is "absurd" to suppose that physical laws "cause the outcome of the observed phenomena."[23] Strangely, Dawkins has written that the work of David Mills is "admirable",[24] yet Dawkins does not even show understanding of this fundamental fact that physical laws are, by definition, descriptive (not causal).

Douglas J. Futuyma likewise shows acceptance of the naturalistic fallacy by assuming physical events (e.g., mutations) can cause physical events, or by assuming a physical law (e.g., natural selection) is causal. For example, Futuyma speaks of mutation and natural selection as if it can "*create* great changes in species over vast periods of time."[25] Also, he writes of the "changes that mutation and natural selection can *bring about* in any one species."[26] In addition, he says "mutations…merely *cause* slight changes in a characteristic."[27] Likewise, "beneficial mutations *alter* species in every imaginable way."[28] In addition, he speaks hypothetically of a "mutation that *caused* the nucleotide sequence UUU."[29] Also, he writes of the "historical *products* of evolution."[30] Futuyma has not provided justification for the claim that entities such as mutation and natural selection possess the causal powers he attributes to them. For him, it is apparently sufficient to reason "a physical law describes it, therefore it is causally explained." Clearly, this reasoning is unsound, even if the law is taken to be true. There is no good reason to suppose descriptive physical laws cause the described events.

Even if some version of a Darwinian natural selection law does correctly describe physical event patterns studied in biology (as recently argued by Michael Ruse), this would entail neither that the law causes the described events, nor that any physical event causes any physical event.[31] Indeed, such a law would in no way be inconsistent with the theistic view that a (very powerful and knowledgeable) person is the cause of such physical event patterns, as even the religiously agnostic Ruse acknowledges.[32]

The point, here, is that the creation/evolution debate is based on a false dichotomy, as both positions are consistent with divine causation of physical events in the world. So, even though I am not personally persuaded that the whole of biological life on Earth has arisen through processes described in terms of Darwinian evolution and natural selection, this is very much beside the major point that even if Darwinian explanations do accurately identify physical laws that describe biological event patterns, the door remains open wide to divine causation of the obtaining of those laws.

Thus, mere proofs by assertion offered by Smith, Dennett, Shanks, Dawkins, Futuyma, Ruse, or, for that matter, the scientific establishment at large, are hardly compelling and wholly without warrant. To justify their position, thinkers such as these must provide evidence that physical events cause physical events, and to my knowledge, this has not been done. Thus, the fact that physical event patterns can be modeled by mathematical equations entails neither that the equations represent natural laws that cause the patterns nor that any physical event modeled by the equations causally determines a subsequent physical event.

Third, it may be assumed that the correlation between prior and subsequent physical events (as described by the laws of physics) is evidence that the laws of physics somehow cause the physical event patterns they describe. This reasoning, however, fallaciously assumes that "Events of type A are correlated with events of type B" entails "Events of type A are causally related to events of type B". For it is possible that events of type C cause events of type A and B such that events of type A are correlated with events of type B, while events of type A and B are, themselves, not causally related (i.e., events of type A do not cause events of type B, and events of type B do not cause events of type A). Correlation does not imply causation. Therefore, the correlation between prior and subsequent physical events (as described by the laws of physics) is not evidence that the laws of physics somehow cause the physical event patterns they describe.

Fourth, it may be assumed that "A is a necessary and sufficient condition of B" implies "A is the cause of B". However, although A may represent the set of conditions necessary and sufficient to guarantee "If A, then B" is true, it does not follow that the conditions represented by A actually produce (bring about) B. The correlation between A and B does not imply that A caused B, for it is possible that both A and B were caused by C, while A did not cause B. Therefore, the cause of a physical event is not necessarily the necessary and sufficient physical conditions of that event.

Fifth, if physical event A logically entails physical event B, then it could be argued that A is, consequently, the cause of B. This reasoning is incorrect, however, since causation is not a logical entailment relation, but is the bringing about (or production) of an event. There is no evidence that if physical event A logically entails physical event B, then A must bring about (or produce) B. Thus, if physical event A logically entails physical event B, it does not follow that A is therefore the cause of B.

Sixth, there is a very large number of cases in which the originating cause of a physical event is the free exercise of a person's power. Since the free exercise of a person's power is a nonphysical event, it follows that each of these cases is one in which a nonphysical event is the originating cause of a physical event.

Seventh, there is no evidence that any caused event is caused by anything other than the free exercise of a person's power. Since the free exercise of a person's power is a nonphysical event, it follows that there is no evidence that any caused event is caused by anything other than the nonphysical event "a person J freely exercising J's power". (Even if, in the future, the free exercise of a person's power will somehow be shown to be a physical event, then it would follow that there is no evidence that any caused event is caused by anything other than the physical event "a person J freely exercising J's power". Those inclined to embrace this view may simply skip down to proposition (10) below.)

The seven considerations above reasonably establish proposition (7). Thus, S is probably not caused by a physical event.

(8) S is probably caused by a nonphysical event.

Proposition (8) follows from (6) and (7). Since propositions (6) and (7) are now established, (8) is also established.

(9) S is probably caused by the nonphysical event "a person J freely exercising J's power".

There are several considerations which support (9). First, as discussed above, the only nonphysical event known to cause physical events is the nonphysical event "a person J freely exercising J's power".

Second, there is no evidence that any caused event is caused by anything other than the free exercise of a person's power.

Third, there is a very large, and increasing, number of cases in which the cause of a physical event is the free exercise of a person's power. The world's human population numbers in the billions, and probably most of these people freely cause physical events on a daily basis. Each of these instances of causation is a case in which the cause of a physical event is the free exercise of a person's power. The cumulative number of such instances increases by many billions each day.

The objection may be raised, here, that the only nonphysical event known to cause physical events is the nonphysical event "a *human* person J freely exercising J's power". Also, it may be argued that there is no evidence that any caused event is caused by anything other than the free exercise of a *human* person's power. Additionally, it could be emphasized that the large, increasing number of cases in which the cause of a physical event is the free exercise of a person's power are all cases in which a *human* person is freely exercising power. One could conceivably argue that the force of these three objections probably establishes (xxiii) in an argument which may be formulated as follows:

(xviii) If a physical event E is known to be caused, then E is known to be caused by the nonphysical event "a human person H freely exercising H's power".

(xix) S is a physical event known to be caused (from (5)).

(xx) S is known to be caused by the nonphysical event "H freely exercising H's power" (from (xviii) and (xix)).

(xxi) Persons of type H do not have sufficient power to be either the exclusive cause or the contributing cause of events of type S (from considerations such as those found in reasoning used to support propositions such as (11) and (12) below).

(xxii) Since (xxi) entails that (xx) is false, (xviii) or (xix) must be false.

(xxiii) Since (xix) and (xxii) are true, (xviii) must be false.

In response to the above objections and associated argument, it should be noted that the fact that (xviii) is false does not entail that (9) is false. Rather, these considerations of the nature of physical events caused by human persons simply lend support for (13) below. Therefore, the disparity between human-caused physical events and physical events of type S establishes not that events of type S are not caused by a person, but that events of type S are not caused by a human person.

There is another line of reasoning that confirms (9). Given space-time regions U and L, where U is defined as the region including all space-time not in L, consider the following:

(xxiv) If each member of a set A of physical events has property Q in L, and if there is no good reason to believe any member of A in U does not have property Q in U, then each member of A in U probably also has property Q in U.

(xxv) Given the set P of physical events known to be caused, each member of P caused by a human person in region E (the vicinity of Earth) has the property C of being caused by a person.

(xxvi) There is no good reason to believe any member of P not in E does not have property C.

(xxvii) Each member of P not in E probably also has property C.

The above argument begins with the principle stated in (xxiv). This principle is a reasonable means by which one may inductively infer the existence of properties possessed by physical entities in a non-local region. The principle is routinely accepted in modern scientific studies. For example, if a particle physics experiment reveals that a specific particle X has a particular property Y under local conditions Z, then it will be assumed that if particle X exists anywhere else in the history of the universe, then X probably also has property Y under conditions Z anywhere else in the history of the universe. This assumption will be embraced so long as no good reason exists for rejecting it.

The statement in (xxv) is logically necessary. If a physical event is caused by a human person, then it is necessarily the case that the event is caused by a person.

If (xxvi) is true, then it follows that (xxvii) is also true. Thus, all physical events known to be caused are probably caused by a person. Since persons are known to cause events only by means of the nonphysical event "a person J freely exercising J's power", it follows that all physical events known to be caused are probably caused by the nonphysical event "a person J freely exercising J's power". We may then conclude that since S is a physical event known to be probably caused (from (5)), S is probably caused by the nonphysical event "a person J freely exercising J's power".

Thus, (9) is shown to be confirmed, if arguments against the truth of (xxvi) fail. How might one argue that (xxvi) is false? If it is claimed that S may be an uncaused physical event, then we may dismiss this claim by referring to (4). If it is argued that S could be caused by a physical event, then we may reject such an argument by referring to (7).

One might object to (xxvi) by claiming that if property C is replaced by property C' in the above argument (where C' is defined as the property *being caused by a human person*), then since probably no human exists in a region not in E, and since the fact that probably no human exists in a region not in E implies that probably no member of P not in E has property C', we may, therefore, conclude that probably no member of P not in E has property C'. In response to this objection, observe that the fact that probably no member of P not in E has property C' does not entail (xxvi) is false. (Somewhat analogously, recall that the fact that (xviii) is false does not entail (9) is false.) So, replacing C with C' does not help to establish (xxvi) is false.

Given the choice between C and C', the simpler and preferable choice is C. The reason C is simpler and preferable is that it leaves less room for error by asserting a less restrictive hypothesis. C' is more restrictive and less preferable in that it hypothesizes that each member of P is caused not merely by a person, but by a human person. This added restriction is neither a necessary nor justified component of a hypothesis regarding the causal origin of physical events. Okham's Razor may, thus, be invoked to favor C over C'.

The objection could be raised that given two hypotheses of the same scope, the simpler hypothesis is not always *a priori* more probable than a more complex hypothesis of the same scope.[33] In response, observe that even if the objection were true, it would not follow that the simpler hypothesis is never *a priori* more probable than a more complex hypothesis of the same scope. In fact, in cases in which the simpler hypothesis leaves less room for error by asserting less than a more complex hypothesis of the same scope, the simpler hypothesis is clearly *a priori* more probable. Both C and C' have the same scope in that they both postulate a causal origin for each of the events in P. C is simpler in that it asserts the less restrictive hypothesis that each member of P is caused not necessarily by a human person, but simply by a person. Therefore, since C is *a priori* more probable than C', C should be favored over C'.

One could object that although C is *a priori* more probable than C', C is just as *a posteriori* probable as C', given that our experience with physical events whose cause is known is limited to cases in which the physical events are caused by human persons. Thus, the objector may infer that the choice between C and C' is arbitrary and consequently can not be made in a manner that does not beg the question. In response, observe that the objection hinges on the assumption that if our experience with physical events whose cause is known is limited to cases in which the physical events are caused by human persons, then C is just as *a posteriori* probable as C'. But if C is just as *a posteriori* probable as C', then the probability Q that any member of P has a non-human cause is zero. It is now evident that the objector is reasoning that if our experience with physical events whose cause is known is limited to cases in which the physical events are caused by human persons, then Q is zero. This objection simply fails to account for the possibility that members of P could have a non-human personal causal explanation. Since it is possible that members of P could have a non-human personal causal explanation, Q must be nonzero, and the *a posteriori* probability of C must be greater than the *a posteriori* probability of C'. Thus, C should be favored over C'.

Since there is no evidence that (xxvi) is false, and since the unwarranted replacement of the simpler C by the more complex C' does not even disconfirm (xxvi), the objections considered here have not established (xxvi) is false. The force of my argument remains in full.

(10) S is probably caused by:
(a) The free exercise of power by a human person(s); or
(b) The free exercise of power by a person(s) who is not a human person(s); or
(c) The combination of the free exercise of power by a human person(s) and a person(s) who is not a human person(s).

Proposition (10) is clearly true. It simply lists what could reasonably be expected to be the different possible causes of S.

(11) The free exercise of power by one or more human persons is probably not the cause of S.

Proposition (11) entails that disjunct (10a) is probably false. Several considerations support (11). First, the most powerful physical event known to be caused by one or more human persons is characterized by a degree of power and knowledge that is much less than that required to cause an event such as S.

Second, there is no evidence that one or more human persons ever has (or ever will) acquire sufficient power and knowledge to cause an event such as S.

Third, the power and knowledge known to be possessed by human persons is insufficient to be a cause of a physical event such as S.

Therefore, proposition (11) is probably true. Disjunct (10a) is, thus, probably false.

(12) The combination of the free exercise of power by a human person(s) and a person(s) who is not a human person(s) is probably not the cause of S.

Proposition (12) entails that disjunct (10c) is probably false. In support of (12), we simply observe that there is no evidence that the free exercise of power by one or more human persons, combined with the free exercise of power of one or more non-human persons, is the cause of S. Since we have no reason to believe any human person(s) participated in the causation of S, we may accept (12). Justification for this acceptance is grounded in the known limitations on human power and knowledge.

(13) S is probably caused by the free exercise of power by a person(s) who is not a human person(s).

Since (11) and (12) are now established, it follows that the remaining disjunct (10b) is now also reasonably established, and, thus, (13) is established.

(14) S is probably caused by the free exercise of power by a person(s) possessing much greater power and knowledge than that possessed by human persons.

The limited nature of human power and knowledge is such that the person(s) who caused S is doubtfully human. There is no reason to believe any human person participated in the causation of S. The nature of the power and knowledge exemplified by S is such that the cause of S would be expected to be a person(s) who has much greater power and knowledge than any human person. Thus, we have now established proposition (14).

One could object to (14) by claiming that the hypothesis that non-human persons exist and cause physical events is a highly improbable, non-simple hypothesis, since there exists no known cause of the existence and nature of the hypothesized non-human person.[34] In response, it should be observed that it is possible that event A may be reasonably identified as the cause of event B, even if the cause and nature of A's existence is not known in great detail, and even if the full nature of A will eventually be discovered to be more complex, in certain respects, than B. It is not necessary that one know, in great detail, the cause and nature of the existence of A when hypothesizing A causes B. Also, it is not necessary that a full accounting of the detailed nature of A be simpler than that of B. Indeed, when A is hypothesized to be the cause of B, precious little may be known of A, save the facts that: (a) it is the hypothesized cause of B; and (b) it has at least one known specific property. We may identify A as the cause of B, even if the question remains unsettled as to whether the detailed nature of A is more complex than B. Therefore, the fact that the cause and/or nature of the hypothesized non-human person in (14) might be unknown does not entail (14) is highly improbable. The mere fact that we may not possess great and extensive knowledge of the origin and/or nature of the non-human person hypothesized in (14) does not entail there exists justification for rejecting the hypothesis. We must also not reject that hypothesis merely on the grounds that A may eventually be shown to be more complex than B. The alternative suggested by Dawkins is that we identify the allegedly more simple natural selection process as the cause of physical events which pertain to biological life.[35] This alternative entails that a physical event can cause a physical event, and this is precisely the assertion which Dawkins has failed to justify, and which has been shown to be unjustified (see (7)). The alternative offered by Dawkins is not a justified causal explanation at all, since he claims to provide a causal explanation (i.e., natural selection), yet fails to justify the claim that a physical event can be a cause. If Dawkins can not even establish that his explanation is a causal explanation, then his alternative is hardly shown to be the cause of the physical events of which he is attempting to provide a causal explanation. Yes, the simplest explanation that best explains all the facts is preferable, but the explanation offered by Dawkins does not square with the critical fact that physical events are not known to cause physical events. Thus, the force of the reasoning up to this point in the AFTLOP establishes that (14) is highly probable, especially given that no known better alternative to (14) exists.

Victor Stenger has argued that it is not necessary to appeal to the existence and action of some external agency as a causal explanation of physical events (e.g., S) which are described by the laws of physics, since the 28 laws of physics simply result from the point-of-view invariant nature of physical reality, as confirmed by all known physical observations.[36] (Point-of-view invariance means that the laws of physics are described using a mathematical model that does not depend on when or where the modeled observations are observed.) In response to this argument, observe that even Stenger acknowledges that not all features of the laws of physics are known to result from point-of-view invariance. Specifically, the relative values of several fundamental forces are not presently calculable from fundamental theory.[37] Therefore, the apparent point-of-view invariant nature of physical reality does not fully explain that reality, and, thus, has not eliminated the plausibility of an external agency being the causal origin of physical events described by the laws of physics.

Lest we be accused of arguing for a God-of-the-gaps, here, it must be strongly emphasized that there is, furthermore, a 29th law of physics which Stenger does not identify or address: existing physical entities continue to exist and evolve in accordance with the other 28 laws. Since point-of-view invariance does not entail that this 29th law of physics obtains, it is evident that point-of-view invariance thoroughly fails to provide a justified alternative to causal explanations such as (14). At most, Stenger has shown that existing physical entities continue to exist and evolve in patterns which may be described using point-of-view invariant mathematical models. This modest result, however, is consistent with (14), as these entities may be fully explained as being caused by an external agency (person) to continue to exist and evolve in accordance with the point-of-view invariant laws of physics.

(15) Therefore God_s probably exists, where God_s is defined such that:
(a) God_s is the person(s) whose free exercise of power is the cause of S;
(b) God_s is not a human person(s); and
(c) God_s's power and knowledge is much greater than that possessed by human persons.

Proposition (15) is simply a statement of what has already been established in (14), where the term "God_s" is introduced to refer to the person(s) described in (14). Proposition (15), therefore, is now established.

(16) Let U represent the set of all physical events such that, given any member U_i of U, U_i may replace S in premises 1 through 15. Therefore God_u probably exists, where God_u is defined such that:
(a) God_u is the person(s) whose free exercise of power is the cause of each member U_i of U;
(b) God_u is not a human person(s); and
(c) God_u's power and knowledge is much greater than that possessed by human persons.

Proposition (16) accounts for the fact that the Crab Nebula is not the only physical event in need of causal explanation. There are many other physical events which, to be causally explained, must be described such that the person(s) who is the cause of those events is identified. At this stage in the argument, it is evident that U consists of a very large number of physical events. The term "God_u" has been introduced to refer to the person(s) described in (16), and (16) is now reasonably established.

(17) Since the members of U minimally include every physical event (excluding any physical events caused by human persons) described by the laws of physics presently known by human persons, God_u is probably the cause of every physical event (excluding any physical

events caused by human persons) described by the laws of physics presently known by human persons.

Proposition (17) more precisely identifies the set of physical events known to be caused by God_u. A physical event E that is described by a known law of physics is a member of U, unless E is a physical event caused by a human person. No member of U is a physical event caused by a human person. Since a significant proportion of the physical events throughout the history of the universe is described by known laws of physics, and since almost none of these events is caused by a human person, a significant proportion of the physical events throughout the history of the universe comprises the members of U. In particular, God_u is thus probably the cause of nearly every physical event described by the laws of physics presently known by human persons. In fact, with the exception of physical events caused by human persons, God_u is probably the cause of every physical event described by the laws of physics presently known by human persons.

(18) Continuing scientific discovery increasingly reveals God_u's enormously great power and knowledge exemplified by the laws of physics that describe the physical events caused by God_u.

Several considerations support proposition (18). First, continuing scientific discovery reveals that the number N of specific known laws of physics continues to increase.

Second, continuing scientific discovery reveals that the number of ways that the N specific known laws of physics can be subsumed into more general, fundamental laws continues to increase.

Third, continuing scientific discovery reveals that the number P of physical events described by the known laws of physics continues to increase.

Fourth, since nearly all of the P physical events are members of U, it follows that continuing scientific discovery increasingly reveals God_u's enormously great power and knowledge exemplified by the laws of physics that describe the physical events caused by God_u. Thus, (18) is established.

The objection may be raised that a human could eat a cheeseburger every Friday afternoon, and this regular pattern of physical events would constitute a law of physics (i.e., a description of a physical event pattern in general terms) which is caused by a human. It could be argued that physical events which comprise a physical event pattern are, therefore, sometimes caused by humans and, thus, laws of physics are sometimes caused not by God$_u$, but by humans.

In response to the above objection, it should be emphasized that although humans can, technically speaking, cause laws of physics by virtue of causing regular physical event patterns which may be described in general terms, the vast majority of the P physical events are not reasonably taken to be human-caused and, thus, are reasonably taken to be caused by God$_u$.

(19) Given some event F of type NE ("NE" denoting "not explained", where events of type NE are defined as physical events not presently known by humans to be explained either: (i) in terms of laws of physics presently known by humans; or (ii) as an event caused by either a human or God$_u$), F will either:

(a) cease to be of type NE by virtue of being known by humans, in the future, to be explained in terms of new physical laws discovered by humans in the future; or

(b) cease to be of type NE by virtue of being known by humans, in the future, as an event caused by a human; or

(c) cease to be of type NE by virtue of being known by humans, in the future, as an event caused by God$_u$; or

(d) always persist as an event of type NE.

Proposition (19) identifies four different future possibilities for events presently of type NE. Other conceivable possibilities are not considered, since other possibilities are not plausible.

Now, let W represent the set of all physical events which satisfies the following conditions:

(e) Each member of W is not presently known by humans to be described by a law of physics presently known by humans.

(f) Each member of W is not presently known by humans as an event caused by either a human or God$_u$.

(g) Each member of W is presently known by humans to be highly unlikely to be caused by any human at any time.

So, conditions (e) and (f) together entail that each member of W is of type NE. Condition (g) further entails that it is highly unlikely that any member of W will cease to be of type NE by virtue of being known by humans, in the future, as an event caused by a human. Since it is, consequently, highly unlikely that disjunct (19b) will apply to any member W_i of W, it follows that one of the following disjuncts will most likely apply to each W_i: (19a), (19c), or (19d). Let *option 1* be the case that either (19a) or (19c) will apply to W_i in the future, and let *option 2* be the case that (19d) will always apply to W_i in the future.

Now, in the case of *option 1*, regardless of whether (19a) or (19c) will apply to W_i in the future, W_i will be known to be caused by God_u in the future. This can be seen as follows. First, members of W to which (19a) will apply in the future will be known to be caused by God_u, since (18) will apply to those members of W. Second, members of W to which (19c) will be known to apply (perhaps by some means presently unknown) in the future will, of course, be caused by God_u. Therefore, in the case of *option 1*, W_i will be known to be caused by God_u in the future.

In the case of *option 2*, the reason for which (19d) will always apply is that humans will never know whether *option 2a* or *option 2b* is best, where *option 2a* is "Disjunct (19a) is probably clearly better than either (19c) or (19d)" and *option 2b* is "Disjunct (19c) is probably clearly better than either (19a) or (19d)". Note, however, that in the case of *option 2*, although humans will never know whether *option 2a* or *option 2b* is best, either *option 2a* or *option 2b* must be best (no other reasonable option remains), and each of *option 2a* and *option 2b* entails that W_i is caused by God_u. This may be seen as follows. First, if *option 2a* were best, then W_i would be explained in terms of new physical laws discovered by humans in the future, and (18) would, thus, apply to W_i, entailing that W_i is caused by God_u. Second, if *option 2b* were best, then W_i would be known by humans, in the future, as an event caused by God_u. So, in the case of *option 2*, W_i is most likely caused by God_u.

Each W_i is, therefore, most likely a member of U. God_u is, consequently, seen to be even more powerful and knowledgeable than previously established, given that W is now seen to be a subset of U. For example, consider some physical behavior B of distant quasars not presently understood by humans in terms of laws of physics known by humans. Initial human consideration of B may render it an event of type NE. Upon further consideration, however, it becomes evident that since B is highly unlikely to be human-caused, B could be explained by humans in the future in terms of: (1) a law of physics presently unknown by humans; or (2) a God_u-caused event, where the means is presently unknown by which B will be known by humans to be God_u-caused. In either case, B would be highly likely to be known by humans to be caused by God_u. If neither of these two cases will ever be known by humans to be the clearly superior explanation, then it is, nevertheless, the case that B is likely caused by God_u, as no other reasonable option remains. Thus, in general, if presently unexplained physical events are probably not human-caused, then they are probably God_u-caused.

The AFTLOP should create a sense of great awe and wonder. Wherever we look, we find evidence of God_u's creative intelligence and sustaining power. Every beat of your heart, each falling drop of rain, and every subatomic particle in every star in every galaxy reveals the power and knowledge of God_u. The psalmist was right…no one can fathom the greatness of the Lord (Psalm 145:3).

NOTES

1.   Kafatos, Minas C. and Henry, Richard B. C. eds. (1985). *The Crab Nebula and Related Supernova Remnants.* Cambridge: Cambridge University Press.
2.   Martin, Michael and Monnier, Ricki (2006). *The Improbability of God.* Amherst, NY: Prometheus Books, p. 144.
3.   Incidentally, Fazale Rana and Hugh Ross have recently argued that the improbability of a naturalistic explanation of the origin of life is a critical factor essential for perceiving that the relevant evidence confirms their creationist model, while disconfirming naturalistic models. See Rana, Fazale and Ross, Hugh (2004). *Origins of Life: Biblical and Evolutionary Models Face Off.* Colorado Springs, CO: Navpress.
4.   Edis, Taner (2002). T*he Ghost in the Universe: God in Light of Modern Science.* Amherst, NY: Prometheus Books, p. 96.
5.   Ibid., p. 94.
6.   Ibid., p. 95.
7.   Ibid., p. 107.
8.   Martin and Monnier (2006), pp. 43-44, 63-64.
9.   Rundle, Bede (2004). *Why there is Something rather than Nothing.* Oxford: Oxford University Press, p. 40.
10. See William R. Stoeger's discussion of contemporary physics and the ontological status of the laws of nature in Russell, Robert John, ed. (1993). *Quantum Cosmology and the Laws of Nature: Scientific Perspectives on Divine Action.* Vatican City State: Vatican Observatory Publications and Berkeley, CA: The Center for Theology and the Natural Sciences, pp. 209-234. See also Hackett, Stuart C. (1984). *The Reconstruction of the Christian Revelation Claim: A Philosophical and Critical Apologetic.* Grand Rapids, MI: Baker Book House, p. 314. The importance of this point can not be underestimated, as failure to grasp its implications is, I suspect, a central reason for which many atheists fail to see the explanatory insufficiency of their natural explanations.
11. Atheist David Mills clearly understands this concept. See Mills, David (2006). *Atheist Universe.* Berkeley, CA: Ulysses Press, pp. 69-70. Unfortunately, Mills later contradicts his own interpretation of physical laws by supposing they can "alone do the job and perform all the work within our universe" (Ibid., p. 103). Rather, Mills should

be consistent and maintain not that physical laws "do the job and perform all the work", but maintain that physical laws describe the job and describe the performed work, thereby leaving open wide the door to theistic causation of physical event patterns described by physical laws, as justified in detail here in my AFTLOP. Physical laws are not known to be a sufficient causal explanation of the described events, but merely a sufficient descriptive explanation of the described events.

12. Martin, Michael ed. (2007). *The Cambridge Companion to Atheism*. Cambridge: Cambridge University Press, p. 184.

13. Ibid., p. 191.

14. Ibid., p. 193.

15. Ibid., p. 194.

16. Ibid., p. 192.

17. Ibid., p. 136.

18. Ibid., p. 146.

19. Shanks, Niall (2006). *God, the Devil, and Darwin: A Critique of Intelligent Design Theory*. Oxford: Oxford University Press, p. 223.

20. Dawkins (2006). *The God Delusion*. Boston: Houghton Mifflin Company, p. 117:15-17, italics mine.

21. Ibid., p. 140:6-7.

22. Ibid., pp. 150:36-151:2, italics mine.

23. Mills (2006), p. 70.

24. Ibid., front cover. See also Dawkins (2006), p. 44.

25. Futuyma, Douglas J. (1995). *Science on Trial: The Case for Evolution*. Sunderland, MA: Sinauer Associates, Inc., p. 204, italics mine.

26. Ibid., p. 204, italics mine.

27. Ibid., p. 203, italics mine.

28. Ibid., p. 207, italics mine.

29. Ibid., p. 205, italics mine.

30. Ibid., p. 207, italics mine.

31. Michael Ruse is a prominent example of an evolutionist who ascribes, without justification, causal powers to physical events and physical laws. See Ruse, Michael (2006). *Darwinism and Its Discontents*. Cambridge: Cambridge University Press, pp. 103-133. Ruse does not understand that physical laws are descriptive (not causal), and he does not account for the personal nature of physical event causation, as defended here in the AFTLOP.

32. Ibid., pp. 285 and 289.

33. Martin, Michael (1990). *Atheism: A Philosophical Justification*. Philadelphia: Temple University Press, p. 111.

34. Dawkins, Richard (2006). *The God Delusion*. Boston: Houghton Mifflin, pp. 120-121.

35. Ibid., p. 151.

36. Stenger, Victor J. (2006). *The Comprehensible Cosmos: Where Do the Laws of Physics Come From?* Amherst, NY: Prometheus Books, Table 5.1, pp. 113-114.

37. Ibid., p. 164.

CHAPTER 2

The Fine-Tuning Argument

A new defense of the theistic implications of anthropic coincidences widely popularized by proponents of fine-tuning teleological arguments is first published here. As mentioned in the Introduction, I did not even originally intend to develop this argument when I began this book, but my fine-tuning arguments here emerged from my contemplation of probabilistic considerations raised by critics of Hugh Ross. Specifically, I developed my fine-tuning arguments in response to the critical online article entitled "The Anthropic Principle Does Not Support Supernaturalism," by Michael Ikeda and Bill Jeffreys.[1] My fine-tuning arguments here rush to the defense of the general line of argumentation presented by Ross,[2] and shore up that defense with a greater measure of philosophical rigor and technical precision.

Although my fine-tuning arguments are also included in the context of my later critique of Ikeda and Jeffreys,[3] they are reproduced here outside that context so that they may be expressed in a stand-alone form that will facilitate their greater ease of interaction with future analyses. My fine-tuning arguments proceed as follows:

(1) $A \rightarrow \sim B$

(2) B

(3) $\sim A$

This line of reasoning is grounded in the well known *modus tollens* inference. Here, A represents the conjunction "N and $(C \in Q)$", and B represents "$P((C \in Q)|N) \approx 0$". N represents naturalism, defined as the hypothesis that the laws M of physics are the impersonal causal explanation of the set Q of physical events, where M represents the set of all presently known laws of physics, and where Q represents the set of all physical events presently known to be described by any member of M. C represents the set of all physical conditions necessary for the naturalistic origin of a planet on which L is true, where L represents the hypothesis "physical Earth-like life exists". As a deductive inference, the reasoning above is valid. However, in the case of the fine-tuning argument, the premises are not known with absolute certainty, and the inductive counterpart to this reasoning may be roughly summarized in probabilistic terms as the inference from $[P(\sim B|A) \approx k]$ to $[P(\sim A|B) \approx k]$ to $[P(\sim A) \approx k]$. Note that the inference from $[P(\sim B|A) \approx k]$ to $[P(\sim A|B) \approx k]$ is justified, in general, only when $P(A|B)$ and $P(B|A)$ are both approximately $1 - k$, since $P(A|B) + P(\sim A|B) = P(B|A) + P(\sim B|A) = 1$ entails that $P(\sim B|A) \approx P(\sim A|B) \approx k$ only if $P(A|B) \approx P(B|A) \approx k - 1$. The further inference to $[P(\sim A) \approx k]$ is justified only if it is also true that $P(B) \approx 1$. In the case of the fine-tuning argument detailed below, since $k \approx 1$ and $P(B) \approx 1$, it follows that $P(\sim A) \approx 1$.

(4) $P((C \in Q)|N) \approx 0$

(5) $P(B) \approx 1$

(6) $P(B|A) \approx 0$

(7) $P(B|A) + P(\sim B|A) = 1$

(8) $P(\sim B|A) \approx 1$

(9) $P(\sim B|A) = P(A \text{ and } \sim B) / P(A)$

(10) $P(A \text{ and } \sim B) / P(A) \approx 1$

(11) $P(A \text{ and } \sim B) \approx P(A)$

(12) $P(A \text{ or } \sim B) = P(A) + P(\sim B) - P(A \text{ and } \sim B)$

(13) $P(B) + P(\sim B) = 1$

(14) $P(\sim B) \approx 0$

(15) $P(A \text{ or } \sim B) \approx 0$

(16) $P(A \text{ or } \sim B) + P(B) - P(A \text{ and } B) = 1$

(17) $0 + 1 - P(A \text{ and } B) \approx 1$

(18) $P(A \text{ and } B) \approx 0$

(19) $P(A \text{ and } B) = P(B \text{ and } A)$

(20) $P(B \text{ and } A) \approx 0$

(21) $P(B \text{ and } A) = P(B) \, P(A|B)$

(22) $P(B) \, P(A|B) \approx 0$

(23) $P(A|B) \approx 0$

(24) $P(A|B) + P(\sim A|B) = 1$

(25) $P(\sim A|B) \approx 1$

(26) $P(\sim A) \approx 1$

(27) $P(\sim(N \text{ and } (C \in Q))) \approx 1$

(28) $P(\sim N \text{ or } \sim(C \in Q)) \approx 1$

Premise (4) is the critical premise supplied by anthropic principle considerations. Premise (5) follows from (4) and the definition of B. Premise (6) is true, since a physical event being a member of Q entails that the probability, given N, of its being caused by M is not vanishingly small, and since any physical event with a vanishingly small probability, given N, of being caused by M is probably not caused by M and, thus, is probably not a member of Q. This follows from the fact that $C \in Q$ is likely (given N) if and only if $P((C \in Q)|N) \approx 1$. In other words, it is unlikely that it would be likely to be very unlikely that $C \in Q$ (given N), if it is given that N and $(C \in Q)$ are both true. Given A, B must be either true or false, and, thus, premise (7) must be true. Premise (8) follows from the substitution of (6) into (7). Premise (9) follows from the definition of conditional probability. Premise (10) follows from substitution of (8) into (9). Premise (11) follows from multiplication of (10) by P(A). Premise (12) follows from the definition of probability with inclusive logical disjunction. Premise (13) must be true, as the sum of the probability space must equal one. Premise (14) follows from substitution of (5) into (13). Premise (15) follows from the substitution of (11) and (14) into (12). The sum in premise (16) must equal 1, since the three terms together account for the full probability space (draw a Venn-Euler diagram to see this.) Premise (17) follows from substitution of (15) and (5) into (16). Premise (18) follows from simplifying and rearranging terms in (17). Premise (19) is true, since the event "A and B" is identical to the event "B and A", in general. Premise (20) follows from substitution of (18) into (19). Premise (21) follows from the definition of conditional probability. Premise (22) follows from substitution of (20) into (21). Premise (23) follows from substitution of (5) into (22). Given B, A must be either true or false, and, thus, premise (24) must be true. Premise (25) follows from substitution of (23) into (24). Premise (26) follows from (5) and (25), and is grounded in the well known *modus ponens* inference. Premise (27) follows from (26) and the definition of A. Premise (28) is the inclusive logical disjunction that results from (27).

Much hinges on premise (4), as the other steps are rather straightforward. The objection might be raised that the smallness of the probability in premise (4) is grounded in the unjustified assumption that the probability space is known to be large. There does appear to be some merit to this objection as it pertains to physical conditions H, where H represents the subset of anthropic coincidences dealing with the alleged improbability of the values of various constants of physics that appear in mathematical physics models. Consider some of the numbers cited by Hugh Ross[4] which describe physical balances accurate to one part in 10^{37}, one part in 10^{40}, one part in 10^{60}, and one part in 10^{120}. Even if it is true that these conditions must be so balanced as a necessary condition for finding a naturalistic explanation of a planet on which L is true, it does not follow that the probability, given N, of these conditions being an element of Q is one part in 10^{37}, one part in 10^{40}, one part in 10^{60}, and one part in 10^{120}, respectively. After all, a probability calculation assumes knowledge of the space of possibilities, and opponents of this category of fine-tuning arguments may object that the space of possible values of these conditions, given N, is not presently known.[5] Even granting this objection, however, it does nevertheless appear odd that such balances do, in fact, obtain. These odd observations might conceivably be the hard data upon which a "Fingerprint of God" argument of some kind could be developed, but consideration of issues relevant to such an argument lies beyond the scope of the present analysis.

More importantly, however, is must be stressed that it is highly unlikely that all other anthropic coincidences have a naturalistic explanation, given N, since the space of possibilities, given N, can be estimated for at least some of these coincidences. For example, consider the estimate of the probability, given N, that $C_p \in Q$, where C_p represents the conditions which are a subset of C and listed in Table 16.2 of the aforementioned book by Hugh Ross.[6] So, although it is not clear how to assess the probability, given N, that $H \in Q$, there exists a distinct subset C_p of anthropic coincidences, where no element of C_p is an element of H, and where the probability of the members of C_p all being an element of Q, given N, can be estimated. Therefore, the unknown probability space objection does not apply to all anthropic coincidences, and fine-tuning arguments that are built on C_p survive against this objection. Furthermore, the AFTLOP establishes that all anthropic coincidences, being physical conditions not caused by humans, are caused by God. (Note that the success of my fine-tuning arguments does not rely on the soundness of the AFTLOP, but the soundness of the AFTLOP does strengthen the degree to which the theistic creation-design hypothesis is confirmed by my fine-tuning arguments.)

The objection may be raised that although the probability may be small that a universe in which L is true could be randomly selected by some natural process, there may nevertheless exist unknown natural processes which entail that the probability is close to 1 that a randomly naturally selected universe would sustain some form of (possibly not carbon-based) life.[7] In response, even if we make the scientifically unjustified concession that the probability is close to one that a naturally selected universe would sustain some form of (possibly not carbon-based) life, there remains the problem of finding a natural explanation of the causal origin of conditions C which facilitate the sustenance of the carbon-based life we actually find on Earth. Therefore, my fine-tuning argument here is immune to this objection.

The following objection has been raised: "Many universes can exist, with all possible combinations of physical laws and constants."[8] Therefore, a multiverse of varied universes (so it may be argued) would contain life in at least some small fraction of the many existing universes. In response, multiverse theory is not scientifically established. The number of known universes is one. Furthermore, even if there is a multiverse, it is not established that it contains universes with varying combinations of physical laws and constants. In addition, even if there is a multiverse with universes that contain varying combinations of physical laws and constants, it is not established that a sufficient number of varied universes exists to render premise (4) false. Also, even if a multiverse is eventually shown to exist and possess a nature such that premise (4) is false, the AFTLOP (chapter 1) remains as a means by which the theistic cause of that multiverse may be identified.

Now the implications of my fine-tuning argument will be explored. Given (28), we have the choice of rejecting N or rejecting C ϵ Q. If we reject N, then since no other naturalistic explanation of physical events (especially C) has been provided, it follows that theistic causal explanations of physical events are seen to be of superior explanatory value, since theistic explanations justifiably identify the source of physical event causation (including the source of the cause of C and Q), whereas no naturalistic causal explanation of physical events is even available as a live option. Thus, rejecting N strongly disconfirms atheism, favoring theism.

Atheists, presumably keenly aware of their intellectual discomfort associated with rejecting N, are instead rather likely to opt to reject the claim "it is presently known that C ϵ Q", pointing out that a scientific discovery at some future time T will establish that C ϵ Q is true at T. This option, however, is simply a naturalism-of-the-gaps tactic, and unless justification is provided for the filling of knowledge gaps with naturalistic explanations, such gaps should not be so filled. Granted, given N, and given that it is not presently known that C ϵ Q, theists are not necessarily justified in inferring that C ϵ Q will not ever be known at some future time, but neither are atheists necessarily justified in assuming C ϵ Q will be known at some future time.

So, given N, and given that C ϵ Q is not presently known, it would be prudent to withhold judgment as to the estimate of P(B), unless there is a good reason to suppose that the estimate may be accurately quantified. In general, knowledge of M may be sufficiently limited such that it may not be possible to calculate a probabilistic estimate of the likelihood (given N) that some specific physical event type R is an element of Q. On the other hand, in cases in which knowledge of M is sufficient to calculate a probabilistic estimate of the likelihood (given N) of R ϵ Q, that estimate represents the degree to which a naturalistic explanation of R is likely. In the case of the fine-tuning argument, since knowledge of M is sufficient to estimate the probability, given N, of C ϵ Q, and since that probability is vanishingly small, it follows that it is very unlikely that there exists a naturalistic explanation of C. It is by default, therefore, that we may arrive at the conclusion that C must have a personal causal explanation, since personally-caused physical events are the only reasonable alternative to naturalistic explanations (this is especially true, given the AFTLOP). The person(s) responsible for causing C is profoundly greater in power and knowledge than humans, and this constitutes strong evidence in support of the theistic hypothesis.

The objection may be raised that a God-of-the-gaps strategy has been employed in the reasoning above. However, the inference to a non-naturalistic personal explanation of C has been made not due to ignorance of unknown naturalistic explanations, but through knowledge of limitations on naturalistic explanations, as quantified by probability estimates grounded in scientific knowledge (not ignorance). We arrive at a justified theistic explanation of C not merely by virtue of observing there is an absence of a presently available naturalistic explanation of C, but by virtue of this observation in conjunction with the knowledge that such an explanation is highly unlikely.

The objection may be raised that since future scientific discoveries are virtually unpredictable, it can not be known that a naturalistic explanation of C will not be forthcoming, implying that theistic explanations ought to be rejected as being unjustifiably dogmatic regarding future unknowns. In response, the objection considered here consists of the arbitrary rejection of possible theistic explanations on the grounds that non-theistic explanations might possibly be discovered in the future, yet no good reason is provided for dismissing the alternative option of rejecting possible non-theistic explanations on the grounds that theistic explanations might always continue to be confirmed in the future. It is logically possible that a naturalistic explanation of C will be forthcoming, but it is also logically possible that a naturalistic explanation of C will always continue to be increasingly unlikely. These bare logical possibilities do not justify rejection of what is presently known with high likelihood, namely, that the probability of a naturalistic explanation of C is vanishingly small. Furthermore, the objection considered here is arguably grounded in the principle "given unknown future discoveries, we do not presently possess knowledge." This principle, however, is self-refuting, since the present nonexistence of knowledge would entail the principle is not presently known, contradicting the assertion that the principle is presently known.

The objection might be raised that many, if not most, physical events have been discovered to be members of Q, and therefore, given continuing scientific progress, the remaining physical events not presently known to be members of Q will likely be known to be members of Q at some future time T. In response, note that this objection simply rejects what is scientifically established. Yes, many physical events not presently known to be members of Q may well be known to be members of Q at T, but this in no way entails that all physical events are likely to be known members of Q at some future time. It is possible that some physical events are not members of Q, and my fine-tuning arguments suggest that this possibility is highly likely. The number of known members of Q may increase for many years to come, and the great majority of physical events might eventually be known to be members of Q, but these facts are also consistent with the existence of some God-caused physical events that are not, and never will be, members of Q. Furthermore, scientific progress is in the direction of increasing knowledge of an increasing quantity of known anthropic coincidences.[9] Given these trends, the theistic hypothesis only continues to be strengthened. Scientific progress is the enemy of the atheist, not the theist.

The objection may be raised that the matter of "whether there are supernatural beings" must be settled "before asking whether in fact one such being actually did design our universe."[10] In response, this objection presumes that entity X must be known to exist prior to examination of evidence of X's existence. Clearly, this is an unreasonable demand, as it would preclude one's capacity to infer the existence of any entity by means of adducing evidence of its existence. Therefore, the objection considered here may be rejected.

The objection may be raised that since we do not understand how a nonphysical mind can cause a physical event, it is unintelligible to claim that physical conditions in the universe are designed by a nonhuman person's nonphysical mind.[11] In response, one may know that R is the cause of T, yet not understand how R causes T. Instances of causation may be known, even if the detailed means are unknown by which the causal relation is effective. Thus, my fine-tuning argument may be used to infer the existence of theistic design of physical conditions, even if it is not understood how the theistic designer actually accomplishes the task of causing physical events by means of the exercise of nonphysical power to produce physical effects.

Observe that throughout my discussion of the fine-tuning argument, I have sought to largely disregard the results of the AFTLOP so as to develop an independent line of natural theology that may be used to confirm theism. In fact, all this concern about whether a physical event will be discovered to be described by M at some future time T is of no concern whatsoever to the theist, since the AFTLOP entails that all physical events not caused by humans are God-caused. Therefore, even multiverse objections to the theistic inference fail, since the AFTLOP entails that all physical events in the multiverse not caused by humans are God-caused. See chapter 1 for details.

The objection may be raised that fine-tuning arguments fail to consider probabilities conditioned upon L. In response to this objection, first note that my fine-tuning argument above is grounded in the assumption that conditions C exist, where C is known to exist by virtue of our observations of physical conditions. Since selection of members of C is made on the basis of our present understanding of the laws of physics and of existing physical life, my argument is seen to be grounded on the condition that life exists.

Also, given N, consideration of probabilities conditioned upon $L \in Q$, in conjunction with the observation that although $C \in Q$ is a necessary condition of $L \in Q$, $C \in Q$ is not a sufficient condition of $L \in Q$, leads to an even stronger fine-tuning argument. I submit that theism is more strongly confirmed by the fine-tuning argument below than by the fine-tuning argument above. Here, V shall represent the conjunction "N and $(L \in Q)$", and W shall represent "$P((L \in Q)|N) \approx 0$".

(29) $P((L \in Q) \mid (N \text{ and } (C \in Q))) < 1$

---

(30) $P((L \in Q)|N) < P((C \in Q)|N)$

(31) $P((C \in Q)|N) \approx 0$

(32) $P((L \in Q)|N) \approx 0$

(33) $P(W) \approx 1$

(34) $P(\sim W|V) \approx 1$

(35) $P(\sim V|W) \approx 1$

(36) $P(\sim V) \approx 1$

(37) $P(\sim(N \text{ and } (L \in Q))) \approx 1$

(38) $P(\sim N \text{ or } \sim(L \in Q)) \approx 1$

Premises (29) and (30) result from the fact that, given N, $C \in Q$ is not a sufficient condition of $L \in Q$ (even though, given N, $C \in Q$ is a necessary condition of $L \in Q$). Premise (31) is from (4). Premise (32) is from substitution of (31) into (30). Note that since the probability in (31) approximates zero, the probability in (32) must even more closely approximate zero. Premise (33) follows from (32) and the definition of W. Premise (34) is true, since a physical event being a member of Q entails that the probability, given N, of its being caused by M is not vanishingly small, and since any physical event with a vanishingly small probability, given N, of being caused by M is probably not caused by M and, thus, is probably not a member of Q. This follows from the fact that $L \in Q$ is likely (given N) if and only if $P((L \in Q)|N) \approx 1$. In other words, it is unlikely that it would be likely to be very unlikely that $L \in Q$ (given N), if it is given that N and $(L \in Q)$ are both true. Premise (35) follows from premises (33) and (34), given that we are able to make the inference from $[P(\sim X|Y) \approx k]$ to $[P(\sim Y|X) \approx k]$, when $k \approx 1$, and when $P(X) \approx 1$ (this inference form has been previously justified, and is generalized from the details shown earlier in premises (5) through (25)). Premise (36) follows from (33) and (35), and is grounded in the well known *modus ponens* inference. Premise (37) follows from substitution of the definition of V into (36). Premise (38) is the inclusive logical disjunction that results from (37).

So, the argument here (premises (29) to (38)) is even stronger than the argument earlier (premises (4) to (28)), since the probability in (32) must even more closely approximate zero than the probability in (4) or (31). Also, we are faced with either rejecting N or rejecting $L \in Q$, yet both options confirm theism. If we reject N, then, by default, this confirms theistic causal explanations of the origin of L (and of Q), as no other reasonable option remains. If we reject L ∈ Q, then this also confirms theistic causal explanations of L, since no other reasonable alternative remains.

Thus, the universe is life-friendly in the sense that conditions that are necessary for L ∈ Q exist, yet the fine-tuning argument in premises (4) through (28) shows that this fact may be used to confirm theism. Also, the universe is not life-friendly in the sense that C ∈ Q is not only exceedingly improbable on N, but is also insufficient for L ∈ Q, and the fine-tuning argument in premises (29) through (38) shows that these facts may be used to confirm theism even more strongly.

This is not the end of problems for atheists, as theists may exploit the implications of (4) from another angle. Consider the following argument:

(39) $P((C \in Q)|N) \approx 0$

(40) $P(((L \in Q) \text{ and } (C \in Q))|N) < P((C \in Q)|N)$

(41) $P(((L \in Q) \text{ and } (C \in Q))|N) \approx 0$

(42) $P((\sim(L \in Q) \text{ or } \sim(C \in Q))| N) \approx 1$

Premise (39) is from (4). Premise (40) is another way to express the fact that, given N, C ∈ Q is not a sufficient condition of L ∈ Q. Premise (41) follows from substitution of (39) into (40). Premise (42) is the conditional disjunction that follows from the conditional conjunction in (41). Here, atheists embracing N are faced with the difficult choice of either rejecting L ∈ Q or rejecting C ∈ Q, yet either choice will leave unexplained what theism justifiably explains as the effect of the causal powers of God. Theism has greater explanatory power (this is especially true given the AFTLOP).

Atheists sometimes resist the implications of compelling theistic evidence by exhibiting an adamant blind faith in the future discovery of presently unknown non-theistic explanations of that evidence. This faith surely rivals, if not exceeds, that of even the most ardent adherents to religious belief systems. However, even if we blindly assume that such future discoveries will be made, then this assumption, along with the presently scientifically established improbability of naturalistic explanations of C and L, nevertheless disconfirms N:

(43) $P(((L \in Q) \text{ and } (C \in Q))|N) \approx 0$

(44) $P((L \in Q) \text{ and } (C \in Q)) \approx 1$

(45) $P(N|((L \in Q) \text{ and } (C \in Q))) \approx 0$

(46) $P(N) \approx 0$

Premise (43) is from (41). Premise (44) is the "blind faith" assumption we grant atheists who, despite presently established scientific evidence to the contrary, withhold from theistic belief on the (unjustified) grounds that C and L will be known at some future time to be members of Q. Premise (45) follows from (43) and (44), using the inference from $[P(X|Y) \approx k]$ to $[P(Y|X) \approx k]$, when $k \approx 0$, and when $P(X) \approx 1$ (this inference form has been previously justified, and is generalized from the details shown earlier in premises (5) through (23)). Premise (46) follows from (44) and (45), and is an instance of the well known *modus ponens* inference.

Thus we have shown that the "blind faith" atheistic assumption actually leads to a disconfirmation of the naturalism to which atheists so desperately cling. Now, it might be objected that the "blind faith" assumption has been misconstrued, since the assumption that (44) is true at future time T entails that (43) is false at T, rendering (45) and (46) both unjustified at T. This objection, however, may be rejected at once, since (43) is *now* presently scientifically established, regardless of whether it will be scientifically disconfirmed at T. We must not reject what is presently scientifically established on the basis of what may conceivably be scientifically discovered in the future. Furthermore, the smallness of the probability in (43) is the reason why (44) is labeled the "blind faith" assumption, since its smallness entails that it is highly unlikely that (43) will ever be scientifically disconfirmed. The "blind faith" assumption is, therefore, seen to be an implicit claim that science is false. If an atheist must reject, on blind faith, what is scientifically established so as to justify the atheistic worldview, then the arguments of that atheist surely ought to be rejected.

The objection may be raised that the argument above is not conditioned upon L. In response, first note that (43) is derived from premises and conditions grounded in the assumption that conditions C exist, and members of C are selected based on knowledge of the laws of physics and of existing *life*. Also, note that if N is replaced with "N and L" in the argument above, then the conclusion becomes $P(N \text{ and } L) \approx 0$. Then, since L is true, and since N is assumed by virtue of the "blind faith" assumption, it follows that "blind faith atheists" hold to the high improbability of (N and L), while also assuming both N and L are true. This does not entail that blind faith atheists believe a contradictory state of affairs actually obtains, but it does show that they embrace a highly improbable alternative to theistic design of L or C, where theistic design of L or C is likely, given the implications of (28), (38), (42) and (46), and given the further confirming implications of the AFTLOP.

In other words, in the face of compelling evidence to the contrary, blind faith atheists embrace a highly improbable naturalistic explanation, where an alternative theistic explanation is far more likely. Granted, improbable events do sometimes occur, and the best explanation may sometimes be that an improbable possibility was in fact actualized.[12] This does not, however, give us license to favor whatever improbable explanation may suit our fancy. For even if it is the case that we know that the best explanation BE is that an improbable possibility was in fact actualized, this knowledge may be acquired and sustained through reflection upon the fact that BE is the most probable good explanation, even though BE entails the occurrence of an improbable event. So, given a set of possible and mutually exclusive explanations, inference to the best explanation does not occur if a probable explanation is rejected in favor of an improbable explanation. Thus, blind faith atheists do not opt for the best explanation when embracing a position that is highly improbable and strongly disconfirmed by justified contrary theistic explanations.

Finally, our entire discussion of the fine-tuning argument has been in the context of consideration of the laws M of physics, which are taken to be the impersonal causal explanation of the set Q of physical events. However, as shown in the AFTLOP (chapter 1), impersonal causes doubtfully exist, and the laws of physics generally describe God-caused physical event patterns. So, my fine-tuning arguments show the inadequacy of naturalistic explanations of certain anthropic coincidences, and they also show the superiority of justified theistic explanations of those coincidences. In addition, my AFTLOP substantially broadens the scope of justified theistic explanations to subsume virtually all physical events.

Therefore, probabilistic fine-tuning arguments derived from anthropic principle considerations confirm theism, and theistic design of physical events relevant to anthropic coincidences is only a small subset of the set of all physical events known to have a justified theistic causal explanation. The fine-tuning argument is alive and well.

NOTES

1. http://quasar.as.utexas.edu/anthropic.html. Reprinted in chapter 3 of part 2 of Martin, Michael and Monnier, Ricki, eds. (2006). *The Improbability of God.* Amherst, NY: Prometheus Books, pp. 150-166.

2. Ross, Hugh (2001). *The Creator and the Cosmos: How the Latest Scientific Discoveries of the Century Reveal God.* Colorado Springs, CO: Navpress, 3rd edition, pp. 175-199.

3. See chapter 4.

4. Ross (2001), pp. 150-153.

5. Shanks, Niall (2006). *God, the Devil, and Darwin: A Critique of Intelligent Design Theory.* Oxford: Oxford University Press, p. 222. See also Young, Matt (2001). *No Sense of Obligation: Science and Religion in an Impersonal Universe.* Bloomington, IN: 1st Books Library, p. 221.

6. Ross (2001), pp. 195-198.

7. Shanks (2006), p. 215.

8. Scott, Eugenie C. (2004). *Evolution vs. Creationism: An Introduction.* Berkeley, CA: University of California Press, p. 160.

9. Ross, Hugh (2006). *Creation as Science: A Testable Model Approach to End the Creation/Evolution Wars.* Colorado Springs, CO: Navpress, p. 179.

10. Shanks (2006), p. 213.

11. Ibid., pp. 212-213.

12. This point is emphasized by Shanks (Ibid., pp. 214-215). His analysis, however, fails to account for the version of fine-tuning argument presented here.

CHAPTER 3

Atheistic Cosmological Arguments Refuted

I now examine the cosmological arguments for atheism found in the book "The Improbability of God" edited by Michael Martin and Ricki Monnier, and published by Prometheus Books in 2006, ISBN: 1-59102-381-5. I urge you to purchase a copy of "The Improbability of God" (IPRG) so that you may fully understand the context of the critical remarks below.

In chapter 1 of part 1 of IPRG, Victor J. Stenger presents an argument against the existence of God. Premise 2 (p. 21:6-8) is false, since it is possible that God could create/sustain the physical world without causing any violations of laws of physics. Premise 3 (p. 21:9-11) is false, as the AFTLOP provides evidence of the creation/sustenance of the physical world. Premise 4 (p. 21:12-13) is false, for if the physical world contains "memory" of the creator in that every physical event not caused by a human is caused by God (as the AFTLOP shows), then every physical event (chaotic or not) that is not caused by a human is caused by (and, thus, has "memory" of) God. Premise 5 (p. 21:14-16) is false, since the AFTLOP shows that cosmological theories, if correct, are descriptions of God-caused physical events that arise from God, not nothingness. Furthermore, it is likely that "from nothing nothing comes", and, therefore, Premise 5 is dubious for this reason as well. Premise 6 (p. 21:17-19) is, therefore, not established, given the falsity of premises 2, 3, 4, and 5.

The AFTLOP establishes that Stenger's assumption is erroneous that physical events described by laws of physics are not caused by God (p. 22:1-9). Since physical laws describe physical events caused by God, God is the cause of the physical events in the assumed creation (p. 24:1-4). Thus, regardless of whether the assumed creation events are consistent with energy conservation principles, the creator hypothesis is not disconfirmed. Also, since the AFTLOP entails that most physical events in the universe are caused by God, most physical events in the universe *are* the creator's imprint (p. 25:20-23).

Stenger claims that quantum events with no evident cause (p. 27:9), and with apparent absence of predetermination by known physical laws (p. 27:32-33), are evidence of uncaused physical events. The assumption is unwarranted, however, that such events are not caused by a person (say, God). In addition, physical events not described by presently known physical laws might be described by future discoveries of presently unknown physical laws. To use Stenger's own words: "…how can we be sure that an explanation will not someday be found?" (p. 22:17-18). Even if quantum events can not be determined from previous physical states, it does not follow that such events are uncaused (p. 27:37-39).

The AFTLOP establishes that no physical event causes a physical event, so if "natural cause" means "a physical event that is a cause", then natural causes do not exist. So, if the universe had a cause, then that cause was a person (p. 28:8-9). Also, regardless of whether the universe began with the big bang, the AFTLOP shows that physical events not caused by humans are caused by God (p. 28:19-21). Additionally, the big bang may not be "miraculous" on Stenger's definition (p. 28:22), but the big bang is, nevertheless, a physical event which, as the AFTLOP implies, is caused by a person, not by a preceding "natural" event (p. 28:23). In fact, Stenger apparently believes that a physical event may be considered supernatural (i.e., caused by God) only if the event is known to be a violation of laws of physics (p. 28:22-30). This belief evidently reveals ignorance of the fact that the results of the AFTLOP suggest that virtually all physical events, whether known to be explained in terms of physical laws or not, are caused by God. Finally, regardless of the number of individuals who embrace the assertion "something can come from nothing" in their cosmological speculations, this assertion remains metaphysically implausible, and remains unjustified, given that uncaused physical events (as shown in the AFTLOP) probably do not exist.

In chapter 2 of part 1 of IPRG, Theodore Schick Jr. assumes vacuum fluctuations in quantum mechanics are uncaused (p. 32:6-20). No evidence is clearly presented to support this assertion. Presumably Schick believes the temporary, apparently spontaneous nature of such fluctuations implies those fluctuations are uncaused (p. 32:16-18). Clearly, the fact that a physical event may appear to be temporary does nothing to establish that it is probably uncaused. Also, the fact that a physical event appears to occur spontaneously does not entail the event is probably uncaused. After all, the hypothesis that God causes vacuum fluctuations to occur in ways that appear spontaneous to humans is not merely a possibly true hypothesis, but a likely true hypothesis, as shown in the AFTLOP.

Schick assumes an actually infinite quantity can physically exist (p. 33:6-7), but this assumption is controversial and in need of support, yet none is provided.

Although examination of the universe itself may not reveal that the creator is all-powerful (p. 33:6-9), it still reveals that the creator is exceedingly more powerful than humans. Likewise, it may not reveal that the creator is omniscient (p. 33:10-14), but it does reveal that the creator's knowledge is exceedingly greater than human knowledge.

If the universe is created by a creator with knowledge, power, and goodness which greatly exceeds that of humans (p. 33:15-35), then no human should assume, without warrant, that he is in a position to determine what such a creator should do, given that the creator could have good, unknown reasons for exercising power such that humans do not know that that exercise of power is good. Likewise, no human should assume, without warrant, that such a creator would create a universe that is supremely desired by all humans (p. 33:34-35).

The possibility that impersonal causes exist (p. 33:36-40) is unlikely, as shown in the AFTLOP. Schick has assumed, without justification, that the existence of impersonal causes is plausible.

Schick examines a common big bang argument for the existence of God. Although this argument is not used in the AFTLOP, a few critical remarks are in order. First, it is assumed that if a physical event is random, then the physical event is uncaused (p. 34:18-22). This assumption is refuted in the AFTLOP. The fact that a physical event occurs randomly (i.e., in accordance with no known law of physics) does not entail the event is uncaused. Second, contra Schick, a cause and effect could occur simultaneously (p. 36:8-9). Third, even if the universe is the result of a vacuum fluctuation (p. 36:24-37:1), the AFTLOP shows that such events are caused by God. Fourth, the AFTLOP shows that the creator is a person with knowledge and power far greater than that of a human (p. 37:2-6). Fifth, Schick assumes it is reasonable to suppose a physical state of the universe could be caused by a prior state of the universe (p. 37:33-35), but does not address the evidence mounted in the AFTLOP against the possibility that a physical event can cause a physical event. Sixth, even if something like Smolin's multiverse hypothesis is true, the AFTLOP shows this still implies the existence of a creator who causes the multiverse to continue to exist and evolve in accordance with the laws of physics which the creator causes. Seventh, it is inconsistent of Schick to assume vacuum fluctuations are uncaused physical events, given Schick's observation that "…our inability to explain a phenomenon may simply be due to our ignorance of the operative laws" (p. 39:1-2). Eighth, Schick assumes that physical events are either caused by God or have a "natural explanation" (p. 39:4-6), but he fails to appreciate that the AFTLOP shows that physical events with "natural explanations" (i.e., explanations in terms of a law of physics) are caused by God. Ninth, appeal to God as the supernatural cause of most physical events *does* increase our understanding in the AFTLOP by identifying the creator as a person who sustains the physical universe (or multiverse, if it exists), in accordance with the laws of physics, with knowledge and power that is far greater than that of humans (p. 39:7-8).

Finally, in the AFTLOP, the theoretical possibility remains open that the God who is shown to exist might actually be an advanced evolved alien(s) of some kind (p. 39:12-21), but Schick's claim that the advanced alien hypothesis is better than the supernatural being (i.e., God) hypothesis is not true. In fact, in the AFTLOP, the term "God" is defined, roughly, as the person(s) who is the cause of the physical events described by the laws of physics. So, if an alien(s) is the cause of the physical events described by the laws of physics, then the alien hypothesis and the supernatural being hypothesis would be identical hypotheses, and Schick would, thus, be wrong in claiming that the alien hypothesis is better.

The alien hypothesis is actually implausible, however, if aliens are taken to be a race of intelligent physical beings whose evolution has occurred in accordance with the laws of physics, since it is unreasonable to suppose that these physical aliens are the cause of the physical laws according to which the aliens evolved. Since these physical laws must have existed prior to the existence of the aliens, the aliens could not be the cause of the physical laws, and, thus, the alien hypothesis should be rejected.

The supernatural being hypothesis, however, does not include the impossible requirement that God cause the laws of physics which have enabled God to evolve to Godhood. Rather, it simply identifies God as the person who causes the physical events which occur in regular patterns known as physical laws. The supernatural being hypothesis is not rendered improbable due to its assumption that nonphysical substances exist (p. 39:18-21), since many kinds of nonphysical substances (abstract entities) exist and are well known. Neither is this hypothesis rendered improbable due to any alleged assumption that this hypothesis entails that natural laws (i.e., laws of physics) are false (p. 39:18-21). In fact, since natural laws are, by definition, a true generalized description of real physical event patterns, existing natural laws are necessarily true. False natural laws can not exist, and the supernatural being hypothesis, if true, would not entail that false natural laws exist. (Also, the fact that existing natural laws are necessarily true does not entail that all physical events are necessarily (or likely) described in terms of natural laws, and does not entail that existing natural laws necessarily exist.) Therefore, the physical alien hypothesis is greatly inferior to the supernatural being hypothesis. Members of the Space Alien Church should convert to the Church of God of the Laws of Physics (p. 39:21-23).

In chapter 3 of part 1 of IPRG, Quentin Smith uses big bang cosmology to argue for the nonexistence of God. Smith assumes Hawking's principle of ignorance in his argument. Hawking's principle of ignorance states that singularities are inherently chaotic and unpredictable (p. 43:9-11). This principle, however, is merely asserted (p. 43:12-18). Proof by assertion is neither persuasive nor compelling. (Smith's claim that the quantity of mass that emerges from a singularity is randomly selected from a range of possibilities (p. 53:23-27) is another grand example of pure speculation without justification.) The fact that classical space-time physical laws presumably break down at a singularity does not necessarily entail that the position and momentum of particles emitted from a singularity are inherently unpredictable. The possibility exists that an unknown law or principle may be discovered in the future which enables human prediction of emissions from singularities. Furthermore, even if singularity emissions can never be predicted by humans, the possibility remains that such emissions could be predicted by other nonhuman persons (say, God). In fact, the AFTLOP establishes that physical events not caused by humans are caused by God. Since both physical singularities and their particle emissions constitute physical events not caused by humans, it follows that both physical singularities and their particle emissions are caused by God. Thus, even if Davies is right in supposing that a singularity is an instance of lawlessness (p. 44:4-6), the singularity and its emission are, nevertheless, physical events caused by God.

Hawking's principle of ignorance entails that even God can not know or predict what will emerge from a singularity. However, since God is the cause of both the singularity and its emissions (as implied by the AFTLOP), and if God knows with certainty every action God will perform, then God causes any singularity that may exist, and God can predict with certainty any particles God may cause to emit from any singularity. Thus, the principle of ignorance must not be asserted unless justification is provided for the assumption that God does not know with certainty every action God will perform. Since such justification has not been provided, the principle of ignorance should be rejected. (It has been assumed that it is intelligible to speak of a singularity as actually physically existing, but this assumption is questionable and will be addressed below.)

Smith's atheistic argument, after eight premises (p. 44-45), concludes that God does not exist. In response, it will first be observed that we may rightly reject premise (2) (p. 44). God might create many universes, only some of which may contain animate creatures. Perhaps God occasionally creates wholly inanimate universes to suit God's own unfathomable purposes. Maybe it's just good fun for God to create inanimate universes every "now and then". Given that God's knowledge, power and goodness far exceed that of any human, it is unclear why Smith assumes he is in a position to know what kind of universe (or universes) God would create, if God exists. Therefore, premise (2) may be rejected.

Premise (4a) (p. 46) may also be rejected. Even if the best possible universe is animate, it is possible that good inanimate universes may also exist. Also, even if God creates the best possible universe (assuming there is a best possible), it is possible that God could also create other good inanimate universes as well. Perhaps there are many possible equally best universes which God could actualize, only some of which are animate. So, even if one of the best possible universe is animate, and even if God is the creator of every equally best possible universe, it is still possible that God could create other good inanimate universes as well. If God creates different kinds of universes for different purposes, then it is possible that God creates some inanimate universes for some good purposes which humans may never know. Therefore, premise (4a) is unsubstantiated.

Premise (7) (p. 45) is grounded in Hawking's principle of ignorance. As discussed above, this principle should be rejected. Premise (7) is, therefore, not established.

Smith claims to know which initial state of the universe God would select, if God created the universe (p. 50:1-6). However, given that God's knowledge, power and goodness far exceed that of any human, it is unclear why Smith assumes he is in a position to know what kind of physical events God would cause, if God exists. Unless Smith justifies that assumption, his inferences grounded in that assumption are unjustified. Smith has not justified that assumption. Therefore, Smith's inferences grounded in that assumption are unjustified. Smith's inferences are, thus, unjustified regarding what kind of initial state of the universe God would select.

Smith asserts (p. 50-53) that the singularity is a physical entity that actually exists. The singularity is interpreted as infinitely compressed mass within a zero-dimensional point that exists for only an instant (p. 53). However, the metaphysical assumption that a zero-volume point can actually physically exist is unreasonable. A zero-volume point necessarily occupies no volume and, thus, assumes no physical location in a region of space-time. Only a nonzero volume can by physically located in a region of space-time. If Smith's assumption that matter exists infinitely compressed in the singularity implies that the singularity is a zero-volume region that occupies a nonzero volume of space-time, then his assumption is evidently self-refuting. If Smith's assumption implies that the singularity is a zero-volume region that occupies zero volume of space-time, then the singularity is not physically located in a region of space-time and, consequently, Smith is seen to be making metaphysical speculations about allegedly physical entities which, in fact, are not *physical* and are not the proper object of investigation by the *physical* sciences. Smith's assumption that matter can exist infinitely compressed into zero volume contradicts the fact that existing physical matter, by definition, must occupy a nonzero volume. If Smith believes that matter can exist when the singularity (a zero-volume region) exists, then Smith is seen to be asserting the existence of nonphysical (and spaceless? timeless?) matter, and this assertion is clearly a metaphysical assumption not properly justified by mere appeal to any purely physical law.

In short, points do not physically exist, but may be mathematically constructed in physical laws which model physical event patterns; physical matter necessarily occupies a nonzero volume of space-time. Therefore, the singularity does not actually exist, and should be rejected as an unjustified metaphysical speculation. The mere fact that cosmologists may widely assume the singularity physically exists lends no support for the assumption that we are not justified in our skepticism regarding the reality of the singularity (p. 53:32-36), especially given the considerations above. Indeed, the thesis that the singularity physically exists is not a thesis in the discipline of the physical sciences, but is a metaphysical (and implausible) thesis which, if true, would entail the existence of nonphysical (i.e., "supernatural") matter/energy, and it is a short jump from supernatural matter/energy to a supernatural God.

Smith considers the possibility that although humans may never know how to predict the outcome of a singularity, God (if God exists) could still make such predictions accurately (p. 54-56). Central to Smith's argument is the assumption that the singularity is unpredictable in principle, which implies that "no natural laws govern the state(s)" (p. 54: 8-10), which, in turn, implies that even God could not compute what emerges from the singularity (p. 54:13-15). In response to this argument it will be noted that the AFTLOP establishes that all physical events not caused by humans are caused by God. Therefore, it is absurd to suppose that God can not predict what will emerge from the singularity, given that God is the person who causes both the singularity and everything that emerges from it! The means by which God knows what will emerge from the singularity need not be God's knowledge of counterfactuals (p. 54:36-37), but may rather be God's knowledge of God's future actions. God need not possess knowledge of what will emerge from a singularity by virtue of God's knowledge of natural laws which describe singularity emissions. Even if there exist no such natural laws, God could know everything about all future singularity emissions by virtue of God's knowledge of God's future actions.

If God exists timelessly "prior" to the first change, and if the first change is God's creation of a physical universe with a singularity, then when God exists timelessly "prior" to creation, God could timelessly know everything about all future singularities and singularity emissions God will cause to exist in the physical universe God knows God will create in time. There need not actually exist an actual world that must serve as a relatum of the similarity relation in some definition of a counterfactual in order for God to know what God will cause to emerge from a singularity in a world God knows God will create (p. 55:19-26).

Smith may assume "God does not know what will emerge from a singularity in a world God will create" only if Smith knows that God does not know God's future actions. Smith has not established that God does not know God's future actions. So, Smith should not assume "God does not know what will emerge from a singularity in a world God will create".

Smith's essay has, therefore, failed to establish that God does not exist, and has not shown that the universe exists without cause and without explanation (p. 56:36-57:1). Also, given the evident existence of our universe, it is clear that it is false that there is possibly no universe (p. 57:1-3). In addition, the AFTLOP shows that God's causal activity is the reason for which our universe exists. Our experience of being profoundly astonished by the actual existence of our universe may, therefore, be grounded in the knowledge that God is the sustaining cause of the continuing existence of the universe.

In chapter 4 of part 1 of IPRG, Quentin Smith provides an atheistic interpretation of the Big Bang and argues that God's nonexistence is entailed by Big Bang cosmology. He begins by discussing Hawking's principle of ignorance. Smith's support of this principle is evidently based on comments such as those he quotes from Stephen Hawking and Paul Davies. The Hawking quote (p. 63:29-34) claims that since known physical laws break down at a singularity, singularity emissions can not be predicted. In response, it should be observed that even if every known physical law breaks down at a singularity, it does not follow that singularity emissions can not be predicted. Perhaps an unknown physical law of some kind will be discovered in the future. Perhaps laws describing singularity emissions are not knowable by humans, but are knowable by other knowledgeable persons (e.g., God). The assumption that singularities are inherently unpredictable and, thus, can be described by no law (p. 63: 24-27) is entirely unsupported by the Hawking quote. The fact that classical physical laws may break down at a singularity does not entail that non-classical laws can not exist which enable prediction of singularity emissions. The Hawking quote does not establish what is claimed, there, by Hawking. So, Smith's unjustified acceptance of Hawking's principle is evidently grounded, in part, in Hawking's unjustified acceptance of the principle. Perhaps Hawking has some other reason for accepting the principle, but Smith does not cite the reason.

Smith also cites a Paul Davies quotation as evidence that a singularity is an entity which is in a state of lawlessness (p. 64:2-6). The quote assumes both that a singularity is an instance of lawlessness, and that it is a case in which something comes from nothing. In response, observe that alleged lawlessness of the singularity is, once again, merely assumed. Proof by assertion is not very compelling! No real evidence is provided. The fact that we may not know any laws describing singularities does not require that no such laws can exist. The assumption that the Big Bang universe is an instance of an uncaused event (in which something comes from the nothingness of a singularity) is also simply assumed in the Davies quote. Once again, proof by assertion is hardly compelling! So, Smith evidently embraces Hawking's principle of ignorance, in part, on the basis of an unjustified assertion made by Davies. Perhaps Davies or Smith have other reasons for accepting the principle, but no other reasons are provided.

Smith apparently believes that prediction of singularity emissions can be made only through knowledge of a law describing singularities. This assumption is, itself, unjustified. It is possible that God could predict singularity emissions by simply knowing what events God will cause in the future. God's knowledge of future physical events need not be grounded in the knowledge of physical laws. After all, the AFTLOP establishes that physical events not caused by humans are caused by God. Furthermore, physical laws not caused by humans are simply descriptions of physical event patterns caused by God. Any physical event not described (or even describable) by a physical law, and not caused by a human, is also caused by God, as shown in the AFTLOP. Therefore, God's knowledge of singularity emissions can be predicted by God by virtue of God's knowledge of the future actions God will perform. Unless Smith establishes that God can not have such knowledge, Hawking's principle of ignorance remains unjustified. Smith's proof by repeated assertion does not accomplish his desired task.

Smith provides a cosmological argument for God's nonexistence. The argument consists of four premises (p. 64: 10-20). Since premise (3) is grounded in Hawking's principle of ignorance, and since acceptance of that principle is shown above to be unjustified, Smith's atheistic cosmological argument is unsound.

Smith claims premise (4) of his argument is inconsistent with the claim that God caused the first state of the universe (p. 64:21-25). But, since (4) is entailed by (1)-(3), and since (3) has been shown to be unjustified, it follows that (4) is also unjustified.

Smith believes that if God is omnibenevolent and creates a universe, then the universe will be animate so that God can exercise his benevolence towards the created animate beings (p. 65:14-21). Smith claims it would be an evil act of God to create an inanimate world (p. 65:40-41). In response, it should first be observed that if God exists, and if God has exceedingly greater knowledge, power, and wisdom than man, then it is not clear why Smith supposes he knows what God would or would not do in some hypothetical case. An omnibenevolent God could have unknown good reasons for performing only good actions, where each of those actions may not appear, at all times, to be obviously good to each of God's created beings.

Smith presumably grants that if God could ensure that a created multiverse (universe of universes) would eventually evolve into an animate state, then God's creation of that multiverse is consistent with God's omnibenevolence. Given this assumption, there would then be nothing evil about God creating a lifeless evolving multiverse, so long as at least one of the universes in the multiverse evolves into an animate state. But, given an evolving multiverse comprised of endlessly forming universes, each with different physical properties, the probability is high that eventually a universe will form that evolves into an animate state. Thus, God's creation of such an evolving multiverse would not be inconsistent with God's omnibenevolence.

If Smith objects that the multiverse is only good if each universe within the multiverse evolves into an animate state, then Smith might as well object that our universe is evil because it contains inanimate rocks. After all, God could have created animate rocks if God so desired! Of course, we are not justified in supposing that our universe is evil because it contains some inanimate entities. Therefore, a multiverse would also not be evil if some of its universes were inanimate.

Also, God could create a universe which is not guaranteed to evolve by natural processes into an animate state, with the plan of later intervening in the universe miraculously to bring about the existence of animate beings. This would also be consistent with the omnibenevolence of God.

Smith believes an animate universe is better than an inanimate one, but why should we suppose an omnibenevolent God would not create both? God could create animate universes to express omnibenevolence to his created animate creatures, and God could create inanimate universes just for fun! Maybe God has created beautiful inanimate universes for the purpose of revealing God's creativity to his animate creatures at some point in the future. We can only wildly speculate what an omnipotent, omniscient, omnibenevolent God might do, especially given our relatively inferior knowledge. Therefore, Smith is hardly justified in claiming to know what such a God would do (p. 66:24-26).

Smith claims it is inefficient of God to create a universe from an unpredictable singularity, since immediately following the singularity emissions, God must intervene in the ensuing physical events to ultimately achieve an animate universe (p. 67:10-12). Smith also believes that inefficiency is of negative aesthetic value (p. 69:26-28), but offers no justification for this belief. Thus, the assertion is unjustified that God's inefficiency would be of negative aesthetic value. Furthermore, if God's method of creation precisely accomplishes God's intended purposes, then God's creation of the universe would not be inefficient, but would be an efficient accomplishment of precisely what God intended to do. Unless Smith shows that God's method of creation of the universe has not precisely accomplished God's intended purposes, then Smith is unjustified in assuming that God's method of creation is inefficient.

Smith then presents an argument that allegedly implies that God does not exist (p. 69:36-70:9). In response, note that the argument assumes that God does not have the goal of creating both S and S'. If God has the goal of creating both as part of a multiverse God creates and sustains, then it is not irrational of God to create that multiverse. Since Smith has not shown that God does not have the goal of creating both, Smith has not shown that God is irrational. More generally, Smith has simply assumed God's goals are not advanced by creating S'. Thus, Smith has shown neither that God is irrational nor that God does not exist.

Smith grants that it is logically possible that God has unknown reasons for creating S', but claims absence of evidence of such reasons entails such reasons probably do not exist (p. 70:15-18). In response, observe that Smith has failed to show why he would probably know God's reasons for creating S', if God created S'. God could have reasons (unknown to Smith) for creating S', and Smith has failed to show why his lack of knowledge of such reasons should be considered justification for the belief that such reasons probably do not exist. Absence of evidence is not necessarily evidence of absence. One's ignorance of evidence for the truth of a proposition does not imply the proposition is false. Unless Smith has other unstated reasons for rejecting the possibility that God has unknown reasons for creating S', it seems Smith is employing the *argument from ignorance* fallacy. Furthermore, the AFTLOP establishes that physical events not caused by a human are caused by God. So, regardless of whether S or S' describes the initial physical state of the universe, that initial state would be a physical event caused by God. Also, the evolution of an animate universe by "random chance and improbable occurrences" may be identified as the result of physical events caused by God (p. 70:26-29), as implied by the AFTLOP. This, in turn, would contradict Smith's inference that God does not exist (p. 70:8-9, p. 70:26-29), implying that Smith's argument is unsound.

Smith makes some additional comments that deserve a response (p. 70:33-40). Smith objects that a rational God would not create a universe that requires God's divine interference with natural tendencies of physical events. In response, note that both natural tendencies of physical events and God's "divine intereference" with physical events *are* God's creative activity, so both are simply descriptions of different sets of physical events caused by God. The claim that God is inefficient is, again, made without justification. Also, even if God were inefficient, it would not follow either that God is irrational or nonexistent, since Smith again fails to justify the claim that such inefficiency would be aesthetically disvaluable. Therefore, God's divine interventions have not been shown to be inconsistent with the God of classical theism.

Smith claims that the singularity actually exists (p. 71:16), but not in the space-time continuum (p. 71:19-23). However, if an object does not exist in that continuum, then it is not physical. It follows that Smith believes that the singularity is an actually existing nonphysical entity. If Smith is open to the existence of such nonphysical entities, then he ought to be open to the existence of other kinds of nonphysical entities for which we have evidence (e.g., God, see the presentation of the AFTLOP in chapter 1 and my fine-tuning arguments in chapter 2).

Smith claims that physicists treat the singularity as if it is real, and he believes this reality follows from the Hawking-Penrose singularity theorems; he also claims there is no reason to deny that the singularity's existence is real (p. 72:5-8). In response, the fact that some physicists may treat the singularity as if it is real does not entail that the singularity is probably real. Furthermore, if a mathematical model accurately represents some physical phenomena, it does not follow that all features of that model must depict actually existing features of physical reality. For example, if time is continuous (and Smith is evidently open to this possibility (p. 68)), then temporal instants do not actually physically exist, but only exist in the abstraction of the mathematical models used to represent physical change. Thus, the fact that mathematical models with spatial points, temporal instants, and pointlike objects can do a fine job of modeling physical reality does not entail that spatial points, temporal instants, and pointlike objects actually exist. Atheist physicist Victor Stenger understands this concept and discusses it in a recent book.[1]

Features of physical models need not be taken to be actually real. Thus, the fact that Special and General Relativity represent "spacetime as a continuum of instantaneous spatial points" (p. 71:28-30) does not entail that temporal and spatial points actually exist. Indeed, the very concept of a continuum of points is contradictory. A continuum is smooth; points are discrete. Change occurs either smoothly/continuously or (exclusive disjunction) in discrete jumps from one point of existence to the next. Mathematical physics can accurately model change regardless of whether change occurs continuously or discretely, and the success of a physical model in describing observables may be useful in many ways, but that success does not solve the problem of determining whether physical change occurs continuously or discretely. Smith is, therefore, seen to be applying, without justification, ontological significance to discrete/pointlike features of mathematical physical models when claiming that points in spacetime models are actual physical events (p. 71:30-72:3).

Smith assumes that denial of the existence of physical points entails that all physical events are equivalent to nothing (p. 72:3-5). This view is mistaken, however, since it has been assumed that a physical event must be a physical state at a point. Physical events may be understood as an element of change in a continuously changing physical state. Physical events need not be considered pointlike, but may be understood as occupying an element of a spacetime region that may be very large or very small, but nonzero. Real spacetime may be viewed as continuous, even though mathematical models can describe spacetime in a more discrete fashion, referring to spatial points, temporal instants, and pointlike objects. Thus, the reality of the singularity may be denied without denying the existence of physical events, and the problem of unpredictability does not remain (p. 73:15-19).

Smith believes that the creation of an unpredictable singularity would be inconsistent with the rational action of the God of classical theism. This claim of inconsistency is grounded in the assumption that singularity emissions are, in fact, unpredictable, even by God. Smith believes this unpredictability problem "would be solved if counterfactuals of singularities were true logically prior to creation" (p. 73:21-22). In response to this issue, observe that the so-called "unpredictability problem" is, itself, grounded in the assumption of the validity of Hawking's principle of ignorance. This principle was earlier shown to be accepted without warrant. Therefore, given the lack of warrant for the belief that Hawking's principle of ignorance applies to singularities, Smith has not even established that there is an unpredictability problem. Theists need not be concerned, here, about such issues as the proper analysis of counterfactuals, the best theory of possible world semantics, the plausibility of truth-maker theory, and which counterfactuals as truth-bearers must have truth-makers. Furthermore, God's knowledge of singularity emissions need not be possessed by virtue of God's knowledge of counterfactuals of singularities. Since the AFTLOP establishes that physical events such as singularity emissions are caused by God, God can know logically prior to creation what will be emitted from singularities simply by virtue of God's knowledge of God's future causal activity. Unless Smith demonstrates that God can not know what physical events God will cause in the future, then the problem of unpredictability has not even been proven to be a problem.

Smith argues that, given certain assumptions, the atheistic hypothesis is simpler than the theistic hypothesis (p. 75:13-76:29). The assumptions, however, are not justified. First, Swinburne's assumption (p. 75:25) is arguably false, given that both simple and complex mathematical truths exist as unexplained (i.e., uncaused) abstract entities, and both are equally likely to exist as unexplained, since all mathematical truths are necessary and uncaused. Second, the atheistic hypothesis entails that an uncaused singularity can exist (p. 76:7-12), but the claim that points (including singularities) can physically exist is unjustified, given that continuously changing physical entities can fully constitute the nature of physical reality without need of reference to points or pointlike objects that may appear in the abstraction of mathematical physical models. Third, it is assumed that the singularity is physical (p. 76:20-24), but a zero volume region is arguably either nonexistent or nonphysical, rendering the atheistic hypothesis less simple. Additionally, the atheistic hypothesis contains the assumption that the four-dimensional physical universe began (i.e., is caused) from "something physical", yet, as shown in the AFTLOP, we have no evidence that any physical event is caused by either another physical event or anything else other than the free action of a person's power to cause a physical event. Therefore, Smith has failed to show that the atheistic hypothesis is simpler than the theistic hypothesis.

Smith considers the question of whether a Big Bang universe is metaphysically necessary (p. 76:30-79:30). Smith presents an argument form which assumes that a physical property can be the cause of other physical properties (p. 78:21-23, p. 78:35-37). In response, it will be emphasized that we have no evidence that any physical event is the cause of a physical event (see discussion of the AFTLOP in chapter 1). Therefore, premise (6) (p. 79:2-3) is not established by Smith's argument.

Smith assumes it would be "irrational and incompetent" (p. 79:22-27) of God to create a universe that requires divine interventions in order to ensure animate states eventually occur. In response, note that Smith does not explicitly state, here, why such divine interventions would imply God would be irrational and incompetent. If Smith has in mind reasons mentioned earlier, such as alleged irrationality, inefficiency, negative aesthetic value, etc., then his argument here is unjustified, as we have previously shown those putative reasons to be, themselves, unjustified. Finally, Smith assumes he knows what actions a rational, omniscient, omnipotent, omnibenevolent God would perform. However, given that Smith's knowledge would be profoundly inferior to that of God (if God exists), Smith is seen to have assumed, without warrant, that he is in a position to know that God does not both exist and have reasons (unknown to Smith) for rationally creating a universe that requires divine interventions in order to ensure animate states eventually occur. Consequently, we have shown that Smith's Big Bang cosmological argument for God's nonexistence is not defended against my objections.

In chapter 5 of part 1 of IPRG, Quentin Smith presents a brief critique of the Kalam Cosmological Argument defended by William Lane Craig. Although the AFTLOP does not depend on the soundness of Craig's argument, it will be shown that the AFTLOP does entail premise (1) (p. 82:11). Smith claims there is no evidence that premise (1) is true (p. 83:38-84:1), and he claims "we have no observation of things coming into existence" (p. 84:4). In response, it is evident that we do observe things coming into existence. For example, on Earth, lightning bolts come into existence on a daily basis. Smith might object that the coming into existence of a lightning bolt is not the coming into existence of material from nothingness, but is simply the transformation of matter/energy from one form or state into another form or state. Even granting this objection, however, the fact remains that a lightning bolt is the coming into existence of a new form or state of matter/energy. We need not assume that the beginning of existence in premise (1) must be the coming into existence of matter from nothingness, as Smith evidently supposes (p. 84:11-12). Rather, the beginning of existence in premise (1) may simply refer to the beginning of existence of a material state, and 'cause' in premise (1) need not necessarily refer to the creation of physical matter from nothingness, but may simply refer to the generation, production, or bringing about of a new material state by an unspecified entity. The state is new in the sense that its beginning of existence occurs in some spatial region during a temporal interval T, where that state did not exist in that spatial region during an immediately prior temporal interval of unspecified length. Therefore, any lack of observations of material being created from nothingness does not count as evidence against premise (1). Furthermore, all physical events do constitute physical beginnings of existence, and the AFTLOP establishes that physical events are caused only by persons. This implies that all physical beginnings of existence are indeed caused, confirming premise (1).

Premise (1) is now seen to be not a baseless assumption (as Smith claims), but an empirical generalization grounded in an analysis of the nature of physical events. Or at least, premise (1) is justified insofar as it refers to beginnings of existence of physical entities or states, as the beginning of existence of nonphysical entities or states is an altogether different category of beginnings of existence. It may be possible to argue successfully that beginnings of existence of nonphysical entities or states are also caused, but such arguments lie outside the scope of the present analysis.

Smith also claims that there do not exist observations of people who have come into existence (p. 84:4-5). In response, if Smith believes presently existing people have not come into existence, then it follows that presently existing people have always existed, or at least, have existed since the time at which the material which comprises their physical bodies was emitted in some primal form from a singularity. Surely presently existing human persons on Earth have not existed as persons for more than perhaps 120 or so years as an upper limit, while the alleged singularity emissions occurred many billions of years ago. Therefore, it must be incorrect to claim that presently existing human persons on Earth have not come into existence.

If the objection is raised that the coming into existence of humans on Earth does occur, but is not directly observed, then we may respond by simply noting that even if it is true that the coming into existence of persons on Earth is not directly observed, the fact of the coming into existence of persons with physical bodies on Earth counts as evidence of the beginning of existence of a physical entity (i.e., a person's physical body). This beginning of existence of a physical human body, in turn, constitutes a physical event, and the AFTLOP establishes that such events are caused by persons. Thus, such events are caused, confirming premise (1).

Smith claims that the wave function law of the universe is a scientific law confirmed by observational evidence which "tells us that the universe began without being caused" (p. 84:36-37). This law entails that a small timeless uncaused four-dimensional hypersphere exploded into our presently existing universe (p. 85:4-11). In response, if a four-dimensional hypersphere is timeless, then presumably time must not be one of the four dimensions, and all four dimensions which comprise the hypersphere must be spatial dimensions. However, since no justification is provided for the belief that there exists a fourth spatial dimension in the hypersphere, the wave function law is seen to be assumed without justification.

Smith's belief that the hypersphere is in need of no cause might be grounded in the assumption that since only beginnings of existence can be caused, timelessly existing entities can not be caused because they have no beginning of existence. In response, first note that no evidence for the timeless existence of the hypersphere is provided. The fact that the timeless existence of a hypersphere may be a feature of a physical event mathematical model that is confirmed by physical observations does not necessarily (or even probably) entail either that such a hypersphere is connected to our expanding universe or that any other feature of that model actually corresponds to a physically existing state of affairs in our universe. As mentioned earlier, features of physical models need not be taken to be actually real, even if those models are useful for accurate modeling of physical event patterns.[2] Thus, the fact that Special and General Relativity represent "spacetime as a continuum of instantaneous spatial points" (p. 71:28-30) does not entail that temporal and spatial points actually exist. Likewise, the fact that a wave function law that accurately models physical events in the universe includes the hypothesized existence of a timeless uncaused hypersphere does not entail the hypersphere is actually a real component of the history of the physical universe. In fact, a timelessly existing entity is arguably nonphysical and, as such, is not properly the object of the laws of physics, since the laws of physics describe regular patterns of *physical* events, not nonphysical events. The claim that a timeless uncaused nonphysical entity exists may not be justified by noting the accurate correspondence between predictions of a mathematical physical model and physically observed events, but may be justified by appeal to metaphysical reasoning which establishes a rational basis for belief in the nonphysical existence claim. Since no such justified metaphysical reasoning is provided, the claim that the universe is connected to a timeless uncaused nonphysical hypersphere stands unjustified. Uncaused events are not proven to exist by merely asserting that a scientific law confirmed by observational evidence obtains, since physical laws simply describe physical event patterns, but do not assert metaphysically speculative claims such as "uncaused physical events transpire in a particular way".

It may be claimed that the hypersphere may be understood as a physical entity by virtue of its small, but nonzero, spatial size, and, therefore, the justification for belief that the wave function law accurately describes observed physical events entails that the hypersphere feature of that law is also real. In response, as mentioned previously, features of physical models need not be taken to be actually real, even if those models are useful for accurate modeling of physical event patterns. Thus, the timelessly existing hypersphere feature of the wave function law need not be taken to be actually real. We may further respond that the hypersphere, even if spatial, is nevertheless nonphysical due to its timeless nature. Therefore, the goal of avoiding the requirement that the existence of the hypersphere be justified by appropriate and relevant metaphysical reasoning has not been achieved.

Smith claims that the timeless hypersphere "no more needs a cause than the timeless god of theism" (p. 85:7-8). This suggests that God, not a timelessly existing hypersphere, may instead be taken to be the possible cause of the beginning of the universe. However, Smith evidently rejects the possibility that God (rather than the hypersphere in the wave function law) is the correct explanation of the origin of the universe by reasoning as follows. He claims the wave function law describes the universe as coming into existence "because of its natural, mathematical properties" (p. 85:15-17). In response, if the mathematical properties of the existing universe are identified as the cause of the beginning of existence of the existing universe, then an existing effect can exist logically (if not also temporally) prior to its cause. However, an effect can not exist prior to its cause. Therefore, the mathematical properties of the existing universe may not be identified as the cause of the beginning of existence of the existing universe. Furthermore, since the AFTLOP establishes that physical laws describe physical events caused by God, the physical events described by the wave function law are also caused by God, which entails that Smith is incorrect in supposing that God is not the creator of the universe. In addition, on theism, God is justifiably identified as the sustaining cause of the continuing existence of physical entities which continue to change in accordance with the laws of physics, whereas Smith's unjustified atheistic version of a wave function law does not identify the cause of the continuing existence of the physical entities described by the law. The theistic hypothesis has greater explanatory power. Also, since mathematical properties of existing entities necessarily exist, Smith is seen to be claiming that necessarily existing properties explain the coming into existence of the universe, which would appear to entail that the coming into existence of the universe is necessary. However, a state of complete nothingness (or, rather, a permanent and complete absence of any physical state of affairs whatsoever) is a conceivable logical possibility and, thus, it can not be true that any physical state is necessary, which implies that the coming into existence of the universe can not be necessary after all. It must be incorrect to assume mathematical properties explain the coming into existence of the universe.

Smith also argues that God can not be the cause of the coming into existence of the universe because the wave function law entails that there is a 95% probability the universe would come into existence, whereas the probability would be 100% if an omnipotent God is the cause of the coming into existence of the universe (p. 85:12-21). In response, there is simply no contradiction in the claim that God causes a universe to come into existence, where the probability of the coming into existence of that universe is perceived by humans to be 95% based on the limited information available to humans. A human with limited knowledge could know that a universe is 95% likely, yet God could know it is 100% likely, since God could know with certainty what actions God will perform in the future. Smith has not explained why we should suppose random physical events are not caused by God to generate humanly-perceived probabilities that God will cause particular physical events. Since the AFTLOP establishes that random physical events are caused by a person, the random coming into existence of the universe in accordance with a wave function law would be caused by a person (i.e., God). So, even if the wave function law is the best physical model of observed physical events, God is, nevertheless, properly identified as the cause of those physical events. Smith's atheistic conclusion (p. 85:22-23) is, therefore, unwarranted.

In chapter 6 of part 1 of IPRG, Quentin Smith argues that Stephen Hawking's quantum cosmological wave function law is inconsistent with classical theism. Classical theism is defined such that God is the cause of any existing universe in any possible world (p. 89:2-18). It is argued that the wave function law, if true, entails that the probability of the universe beginning to exist is less than 1, whereas that probability is equal to 1 on classical theism (p. 88:14-16). In response, note that it is assumed that the wave function law gives the probability "for the Universe to appear from nothing" (p. 87:20-23). This assumption entails that uncaused physical events are plausible, and it is this very assumption that remains unjustified. Since the AFTLOP establishes that uncaused physical events probably do not exist, we may reject the feature of the wave function law that assumes uncaused physical events probably exist. In addition, the fact that a mathematical model of physical events may be confirmed by observational evidence does not entail that unjustified metaphysical assumptions attached to that model are probably also consequently confirmed. Specifically, we need not suppose that observational evidence (p. 91:37-92:4) that confirms Hawking's wave function model of physical changes in the universe probably entails the unjustified metaphysical assumption that uncaused physical events probably exist (p. 92:5). We have, thus, stopped this atheological cosmological argument dead in its tracks, for before it can even get off the ground, the implausible assumption must be made that uncaused physical events probably exist. Furthermore, after this unjustified assumption is removed from physical models, the models simply reduce to a mathematical description of regular physical event patterns, and there is evidence (see the AFTLOP) that most such patterns are caused by God. As mentioned earlier, since the AFTLOP establishes that random physical events are caused by a person, the random coming into existence of the universe in accordance with a wave function law would be caused by a person (i.e., God).

Additionally, as mentioned earlier, Smith has not explained why we should suppose random physical events are not caused by God to generate humanly-perceived probabilities that God will cause particular physical events. God could cause quantum events to occur such that humans can only probabilistically determine future possible physical events from prior physical states, yet God could be the sole cause of each such event. Thus, there could exist the humanly-perceived probability of 95% that God would cause quantum event Q at time T, yet God would always have known with 100% certainty that God would cause Q at T. It is incorrect, therefore, to suppose probabilistic quantum events are inconsistent with God's continuous causation of physical events (p. 90:9-15).

Smith identifies some causal versions of nonclassical theism, in which God is the originating and sustaining cause of the universe, but is not the cause of every universe in every possible world (p. 90:25-92:13). He then argues that if God desires to cause our universe to begin to exist, then God has no reason for actualizing the wave function law that makes it 95% probable that our universe would begin to exist uncaused (p. 91:26-35). In response, since the AFTLOP establishes that physical events not caused by a human are probably caused by God, Smith is seen to be mistaken in supposing that the obtaining of the wave function law entails that uncaused physical events probably exist. We may not claim God is irrational for actualizing a law that makes uncaused events probable, since all laws of physics are descriptions of physical event patterns caused by a person (i.e., God). If the wave function law entails the existence of uncaused physical events, then that law may be rejected, given the absence of a rational basis for the belief that uncaused physical events exist. If the wave function law is freed from its unnecessary and unjustified metaphysical attachment (i.e., the supposition that a universe could begin to exist uncaused), then the law is simply a description of physical event patterns caused by God. Furthermore, the knowledge possessed by God is immensely superior to that of a human, as established in the AFTLOP. Therefore, Smith has not established why he (a finite being with limited knowledge) should suppose that God would enable Smith to know God's reasons for performing the actions God performs.

Smith argues that it would not be good of God, but rather deceptive of God to permit the human perception that the universe began to exist uncaused in accordance with the wave function law, if God actually caused the universe to begin to exist (p. 91:36-92:13). Smith's position is unwarranted for a number of reasons. First, Smith has not clearly defined the term "good", nor has he clearly shown how God's actions are inconsistent with that definition. Second, Smith has not shown why we should suppose he is in a position to know which of God's actions are good, given that God's knowledge is immensely superior to Smith's knowledge. Third, all of Smith's views have not remained constant over time, and if Smith discovers in the future that his perceptions relevant to wave function laws have been false, then it is far from clear whether the period of inaccurate perceptions earlier in Smith's life would not have served good purposes. Fourth, given the limited nature of human knowledge and the general complexity of reality, it is doubtful that any human on Earth possesses only and always true perceptions, and this fact entails neither that God is not good nor that "the quintessentially human project of rational scientific inquiry" is defeated (p. 92:8-9). Fifth, it does not appear that God created the universe with the appearance of it beginning to exist uncaused, so rather than infer God is not good, we may infer Smith's understanding is incorrect.

Smith has provided an account of both classical and nonclassical versions of causal and acausal theism as they relate to the wave function law. Perhaps Smith's most fundamental mistake is his view that the obtaining of the wave function law does not entail that some mind wills that the law obtain (p. 92:21-22). This view reveals a serious misunderstanding of the nature of physical laws and physical event causation. Therefore, Smith's account fails to justify his conclusion that the wave function alone "is responsible for the existence of the universe" (p. 92:33-34).

In chapter 7 of part 1 of IPRG, Quentin Smith explains why he believes quantum cosmological theories imply God does not exist (p. 95:11-13). Smith begins with an explanation of why he believes the probability amplitude derived from the wave function is an unconditional probability that is not conditional upon the existence or action of a person (p. 96:6-27). This explanation entails the unsupported assertion that uncaused physical events exist, and it is precisely this assertion that is strongly disconfirmed by the AFTLOP. Proof by assertion is not compelling, especially given evidence to the contrary. To support his claim, Smith needs to explain why this mathematical description of all possible four-dimensional finite spacetimes entails that a universe can begin to exist uncaused. Smith needs to explain why we should suppose physical events can occur uncaused, given the evidence (see the AFTLOP) that physical events are caused by persons. The mere mathematical identification of all physical possibilities does not entail that physical events are not caused by a person. Furthermore, even if the probability of every subsequent state of the universe can be derived from the initial three-geometry S (p. 95:30-32), this does not entail that any subsequent state is caused by any prior state. As explained in the AFTLOP, the mere existence of a correlation between prior and subsequent physical events does not entail that any prior physical event actually caused any subsequent physical event.

Smith claims the probability amplitude derived from the wave function is inconsistent with classical theism, since classical theism entails that the existence of the universe is dependent on the actions of a person (i.e., God). He assumes that since the probability amplitude calculation does not "sum over anything supernatural" (p. 97:5-8), the probability is unconditional and entails that a universe can exist uncaused. In response, observe that the probability *is* conditional in that it is assumed that physical events can exist. After all, if no physical event could possibly exist, then the nonzero "unconditional" probability calculation of an uncaused physical universe is necessarily an incorrect calculation, since the probability (given the impossibility of physical events) of a physical universe could not possibly be nonzero. Now that we have established that the allegedly unconditional probability is, in fact, conditional upon the possibility of physical events, it is seen that the calculation does not rule out the possibility that physical events are caused by a person. Indeed, the AFTLOP establishes that physical events not caused by a human are caused by God. Therefore, since the beginning of the universe was surely not caused by a human, we may infer that it was caused by God, Hartle-Hawking probability calculations notwithstanding.

Smith fails to understand both the conditional nature of the probability amplitude calculations and the personal nature of physical event causation. The inconsistency between classical theism and the wave function, therefore, exists only in his misunderstanding, not in reality (p. 97:11-13). There is not a 99% chance that a universe begin to exist uncaused, given that the probability calculation is conditional upon the possibility that physical events can exist, and given that the AFTLOP has established that the possibility of physical events is actualized by the action of persons (p. 97:14-19, 30-32).

Smith claims that the 99% probability of a Hartle-Hawking universe is inconsistent with the fact that there is a 100% probability of a Hartle-Hawking universe, given God's knowledge that God will cause a Hartle-Hawking universe to exist (p. 97:9-11, 36-38). In response, even if it is true that the probability of a Hartle-Hawking universe is 99%, we have shown that that probability is conditional upon the possibility of the existence of physical events, where that possibility is actualized by the action of persons. Therefore, the 99% probability of God causing a Hartle-Hawking universe may be viewed as being based on human perception of the nature of physical and mathematical reality, whereas the 100% probability of God causing a Hartle-Hawking universe is grounded in God's knowledge of the actions God will perform. The differing values of these probabilities do not establish a contradiction between classical theism and the wave function law, since there is no contradiction in the idea that physical events are caused by God to generate humanly-perceived probabilities that God will cause particular physical events, where God knows with 100% certainty the physical events God will cause. Thus, Smith's atheistic conclusion (p. 98:4-5) is unjustified.

Smith again claims that the Hartle-Hawking probability is unconditional (p. 99:39-100:2). However, as discussed earlier, the probability is, in fact, conditional upon the possibility of existing physical events, where that possibility is actualized by the action of persons. So, if theism and quantum gravity cosmology are inconsistent (p. 100:6-102:5), and if it is quantum gravity cosmology that is grounded in an unjustified interpretation of the Hartle-Hawking probability, then we may reject the Hartle-Hawking interpretation and favor the theistic interpretation, only the latter of which is consistent with the results established in the AFTLOP.

Smith then expresses the view that theistic conservation (causation) of successive physical states of the universe entails that science is false (p. 102:6-105:34). The conjunction of propositions 3a and 4a (p. 102:26-30) implies that Smith considers a cause to be a sufficient condition. However, if C is a sufficient condition for E, this does not entail that C is the cause of E. It is possible that some entity G always causes events of type C to precede events of type E such that knowledge of C is sufficient to accurately predict that E will follow, yet C is never the cause of E. Causes are not sufficient conditions. Rather, a cause brings about or produces its effect. Therefore, Smith's argument (p. 102:18-30) is unsound, being grounded in a mistaken understanding of causation.

Smith concludes that theism implies that natural laws (e.g., the Hartle-Hawking quantum cosmological law) are false, but this conclusion is based on the unjustified assumption that natural laws cause the physical event patterns they describe. Natural laws are simply descriptions of regular physical event patterns. There is no good reason to suppose natural laws somehow cause the physical event patterns they describe. Thus, natural laws may be understood as descriptions of regular physical event patterns caused by a person (i.e., God). This understanding does not entail that science is false, but only that naturalistic science is false. If naturalistic science entails that natural laws cause the physical event patterns they describe, and if theistic science entails that natural laws describe physical event patterns caused by God, then Smith's conclusion "science is false" may be interpreted as meaning that naturalistic science if false. We need not conclude that theistic science is false, especially since the conclusions of the AFTLOP strongly suggest it is true.

Smith then claims that if probabilistic quantum effects are caused by God, then natural laws describing probabilities of subsequent physical states (given prior physical states) never yield the correct probabilities, since God may never cause quantum event patterns to occur in precisely the ways predicted by the natural laws (p. 103:15-41). In response, although on theism the correct probabilities may not be exactly yielded, the probabilities may, nevertheless, be approximately true and practically useful. Theists need not reject quantum mechanics outright, but merely leave open the possibility that God may occasionally cause quantum effects in ways not predicted by the laws of quantum mechanics. Also, if God generally causes quantum effects in predictable ways that may be probabilistically determined from an earlier 3-space and the background knowledge of the wave function, then Smith's assumption that e and b are irrelevant conditions of p(h) is unwarranted (p. 103:29-41).

Smith is wrong, therefore, in supposing that theists ought to be forthright in their view that "science is false and religion is true" (p. 104:7-9), since theists may rather assert that theistic science and religion are both true. Smith's suggestion that theists are "beyond the pale of academic respectability" (p. 104:7-9) is not taken seriously, given that Smith is surely aware that nothing short of a religious revival has occurred amongst professional philosophers of religion over the past few decades, many of whom are of the highest intellectual caliber. Furthermore, "academic respectability" may be defined in terms of the general consensus amongst academics, and there is no reason to suppose that the prevailing view amongst academics is always best. So, even if theists were not in the academic mainstream, this fact would not entail theism is false. Truth is not determined by vote.

Smith's conclusion that Alston is mistaken is, in a sense, true (p. 104:12-13). If Alston is taken to believe: (1) classical deterministic natural laws describe a closed system in which those laws (not God) cause the physical event patterns they describe; and (2) quantum mechanical probabilistic laws describe physical events which may be caused by God, then Alston has erroneously assumed there exists a rational basis for supposing that natural laws actually cause the events they describe. (I'm not sure whether Alston actually takes this position.) Both classical deterministic laws and quantum probabilistic laws are descriptions of regular physical event patterns, and these laws are reasonably taken to be caused by God, as shown in the AFTLOP. So, both quantum mechanics and classical mechanics may be viewed as descriptions of regular physical event patterns caused by God.

Smith claims that if theism is true, then quantum mechanical laws are false, since the laws provide calculations based on prior physical states, not on God's beliefs, actions, intentions, etc. Also, Smith claims that if quantum mechanical laws are true, then God can not be the cause of physical events described by those laws, since the laws provide calculations based on prior physical states, not on God's beliefs, actions, intentions, etc. (p. 104:20-24). In response, observe that Smith has assumed, without justification, that regular physical event patterns are not, themselves, God's action in the world. The AFTLOP establishes that physical event patterns are God's action in the world. If God causes quantum effects to occur in sufficiently regular patterns such that probabilistic relationships between prior and subsequent physical states are approximately accurate and practically useful, then theists may accept that quantum mechanical laws are generally correct, knowing that God may occasionally cause quantum effects in ways not predicted by the laws. On this interpretation, both quantum mechanics and theism may be true.

Smith claims that quantum cosmological laws entail that "there are no other possible outside influences" (p. 104:33-34), meaning that if these laws are true, then God could not possibly be the cause of the physical events described by the laws. Needless to say, this interpretation of quantum cosmology is loaded with the unjustified metaphysical assumption that nonphysical (i.e., supernatural) entities can not both exist and cause effects in the physical world. What is the rational basis for this assumption? Given the AFTLOP, it is difficult to imagine what it might be. Smith does not even appear to provide that rational basis, but simply resorts to proof by assertion. He simply asserts that "this law in fact has no limits to its domain of quantification" (p. 105:1-2). Why accept this assertion? After all, physical laws describe regular patterns of physical events, and the metaphysical assertion that supernatural entities can not affect the physical world is not based on observations of physical events, but is pure metaphysical speculation, and its unjustified to boot. It may be appropriate to view the quantum cosmological wave function as ranging over all physical variables, but not over all possible physical and nonphysical (supernatural) variables. Natural laws are laws of physics which describe physical event patterns, not nonphysical (supernatural) event patterns.

The natural/supernatural distinction is not an unnecessary distinction created by the theist (p. 104:40-105:1), but results from the proper identification of the nature of physical laws. Laws of physics describe physical event patterns, and if there exist supernatural nonphysical entities (e.g., God, heaven, hell, angels, demons, etc.) in some kind of supernatural nonphysical domain, then event patterns in that domain may be described by entirely different nonphysical laws no matter how strongly Smith asserts (without justification) that such entities, if they exist, must be described by a physical quantum cosmological wave function law. There is no good reason to suppose nonphysical entities must be described by a physical law, even if nonphysical entities have the capacity to cause physical events.

So, if Hawking's cosmology entails that the physical wave function law be attached to the unjustified metaphysical assumption that the law apply to any possibly existing nonphysical entities, then Hawking's cosmology is surely unjustified. Thus, the wave function is probably false, given that we have no rational basis for the belief that it truly applies to any possibly existing nonphysical entities, and given the AFTLOP and my fine-tuning arguments which together establish that natural laws (including any wave function law) describe physical event patterns caused by a person who may exist and operate in a realm outside the range of events described by the law.

We need not suppose that God's actions must be constrained to comply with a complete wave function that includes *all* events (p. 105:21-25). Rather, a complete *physical* wave function may be identified as a fairly good model of physical events, where those physical events not caused by a human person are caused by a nonhuman person. Indeed, it is rather absurd to suppose that an omnipotent God who causes a physical universe to exist and evolve generally in accordance with a wave function of that universe (with occasional physical events possibly being caused by God or other persons to occur in ways that may not be predicted by the wave function probability) should be demanded by Smith (a person created by God) to exist and act in full and complete compliance with that wave function! The creature is not in a position to make such a demand of the Creator. So, although classical theism may be inconsistent with an unjustified version of Hawking's cosmology, there is no good reason to suppose theism is inconsistent with a revised version of quantum cosmology that allows for the possibility that physical events are caused by God or other persons.

It is a false dichotomy to suggest that we must choose between embracing atheism and rejecting science (p. 105:32-33), since theists need not argue that science is false, but may argue that naturalistic science ought to be rejected in favor of theistic science that accounts for the results of the AFTLOP and my fine-tuning arguments. Accepting theistic science would indeed be wise, given that any time man would oppose God, man would surely lose.

NOTES

1. Stenger, Victor J. (2006). *The Comprehensible Cosmos: Where Do the Laws of Physics Come From?* Amherst, NY: Prometheus Books, p. 175:26-32, p. 176:19-37.

CHAPTER 4

Atheistic Teleological Arguments Refuted

I now examine the teleological arguments for atheism found in the book "The Improbability of God" edited by Michael Martin and Ricki Monnier, and published by Prometheus Books in 2006, ISBN: 1-59102-381-5. I urge you to purchase a copy of "The Improbability of God" (IPRG) so that you may fully understand the context of the critical remarks below.

In chapter 1 of part 2 of IPRG, Nicholas Everitt presents an "argument from scale" which he believes provides evidence against the existence of God. The general argument form may be considered valid (p. 111:13-17). My response to Everitt's assertion that his argument is sound will be to challenge the claim that it is reasonable for us to expect that if God exists, then God will cause the changes Everitt represents by C (p. 111:13-14).

First, Everitt considers a Crusoe analogy (p. 112:1-40) to help illustrate his argument. This analogy, however, is not good, since before we even start our empirical investigation of the implications of scale in the universe (p. 112:26-28), we already have evidence for the existence of God (see chapters 1 and 2), whereas Crusoe, prior to his empirical investigation of the island, has no reason to believe any other survivors such as himself have been roaming the island seeking to make contact with any other survivors.

Everitt assumes that if theism is true, then there are some physical events that God would likely cause. Everitt does not really shoulder the burden of proof, however, as he often simply resorts to unanswered questioning tactics (p. 113:27-30; 113:34-37; 114:7-8; 115:36; 115:41-116:2), and he makes many assertions for which no justification is provided (p. 113:9; 113:30-37; 113:37-114:7, 114:32-34; 115:8-9; 115:15-17; 115:26-27; 116:2-4; 116:14-15; 116:20-22; 116:23-35; 116:28-31). Proof by assertion is hardly compelling.

Then Everitt considers five possible theistic replies to his argument (p. 116:33-123:30). The last of these replies is especially in need of examination, as it fails to adequately respond to successful objections theists may raise. Everitt construes this theistic reply as being the claim that although the scale of the universe provides prima facie evidence against theism, this fact does not actually diminish the probability of theism, given that N is true, where N represents "God's ways are largely inscrutable" (p. 122:3-15). Everitt's response is to challenge the theist to provide a good reason for believing N, where that reason is not ad hoc or unsupported by evidence. Since Everitt believes there is no good reason for believing N, he thinks that his argument from scale reduces the probability of theism.

Theists may respond to Everitt's argument in several ways. First, even if theists concede that consideration of scale in the universe provides prima facie evidence against theism, theists may provide independent evidence for the existence of God which confirms theism more strongly than Everitt's argument disconfirms theism. Thus, theists may still be justified in holding that theism is true.

Second, theists need not even concede that consideration of scale in the universe provides prima facie evidence against theism. The AFTLOP establishes that the physical events which comprise the scale considerations are caused by God. It is simply wrong to suppose that physical events known to be caused by God provide evidence against theism!

Third, theists may reject Everitt's view that if theists have no good reason for believing N, then the argument from scale reduces the probability of theism. Theists may offer an argument for the existence of God (e.g., my AFTLOP or my fine-tuning arguments) as the basis for supposing that God exists and possesses much greater power and knowledge than that of man. Given God's far superior knowledge, it becomes evident that there is indeed no reason (apart from divine revelation) to suppose mere humans are in a position to say much at all about what God might desire, know, or cause. This may not show that N is true, but it is evident that we have no good reason to believe N is false. Although our considerations here do appear to suggest that N is more likely true than false, they do seem insufficient to establish whether N is probably true or false, and it follows that we do not know N is false. Since we know Everitt's consideration of scale decreases the probability of theism only if we know N is false, and since we do not know N is false, it follows that we do not know whether Everitt's consideration of scale in the universe actually decreases the probability of theism. So, it is not the case that if theists have no good reason for believing N, then the argument from scale reduces the probability of theism. To make his case, therefore, it is not enough for Everitt to object that theists have not established that N is true, but Everitt must establish that N is false, and this he has not done. It is difficult to imagine how Everitt can accomplish that task, since N appears more likely true than false, given that my theistic arguments (chapters 1 and 2) establish that God's knowledge is immensely superior to that of mere humans.

Fourth, theists who justify the claim that biblically derived theology is divinely authoritative may show that although God's ways are generally inscrutable apart from divine revelation (Psalm 145:3; Psalm 147:5; Isaiah 40:28; Isaiah 55:8-9; Romans 11:33), our capacity to discover truth through reasoning (Isaiah 1:18) and arguments (Isaiah 43:26), assuming we positively respond to truth with honesty and humility (Psalm 25:9), may lead to such knowledge as that God's ways are just (Deuteronomy 32:4), righteous and loving (Psalm 145:17), good and upright (Psalm 25:8), and worthy of praise (Psalm 145:3). Thus, such theists may respond to Everitt's unanswered questions about scale not merely by responding that the AFTLOP entails that the physical events in question are caused by God, but by responding that the character of God is such that God surely has good reasons for having caused those physical events, even though we may not be certain what those reasons are. A full exploration of the issues involved in this kind of theistic perspective is, however, beyond the scope of the present analysis.

Therefore, given the four theistic responses above, it is simply incorrect to characterize theists as arbitrarily and unreasonably attributing further intentions to God (p. 123:18-20), since theists can provide independent grounds for believing that God exists and is the cause of the physical events on which the argument from scale focuses. God's ways may be inscrutable to some degree, but this fact should not be surprising (given that God's knowledge is so immensely superior to that of mere humans), and this fact may indeed result in strange discoveries on occasion (p. 123:28-30). Everitt has, therefore, failed to show that his argument from scale is sound, especially since his attempted support for proposition (1) (p. 123:35-124:3) consisted of frequent use of unanswered questioning tactics and proof by assertion, and since the theistic responses outlined above refute his conclusion.

In chapter 2 of part 2 of IPRG, Victor Stenger attempts to provide a natural explanation for the anthropic coincidences. Stenger makes the assumption that natural laws actually cause the physical events they describe (p. 126:13-17). No justification for this assumption is provided, and the AFTLOP (see chapter 1) confirms that this assumption is unjustified.

Stenger claims that scientific journals successfully operate on the presupposition of naturalism (p. 127:4-6). In response, observe that such a journal could not possibly accept a theistic causal explanation of physical events, since that possibility is rejected due to naturalistic presuppositions. It is hardly surprising that such journals do not accept theistic explanations of physical events. This fact does not establish that theistic explanations are unjustified, but only establishes that such journals reject, without justification, theistic explanations by virtue of a prior commitment to naturalistic presuppositions. Furthermore, if a scientific journal can "successfully operate" even when it consists of publications which use unjustified naturalistic presuppositions to deny justified theistic inferences, then such journals are clearly not maximally successfully operational. Also, the success of journals in which publications are committed to naturalism is grounded in the fact that physical events are very often explainable in terms of descriptive physical laws, but my theistic arguments (see chapters 1 and 2) establish that such descriptive explanations are made possible by virtue of the fact that God is the continuous sustaining cause of the existence of physical entities which God causes to change in accordance with the descriptive physical laws God causes to obtain. Therefore, naturalism-presupposing journals could not "successfully operate" apart from this divine action in the physical world, and the naturalism presupposed in those journals neither justifies that naturalism, nor disconfirms theism. Many scientists successfully integrate their scientific and religious beliefs such that dogmatic and unjustified naturalism is not presupposed as a component of their worldview. Perspectives on Science and Christian Faith (the Journal of the American Scientific Affiliation) consists of publications which explore such issues in detail.[1]

Stenger mentions what appear to him to be cosmic waste, inefficiency, and jerry-building (p. 135:12-21), but does not consider the implications of the possibility that God has good reasons for having caused physical events to occur such that they presently appear to Stenger to be wasteful, inefficient, and jerry-building, when in fact they are not. So, such appearances have not been shown to lend support for atheism. In fact,

Stenger has not even shown that there exist such appearances, since a God whose ways are at least partially inscrutable may have good unknown reasons for having caused physical events to occur such that Stenger does not know those good reasons, in which case we may infer not that such appearances actually exist, but that God's unknown good reasons appear to exist. Furthermore, the AFTLOP establishes that the physical events to which Stenger refers are caused by God. Thus, given the AFTLOP, Stenger has not shown why we should conclude that there exists the appearance of waste, inefficiency and jerry-building, rather than conclude that there exists the appearance of God's good unknown reasons for having caused physical events to be as they are.

In his explanation of how our particular universe could arise with its anthropic coincidences, Stenger considers the possibility that there exists an ensemble of universes with varying physical constants (p. 135:24-26). However, in this passage, he does not provide evidence that multiple universes exist, so his explanation of the possible origin of the anthropic coincidences is unjustified.

Stenger claims that some theists are inconsistent in that they argue that natural physical events are both too uncongenial for life and exquisitely congenial to life (p. 136:11-16). However, such theists need not be viewed as inconsistent if P (defined as natural physical events) is viewed as too uncongenial for life in the sense that P is insufficient to guarantee L (defined as Earth-like life in the universe) is probable, yet P is viewed as being exquisitely congenial to life in the sense that P, being necessary and insufficient for L, is nevertheless highly unlikely on atheism (I explore this issue in greater depth later in this chapter, where a detailed set of teleological fine-tuning arguments for the existence of God is presented during the course of my critique of the essay by Michael Ikeda and Bill Jefferys.) More importantly, Stenger objects that we are not justified in assuming P is insufficient to guarantee L is probable (p. 136:17-19). However, given my fine-tuning arguments presented later in this chapter, and given the AFTLOP, P is sufficient to guarantee theism is probable, so Stenger's considerations here need not worry the theist.

The anthropic coincidences are physical events caused by God, as shown in the AFTLOP and in my fine-tuning arguments, regardless of whether any form of life is possible for only a small improbable range of physical parameters (p. 136:17-19). Stenger is apparently unaware of this fact and, thus, incorrectly concludes that the arguments used to support option (A) are weak (p. 136:20-22).

Stenger's rejection of option (B) appears justified (p. 136:24-137:27). There appears to exist no good reason for accepting option (B).

Stenger considers option (C), and claims that "all scientific explanations until now have been natural" (p. 137:33-34). However, all scientific explanations may be understood in supernaturalistic terms rather than naturalistic terms. Scientific explanations (the laws of physics) may be understood as regular physical events patterns caused by God, as shown in the AFTLOP. Therefore, Stenger's assumption is incorrect that the best explanation of the laws of nature is a natural explanation that does not consist of entities which exist and operate in a spirit world (p. 137:35-37).

Likewise, Stenger's assumption that the laws of nature "do not require an agent to bring them into being" reveals his ignorance of the AFTLOP (p. 138:11-12). Thus, in the absence of an agent, we would not expect any laws of nature at all, since we would not even expect any physical events to exist, contrary to Stenger's view (p. 138:12-13).

Stenger supposes that global conservation laws in a universe are expected if no agent acts on the universe (p. 139:22-23). However, this view implies that the laws describe physical events that are not caused by a person, whereas the AFTLOP establishes that physical events are caused by persons. Given the AFTLOP, and given Stenger's failure to justify his claim that physical events with no personal cause can exist, we may infer that he is wrong in claiming that the data "are consistent with no agent" (p. 139:24). Similarly, he is incorrect in claiming that a symmetry-breaking physical event can occur undesigned (p. 140:22-24), since physical events are caused by persons, as shown in the AFTLOP. Also, he erroneously asserts that the inflationary big bang model offers a "plausible, natural scenario for the uncaused origin and evolution of the universe" (p. 140:29-31), as the AFTLOP shows that such physical event models describe physical events caused by God.

Stenger asserts "no rational basis exists" (p. 140:35-38) for the belief that God created the universe. However, he is evidently unaware of the AFTLOP and my fine-tuning arguments, which together establish not only the rational basis for the belief that God created the universe, but also entail that no rational basis exists for the belief that God did not create the universe. Specifically, we have no rational basis for the following beliefs: (1) uncaused physical events exist; (2) a physical event is a cause of a physical event; and (3) a physical event is not caused by a person. Thus, his quantum tunneling explanation (p. 141:1-18) of the origin of the universe, as a natural explanation, stands unjustified. Additionally, that explanation simply assumes (without justification) that something physical can come from nothing, when the AFTLOP entails this assumption is unjustified.

Stenger also assumes (without proof) that chance can arrange a physical event (p. 141:20-23), yet appears unaware that the AFTLOP establishes that such physical events are caused by God. Stenger should be open to the idea that God is the cause of physical events described by natural laws. After all, he emphasizes "we have no reason to assume that ours is the only possible form of life" (p. 141:20-23). Nevertheless, he persists in maintaining the unjustified view that symmetry breaking can "produce the fundamental laws and constants we still observe today" (p. 141:35-37), despite the evidence (AFTLOP) to the contrary. Also, he simply asserts (without proof) that the existence of a lawgiver need not be invoked to explain the physical laws of broken symmetry (p. 141:41-142:5). This proof by assertion is hardly compelling, especially given evidence (the AFTLOP) to the contrary.

Stenger reveals a confused understanding of the concept of "nothing". Either "nothing" refers to an existing entity or "nothing" refers to the absence of any existing entity. If "nothing" refers to an existing entity, then this "nothing" is, technically speaking, something, and Stenger claims it possesses the property of being symmetric with zero information (p. 142:10-13), and he claims that an action by an outside agent would cause it to no longer possess those properties (p. 142:13-14). In response, observe that Stenger has simply assumed (without proof) that there could not exist an outside agent who is the cause of this entity's possession of those properties. Now, if "nothing" is instead taken to refer to the absence of any existing entity, then Stenger has made the unjustified assumption that properties can be possessed by a state of nonexistence. Furthermore, if the arguments for the claim "something necessarily exists" are sound, then Stenger's hypothesized state of nonexistence could never be actualized, and Stenger has not even considered such arguments. His discussion of "nothing", therefore, contains nothing about which the theist ought to be concerned. In particular, theists need not be concerned by his unjustified reference to "the uneconomical hypothesis of a creator" (p. 142:15-16), which flies in the face of the results established in the AFTLOP and in my fine-tuning arguments.

Stenger's proofs by assertion continue. He asserts (without proof) that spontaneous, causeless, random, unpredictable physical events exist (p.

142:17-25). Needless to say, proof by assertion is not very compelling, especially given evidence (AFTLOP) to the contrary. Stenger's attempt to deflect the accusation of "simply assuming" (p. 142:32-35) is based on his naturalistic interpretation of scientific knowledge, and the AFTLOP and my fine-tuning arguments together establish that this interpretation is unjustified. We should not blindly assume constants and forces can be "selected by accident" (p. 142:39-41), when the AFTLOP entails that physical constants and forces are references to physical events caused by God.

Stenger assumes that the results of symmetry breaking are "not determined ahead of time" (p. 142:26-28). However, given the AFTLOP, it is not obvious why we should assume God does not determine ahead of time the physical events God intends to cause.

Theistic proponents of teleological arguments are sometimes criticized for assuming that the allegedly narrow range of life-permitting values of physical constants is truly narrow, given the possibility that there may exist unknown natural explanations which entail that the range is either: (1) necessarily narrow; or (2) highly probably narrow. Stenger evidently rejects this criticism, however, given his claim that a "huge range of values" is possible (p. 142:37-38). Although this concession on Stenger's part might seem to conceivably strengthen theistic fine-tuning arguments based on the improbability of life-permitting values of physical constants, it is not actually clear why we should accept Stenger's concession.

Stenger claims "we have no reason to assume life only exists on earth" (p. 143:7-9). However, given the very small probability[2] (on naturalism) of finding a planet in our universe which would have the necessary parameters for carbon-based life support, and given Stenger's failure to respond to this calculation, his discussion is clearly incomplete. Yes, Stenger refers to Tegmark's calculation of the "parameter space where ordered structures can form" (p. 146:34-38), but does not explain how to square Tegmark's results with those of Ross. So, Stenger's discussion is indeed incomplete. Granted, the likelihood of some form of life in our universe "is not necessarily small" (p. 144:17-19), but logical possibility does not entail high probability, and the calculation by Ross suggests the probability (on naturalism) of carbon-based life is low, even vanishingly small. Yes, it is possible that an altogether different or unimaginable life form may exist in some other universe (p. 144:24-26), but this bare logical possibility is insufficient as a plausible causal explanation of the origin of life, especially since the number of known universes is one. Given that we have no reason, on naturalism, to suppose non-carbon-based molecules can become sufficiently complex to support life, these considerations do appear to provide a reason for believing physical life probably only exists where it is presently known to have physically existed (i.e., on Earth, or perhaps also Mars).

Stenger's explanation for the origin of life, however, is evidently not grounded in the idea that life has arisen through chance and natural causes in our universe, where our universe is the only universe which exists. Rather, he seems to rely more heavily on the idea that there exist multiple universes with different physical conditions, where our universe happens to be a universe in which conditions have been favorable for the evolution of life through natural processes. Given that only one universe (our own) is known to exist, however, Stenger appears to be relying on a theory that postulates the existence of entities for which no evidence exists, and it is the postulating of such entities that violates the Ockham's Razor principle of parsimony. Stenger seeks to deflect the charge of having violated this principle by considering an analogous case in which the atomic theory of matter was developed (p. 144:27-34). The analogy is not good, however, since the atomic theory is grounded in testable, observable physical events, whereas the theoretically hypothesized multiple universes are neither testable nor observable. Note, also, that we are discussing theoretical hypotheses that contain the assumption that multiple universes exist, and since hypotheses should not be "multiplied beyond necessity", neither should the assumptions (universes) entailed by the hypotheses be multiplied beyond necessity (p. 144:27-38). Therefore, Stenger's assertion that "a theory of many universes contains fewer hypotheses than a theory of one" (p. 146:21-24) is mistaken. Also, Stenger's hypotheses/universes distinction (p. 144:28-30) does not assist his efforts to avoid the charge of having provided an explanation that fails to be appropriately parsimonious.

As for Stenger's view that Tegmark's Ultimate Ensemble Theory is more parsimonious than the theory that only one universe exists (p. 144:35-36), it is true, as discussed in chapter 1, that one could conceivably construct a Theory of Everything that identifies the fundamental laws of physics according to which every universe that exists in a hypothesized multiverse evolves, where the statement of the Theory of Everything has less algorithmic complexity than that of the conjunction of that statement and the specific conditions that determine the particular universe we inhabit. (The term "algorithmic complexity" simply denotes a particular formal way of precisely representing the information content of a statement or hypothesis.) However, it is a faulty comparison which grounds the assumption that a hypothesized multiverse that evolves in accordance with such a Theory of Everything is simpler and ought to be favored over the anti-multiverse hypothesis that only our particular universe exists/evolves in accordance with that theory. Since a full explication of the anti-multiverse hypothesis has the algorithmic complexity needed to state the Theory of Everything and identify merely the conditions that determine our particular physical universe, whereas a full explication of the hypothesis that a multiverse actually exists has the algorithmic complexity needed to describe the Theory of Everything *and* identify all the conditions that determine the many allegedly existing actual physical universes, the anti-multiverse hypothesis is, thus, shown to be *much* simpler.

Relative simplicity of competing hypotheses is determined not by comparing, for each hypothesis, the ratio of information content represented by the symbolism expressing the hypothesis to the information content of the symbolic expression itself. The ratio of "information" to "number of characters" alluded to by Stenger (p. 145:2-4) is, therefore, completely irrelevant. It is the number of theoretical hypotheses that are invoked to explain a body of evidence, and especially the degree to which those hypotheses are justifiably invoked, that helps to determine relative simplicity. Stenger's analogy (p. 145:1-5) is not a good one, and he has not explained why we should accept his definition of "simple" rather than some other definition.

The fact that a theory is consistent with available evidence (p. 145: 6-7) is not sufficient to establish that the theory is the best explanation of the available evidence. The claim that ours is the only physical universe that exists is not uneconomical (p. 145:9), but is grounded in the evidence which may be used to show that only our universe is known to exist. The claim that multiple universes exist is uneconomical in that we do not have evidence that establishes that we know that other universes exist. Thus, we may reject White's line (p. 145:9-11), aligning our analyses instead with the idea that everything supported by evidence and not forbidden is compulsory. Tegmark's Ultimate Ensemble Theory, in which "all structures that exist mathematically exist also physically"[3] may be rejected on the grounds that there is no evidence for the existence of physical universes other than our own. This rejection is especially prudent, given both the confused understanding of simplicity and economy (as discussed above), and given that no good reason is given for rejecting the assumption that some logically possible universes may not actually physically exist.

Incidentally, theism does not entail that our universe is the only physical universe that exists, although lack of evidence for other physical universes does establish that multiverse hypotheses are not justified. So, theists need not necessarily be opposed to such theories as the multiverse hypotheses to which Stenger refers (p. 145:12-146:15). However, since Stenger does not provide justification for the belief that any of these hypotheses is the best explanation of available evidence, he has in no way established that a multiverse hypothesis is the best explanation. Stenger merely suggests that "natural selection may offer a natural explanation" (p. 146:14-15). The mere suggestion that a theory is possible is a far cry from establishing that a theory is the best explanation. These multiverse theories, therefore, are interesting, but speculative and unjustified. Furthermore, since any supposed "natural explanation" would be a description of regular physical event patterns caused by God (see the AFTLOP), theists need not be concerned about whether a multiverse theory eventually wins the day in the court of scientific opinion.

Stenger assumes that contemporary theistic design arguments contain the erroneous assumption that "only one kind of life, ours, is possible in every configuration of possible universes" (p. 147:16-17). Proponents of theistic design arguments, however, need not make this assumption, for example, when using anthropic coincidences in demonstrating that theistic explanations are best. Stenger has not established that all contemporary proponents of theistic design arguments make the erroneous assumption, and he does not even mention what other flaws, unjustified assumptions, or inconsistencies he may have in mind (p. 147:14-16).

Furthermore, Stenger's summary of his examination of possible natural explanations for anthropic coincidences concludes "human life would certainly not exist in such universes" (p. 147:24-27). This implies that even Stenger believes human life probably has no known natural explanation, which, by default, confirms the hypothesis of a non-natural (supernatural) theistic explanation. (Perhaps I have misread Stenger on this point, and I will gladly stand corrected if I discover a reason to believe such correction is needed.)

Stenger mentions conservation laws of physics which derive from "symmetries of nothing" that would exist even in the absence of design (p. 147:28-30). This statement implies that it is reasonable to believe an existing physical universe can continue to be sustained in existence apart from the action of a personal cause of that physical sustenance, and it is precisely this assertion that not-personally-caused physical events exist that remains unjustified.

In addition, Stenger has not even established that the conservation laws are the most powerful. The physical law L which states "physical entities in the universe continue to exist and change in accordance with the other laws of physics" is arguably the most powerful physical law (and is a law which Stenger fails to even identify), since only L facilitates the continuous obtaining of the other laws, and since only L explains why the universe continues to exist rather than cease to exist. Furthermore, the AFTLOP establishes that God is the cause of L's obtaining, which entails that the conservation laws mentioned by Stenger are identifiable because of the exercise of God's causal sustaining power, contradicting the supposition that the conservation laws could exist independent of the action of a designer-sustainer.

Additionally, "nothing" has no symmetries, since only something can possess a property. Even Max Tegmark claims "Physical Nonexistence Is a Scientifically Meaningless Concept" as the heading of a subsection in his article[4] and Stenger does not explain how to square his conception of "nothing" with Tegmark who apparently rejects such theoretical concepts on the grounds that they do not qualify as a physical theory.

Stenger claims that the design/creation hypothesis is disconfirmed by the fact that physical structure in the universe may be explained by "accidental, or spontaneous, breaking of symmetries" (p. 147:30-33). In response, Stenger has not explained why random symmetry-breaking events should be considered inconsistent with theism. The AFTLOP establishes that such physical events are caused by God. Also, these physical events may not be truly random in the sense that although the outcome of such events may not be predictable by humans, the outcome may, nevertheless, be foreknown and caused by God, in which case the symmetry-breaking events are consistent with the design-creation hypothesis.

Stenger presents a few final concluding comments (p. 147:34-148:3). These comments are strongly disconfirmed by the arguments presented above.

In chapter 3 of part 2 of IPRG, Michael Ikeda and Bill Jefferys argue that the anthropic principle does not support supernaturalism. They present a technical critique of the fine-tuning argument widely popularized by theists such as Hugh Ross. Their argument rests on the assumption that proponents of fine-tuning arguments would accept assumptions (a), (b), and (c) (p. 150:18-151:5). Proponents of fine-tuning arguments, however, may be likely to reject (b), since the question of whether physical events (including those physical events identified as "physical life") can exist naturalistically is generally a point of dispute between theists and atheists. Prior to presenting a fine-tuning argument, it is not necessary to presuppose that life can exist naturalistically. Jefferys and Ikeda claim to not assume at the outset whether N is likely true or false (p. 152:33-35), but assumption (b) reveals prior acceptance of naturalistic explanations for at least some physical events. Furthermore, the AFTLOP (see chapter 1) establishes that physical events are caused by persons, which implies that assumption (b) is incorrect. Thus, the unjustified assumptions made by Ikeda and Jefferys render their entire analysis inconclusive.

A brief reference is made to the allegedly valid multiverse objection to the fine-tuning argument (p. 151:24-36), but no justification is provided there for the belief that the multiverse hypothesis ought to be favored over the anti-multiverse hypothesis. Reference is also made to the fact that it is logically possible that good unknown reasons exist for believing that the probability of life is not small, given naturalism (p. 152:1-14). Indeed it is logically possible that good unknown reasons exist, but it is also logically possible that good unknown reasons do not exist. If belief B is rejected on the grounds that it is logically possible that good unknown reasons will be discovered in the future which will establish B is probably false, then virtually all beliefs would need to be rejected for the same kind of reason. Nay, the situation would be even worse, for then we would need to reject the belief that virtually all our beliefs would need to be rejected. And then we would need to reject the belief that we would need to reject the belief that virtually all our beliefs would need to be rejected, etc., leading to an infinite regress which, I submit, shows that belief B may be accepted if it is a justified belief, despite the fact that it is logically possible that future discoveries may render B unjustified. Specifically, the theistic implications of theistic arguments ought not be rejected merely on the grounds that it is logically possible that future unknown discoveries will render present theistic beliefs no longer justified. Proponents of the fine-tuning argument need not insist that it is necessarily the case that "only universes very like our own could support life" (p. 152:8-10), but may simply infer that, based on presently available evidence, it is reasonable to believe that physical life, if it exists anywhere, probably is much like life on Earth on a planet much like Earth in a universe much like our universe. The reasonable inference that any existing physical life is probably Earth-like is grounded in presently available scientific knowledge. The mere logical possibility that this reasonable belief may be shown unjustified in the future does not provide adequate justification for the belief that it is presently unjustified. Even if universes much different than our own could support life, fine-tuning arguments may be developed which confirm theism (this will be shown later in this chapter). Also, Ikeda and Jefferys do not explain why we should not suppose that it is logically possible that future discoveries will elevate the theistic implications of theistic arguments to an even higher degree of justification than they presently enjoy, and they have not explained why we should not suppose that this logical possibility entails that any allegedly atheistic implication of any argument should be rejected.

It is claimed that Ross assumes that F is true (p. 152:26), but F follows from assumption (b) which, as mentioned above, entails that naturalistic explanations of at least some physical events are accepted. I doubt Ross accepts naturalistic explanations, and, thus, Ross is doubtfully committed to the claim that F is true. No reason has been given to justify the claim that proponents of fine-tuning arguments must accept F.

As shown above, the analysis of Ikeda and Jefferys is grounded in unjustified assumptions. The analysis also fails to depict how a proponent of a fine-tuning argument may reason. Such proponents need not argue that $P(F|N) << 1$ entails $P(N|F) << 1$ (p. 153:15-16). In fact, $P(F|N)$ must be close to one, for it is quite evident that a universe which is governed solely by naturalistic law *must* be compatible with observed life existing naturalistically. That is, given that all physical events may be explained in terms of naturalistic causes, then it follows that all physical events associated with physical life have naturalistic causes. In other words, N entails F, and this is why $P(F|N)$ must be one (or at least, close to one). Even if it is not true that $P(F|N) \approx 1$, the fact remains that proponents of fine-tuning arguments need not argue that $P(F|N) << 1$ entails $P(N|F) << 1$.

The objection may be raised that my claim above that $P(F|N)$ must be close to one is really better construed as the claim that $P(F|(N \text{ and } L))$

must be close to one. Even granting this objection, N and L together entail F, and this is why P(F|(N and L)) must be one (or at least, close to one). Even if it is not true that P(F|(N and L)) ≈ 1, it is nevertheless the case that proponents of fine-tuning arguments need argue neither that P(F|N) << 1 entails P(N|F) << 1, nor that P(F|(N and L)) << 1 entails P((N and L)|F) << 1.

The poker counterexample (p. 153:23-29) is incomplete, since the mere citing of a counterexample to a probabilistic inference is not sufficient to establish the inference is unjustified. After all, probabilistic inferences are consistent with the existence of counterexamples. It is possible that although a probabilistic inference does not necessarily obtain, it usually does obtain. The fact that a probabilistic inference may not always obtain is consistent with it often obtaining. The implications of the poker analogy will be examined below in greater detail. In particular, it will be shown that the poker analogy need not be considered a good analogy to fine-tuning arguments.

Ikeda and Jefferys explain why they believe certain interpretations of fine-tuning arguments are invalid, yet they do not respond to the fact that the AFTLOP establishes that the physical events represented by F and L are reasonably taken to be caused by God. They have written: "for an inference to be valid, it is necessary to take into account *all* known information that may be relevant to the conclusion" (p. 153:30-154:1). This failure to account for the implications of the AFTLOP (or, for that matter, the implications of a host of other theistic arguments) suggests their analysis is grounded in incomplete and invalid reasoning, given that their analysis is not in compliance with their own requirement that valid inferences account for all known information.

As a counter-argument to the interpretation of anthropic coincidences as accepted by Ikeda and Jefferys, I will reproduce here my fine-tuning arguments from chapter 2 of this book:

(1) $A \rightarrow \sim B$

(2) B

(3) $\sim A$

This line of reasoning is grounded in the well known *modus tollens* inference. Here, A represents the conjunction "N and (C ε Q)", and B represents "P((C ε Q)|N) ≈ 0". N represents naturalism, defined as the hypothesis that the laws M of physics are the impersonal causal explanation of the set Q of physical events, where M represents the set of all presently known laws of physics, and where Q represents the set of all physical events presently known to be described by any member of M. C represents the set of all physical conditions necessary for the naturalistic origin of a planet on which L is true, where L represents the hypothesis "physical Earth-like life exists". As a deductive inference, the reasoning above is valid. However, in the case of the fine-tuning argument, the premises are not known with absolute certainty, and the inductive counterpart to this reasoning may be roughly summarized in probabilistic terms as the inference from $[P(\sim B|A) \approx k]$ to $[P(\sim A|B) \approx k]$ to $[P(\sim A) \approx k]$. Note that the inference from $[P(\sim B|A) \approx k]$ to $[P(\sim A|B) \approx k]$ is justified, in general, only when $P(A|B)$ and $P(B|A)$ are both approximately $1 - k$, since $P(A|B) + P(\sim A|B) = P(B|A) + P(\sim B|A) = 1$ entails that $P(\sim B|A) \approx P(\sim A|B) \approx k$ only if $P(A|B) \approx P(B|A) \approx k - 1$. The further inference to $[P(\sim A) \approx k]$ is justified only if it is also true that $P(B) \approx 1$. In the case of the fine-tuning argument detailed below, since k ≈ 1 and $P(B) \approx 1$, it follows that $P(\sim A) \approx 1$.

(4) $P((C \in Q)|N) \approx 0$

(5) $P(B) \approx 1$

(6) $P(B|A) \approx 0$

(7) $P(B|A) + P(\sim B|A) = 1$

(8) $P(\sim B|A) \approx 1$

(9) $P(\sim B|A) = P(A \text{ and } \sim B) / P(A)$

(10) $P(A \text{ and } \sim B) / P(A) \approx 1$

(11) $P(A \text{ and } \sim B) \approx P(A)$

(12) $P(A \text{ or } \sim B) = P(A) + P(\sim B) - P(A \text{ and } \sim B)$

(13) $P(B) + P(\sim B) = 1$

(14) $P(\sim B) \approx 0$

(15) $P(A \text{ or } \sim B) \approx 0$

(16) $P(A \text{ or } \sim B) + P(B) - P(A \text{ and } B) = 1$

(17) $0 + 1 - P(A \text{ and } B) \approx 1$

(18) $P(A \text{ and } B) \approx 0$

(19) $P(A \text{ and } B) = P(B \text{ and } A)$

(20) $P(B \text{ and } A) \approx 0$

(21) $P(B \text{ and } A) = P(B) P(A|B)$

(22) $P(B) P(A|B) \approx 0$

(23) $P(A|B) \approx 0$

(24) $P(A|B) + P(\sim A|B) = 1$

(25) $P(\sim A|B) \approx 1$

(26) $P(\sim A) \approx 1$

(27) $P(\sim(N \text{ and } (C \in Q))) \approx 1$

(28) $P(\sim N \text{ or } \sim(C \in Q)) \approx 1$

Premise (4) is the critical premise supplied by anthropic principle considerations, not $P(F|N) \ll 1$ as supposed by Ikeda and Jefferys (p. 153:6-9), as $P(F|N)$ is not small at all, since N (on their definition, p. 152:30-32) entails F is likely, as has been discussed above. Premise (5) follows from (4) and the definition of B. Premise (6) is true, since a physical event being a member of Q entails that the probability, given N, of its being caused by M is not vanishingly small, and since any physical event with a vanishingly small probability, given N, of being caused by M is probably not caused by M and, thus, is probably not a member of Q. This follows from the fact that $C \in Q$ is likely (given N) if and only if $P((C \in Q)|N) \approx 1$. In other words, it is unlikely that it would be likely to be very unlikely that $C \in Q$ (given N), if it is given that N and $(C \in Q)$ are both true. Given A, B must be either true or false, and, thus, premise (7) must be true. Premise (8) follows from the substitution of (6) into (7). Premise (9) follows from the definition of conditional probability. Premise (10) follows from substitution of (8) into (9). Premise (11) follows from multiplication of (10) by $P(A)$. Premise (12) follows from the definition of probability with inclusive logical disjunction. Premise (13) must be true, as the sum of the probability space must equal one. Premise (14) follows from substitution of (5) into (13). Premise (15) follows from the substitution of (11) and (14) into (12). The sum in premise (16) must equal 1, since the three terms together account for the full probability space (draw a Venn-Euler diagram to see this.) Premise (17) follows from substitution of (15) and (5) into (16). Premise (18) follows from simplifying and rearranging terms in (17). Premise (19) is true, since the event "A and B" is identical to the event "B and A", in general. Premise (20) follows from substitution of (18) into (19). Premise (21) follows from the definition of conditional probability. Premise (22) follows from substitution of (20) into (21). Premise (23) follows from substitution of (5) into (22). Given B, A must be either true or false, and, thus, premise (24) must be true. Premise (25) follows from substitution of (23) into (24). Premise (26) follows from (5) and (25), and is grounded in the well known *modus ponens* inference. Premise (27) follows from (26) and the definition of A. Premise (28) is the inclusive logical disjunction that results from (27).

Much hinges on premise (4), as the other steps are rather straightforward. The multiverse objection and the unknown-future-discovery objection have both been mentioned earlier, and do not entail (4) is false, since the number of known universes is one, and since presently justified beliefs should not be rejected merely on the grounds that they may possibly be shown unjustified in the future.

The objection might be raised that the smallness of the probability in premise (4) is grounded in the unjustified assumption that the probability space is known to be large. There does appear to be some merit to this objection as it pertains to physical conditions H, where H represents the subset of anthropic coincidences dealing with the alleged improbability of the values of various constants of physics that appear in mathematical physics models. Consider some of the numbers cited by Hugh Ross[5] which describe physical balances accurate to one part in 10^{37}, one part in 10^{40}, one part in 10^{60}, and one part in 10^{120}. Even if it is true that these conditions must be so balanced as a necessary condition for finding a naturalistic explanation of a planet on which L is true, it does not follow that the probability, given N, of these conditions being an element of Q is one part in 10^{37}, one part in 10^{40}, one part in 10^{60}, and one part in 10^{120}, respectively. After all, a probability calculation assumes knowledge of the space of possibilities, and opponents of this category of fine-tuning arguments may object that the space of possible values of these conditions, given N, is not presently known.[6] Even granting this objection, however, it does nevertheless appear odd that such balances do, in fact, obtain. These odd observations might conceivably be the hard data upon which a "Fingerprint of God" argument of some kind could be developed, but consideration of issues relevant to such an argument lies beyond the scope of the present analysis.

More importantly, however, is must be stressed that it is highly unlikely that all other anthropic coincidences have a naturalistic explanation, given N, since the space of possibilities, given N, can be estimated for at least some of these coincidences. For example, consider the estimate of the probability, given N, that $C_p \in Q$, where C_p represents the conditions which are a subset of C and listed in Table 16.2 of the aforementioned book by Hugh Ross.[7] So, although it is not clear how to assess the probability, given N, that H ∈ Q, there exists a distinct subset C_p of anthropic coincidences, where no element of C_p is an element of H, and where the probability of the members of C_p all being an element of Q, given N, can be estimated. Therefore, the unknown probability space objection does not apply to all anthropic coincidences, and fine-tuning arguments that are built on C_p survive against this objection. Furthermore, the AFTLOP establishes that all anthropic coincidences, being physical conditions not caused by humans, are caused by God. (Note that the success of my fine-tuning argument does not rely on the soundness of the AFTLOP, but the soundness of the AFTLOP does strengthen the degree to which the theistic creation-design hypothesis is confirmed by my fine-tuning arguments.)

The objection may be raised that although the probability may be small that a universe in which L is true could be randomly selected by some natural process, there may nevertheless exist unknown natural processes which entail that the probability is close to 1 that a randomly naturally selected universe would sustain some form of (possibly not carbon-based) life.[8] In response, even if we make the scientifically unjustified concession that the probability is close to one that a naturally selected universe would sustain some form of (possibly not carbon-based) life, there remains the problem of finding a natural explanation of the causal origin of conditions C which facilitate the sustenance of the carbon-based life we actually find on Earth. Therefore, my fine-tuning argument here is immune to this objection.

Now the implications of my fine-tuning argument will be explored. Given (28), we have the choice of rejecting N or rejecting C ∈ Q. If we reject N, then since no other naturalistic explanation of physical events (especially C) has been provided, it follows that theistic causal explanations of physical events are seen to be of superior explanatory value, since theistic explanations justifiably identify the source of physical event causation (including the source of the cause of C and Q), whereas no naturalistic explanation of physical events is even available as a live option. Thus, rejecting N strongly disconfirms atheism, favoring theism.

Atheists, presumably keenly aware of their intellectual discomfort associated with rejecting N, are instead rather likely to opt to reject the claim "it is presently known that C ∈ Q", pointing out that a scientific discovery at some future time T will establish that C ∈ Q is true at T. This option, however, is simply a naturalism-of-the-gaps tactic, and unless justification is provided for the filling of knowledge gaps with naturalistic explanations, such gaps should not be so filled. Granted, given N, and given that it is not presently known that $C \in Q$, theists are not necessarily justified in inferring that $C \in Q$ will not ever be known at some future time, but neither are atheists necessarily justified in assuming $C \in Q$ will be known at some future time.

So, given N, and given that $C \in Q$ is not presently known, it would be prudent to withhold judgment as to the estimate of P(B), unless there is a good reason to suppose that the estimate may be accurately quantified. In general, knowledge of M may be sufficiently limited such that it may not be possible to calculate a probabilistic estimate of the likelihood (given N) that some specific physical event type R is an element of Q. On the other hand, in cases in which knowledge of M is sufficient to calculate a probabilistic estimate of the likelihood (given N) of $R \in Q$, that estimate represents the degree to which a naturalistic explanation of R is likely. In the case of the fine-tuning argument, since knowledge of M is sufficient to estimate the probability, given N, of $C \in Q$, and since that probability is vanishingly small, it follows that it is very unlikely that there exists a naturalistic explanation of C. It is by default, therefore, that we may arrive at the conclusion that C must have a personal causal explanation, since personally-caused physical events are the only reasonable alternative to naturalistic explanations (this is especially true, given the AFTLOP). The person(s) responsible for causing C is profoundly greater in power and knowledge than humans, and this constitutes strong evidence in support of the theistic hypothesis.

The objection may be raised that a God-of-the-gaps strategy has been employed in the reasoning above. However, the inference to a non-naturalistic personal explanation of C has been made not due to ignorance of unknown naturalistic explanations, but through knowledge of limitations on naturalistic explanations, as quantified by probability estimates grounded in scientific knowledge (not ignorance). We arrive at a justified theistic explanation of C not merely by virtue of observing there is an absence of a presently available naturalistic explanation of C, but by virtue of this observation in conjunction with the knowledge that such an explanation is highly unlikely.

The objection may be raised that since future scientific discoveries are virtually unpredictable, it can not be known that a naturalistic explanation of C will not be forthcoming, implying that theistic explanations ought to be rejected as being unjustifiably dogmatic regarding future unknowns. In response, the objection considered here consists of the arbitrary rejection of possible theistic explanations on the grounds that non-theistic explanations might possibly be discovered in the future, yet no good reason is provided for dismissing the alternative option of rejecting possible non-theistic explanations on the grounds that theistic explanations might always continue to be confirmed in the future. It is logically possible that a naturalistic explanation of C will be forthcoming, but it is also logically possible that a naturalistic explanation of C will always continue to be increasingly unlikely. These bare logical possibilities do not justify rejection of what is presently known with high likelihood, namely, that the probability of a naturalistic explanation of C is vanishingly small. Furthermore, the objection considered here is arguably grounded in the principle "given unknown future discoveries, we do not presently possess knowledge." This principle, however, is self-refuting, since the present nonexistence of knowledge would entail the principle is not presently known, contradicting the assertion that the principle is presently known.

The objection might be raised that many, if not most, physical events have been discovered to be members of Q, and therefore, given continuing scientific progress, the remaining physical events not presently known to be members of Q will likely be known to be members of Q at some future time T. In response, note that this objection simply rejects what is scientifically established. Yes, many physical events not presently known to be members of Q may well be known to be members of Q at T, but this in no way entails that all physical events are likely to be known members of Q at some future time. It is possible that some physical events are not members of Q, and my fine-tuning arguments suggest that this possibility is highly likely. The number of known members of Q may increase for many years to come, and the great majority of physical events might eventually be known to be members of Q, but these facts are also consistent with the existence of some God-caused physical events that are not, and never will be, members of Q. Furthermore, scientific progress is in the direction of increasing knowledge of an increasing quantity of known anthropic coincidences.[9] Given these trends, the theistic hypothesis only continues to be strengthened. Scientific progress is the enemy of the atheist, not the theist.

The objection may be raised that the matter of "whether there are supernatural beings" must be settled "before asking whether in fact one such being actually did design our universe."[10] In response, this objection presumes that entity X must be known to exist prior to examination of evidence of X's existence. Clearly, this is an unreasonable demand, as it would preclude one's capacity to infer the existence of any entity by means of adducing evidence of its existence. Therefore, the objection considered here may be rejected.

The objection may be raised that since we do not understand how a nonphysical mind can cause a physical event, it is unintelligible to claim that physical conditions in the universe are designed by a nonhuman person's nonphysical mind.[11] In response, one may know that R is the cause of T, yet not understand how R causes T. Instances of causation may be known, even if the detailed means are unknown by which the causal relation is effective. Thus, my fine-tuning argument may be used to infer the existence of theistic design of physical conditions, even if it is not understood how the theistic designer actually accomplishes the task of causing physical events by means of the exercise of nonphysical power to produce physical effects.

Observe that throughout my discussion of the fine-tuning argument, I have sought to largely disregard the results of the AFTLOP so as to develop an independent line of natural theology that may be used to confirm theism. In fact, all this concern about whether a physical event will be discovered to be described by M at some future time T is of no concern whatsoever to the theist, since the AFTLOP entails that all physical events not caused by humans are God-caused. Therefore, even multiverse objections to the theistic inference fail, since the AFTLOP entails that all physical events in the multiverse not caused by humans are God-caused. See chapter 1 for details.

The objection may be raised that fine-tuning arguments fail to consider probabilities conditioned upon L (p. 154:8-9). In response to this objection, first note that my fine-tuning argument above is grounded in the assumption that conditions C exist, where C is known to exist by virtue of our observations of physical conditions. Since selection of members of C is made on the basis of our present understanding of the laws of physics and of existing physical life, my argument is seen to be grounded on the condition that life exists.

Also, given N, consideration of probabilities conditioned upon $L \in Q$, in conjunction with the observation that although $C \in Q$ is a necessary condition of $L \in Q$, $C \in Q$ is not a sufficient condition of $L \in Q$, leads to an even stronger fine-tuning argument. I submit that theism is more strongly confirmed by the fine-tuning argument below than by the fine-tuning argument above. Here, V shall represent the conjunction "N and $(L \in Q)$", and W shall represent "$P((L \in Q)|N) \approx 0$".

(29) $P((L \in Q) \mid (N \text{ and } (C \in Q))) < 1$

(30) $P((L \in Q)|N) < P((C \in Q)|N)$

(31) $P((C \in Q)|N) \approx 0$

(32) $P((L \in Q)|N) \approx 0$

(33) $P(W) \approx 1$

(34) $P(\sim W|V) \approx 1$

(35) $P(\sim V|W) \approx 1$

(36) $P(\sim V) \approx 1$

(37) $P(\sim(N \text{ and } (L \in Q))) \approx 1$

(38) $P(\sim N \text{ or } \sim(L \in Q)) \approx 1$

Premises (29) and (30) result from the fact that, given N, C ∈ Q is not a sufficient condition of L ∈ Q (even though, given N, C ∈ Q is a necessary condition of L ∈ Q). Premise (31) is from (4). Premise (32) is from substitution of (31) into (30). Note that since the probability in (31) approximates zero, the probability in (32) must even more closely approximate zero. Premise (33) follows from (32) and the definition of W. Premise (34) is true, since a physical event being a member of Q entails that the probability, given N, of its being caused by M is not vanishingly small, and since any physical event with a vanishingly small probability, given N, of being caused by M is probably not caused by M and, thus, is probably not a member of Q. This follows from the fact that L ∈ Q is likely (given N) if and only if $P((L \in Q)|N) \approx 1$. In other words, it is unlikely that it would be likely to be very unlikely that L ∈ Q (given N), if it is given that N and (L ∈ Q) are both true. Premise (35) follows from premises (33) and (34), given that we are able to make the inference from $[P(\sim X|Y) \approx k]$ to $[P(\sim Y|X) \approx k]$, when $k \approx 1$, and when $P(X) \approx 1$ (this inference form has been previously justified, and is generalized from the details shown earlier in premises (5) through (25)). Premise (36) follows from (33) and (35), and is grounded in the well known *modus ponens* inference. Premise (37) follows from substitution of the definition of V into (36). Premise (38) is the inclusive logical disjunction that results from (37).

So, the argument here (premises (29) to (38)) is even stronger than the argument earlier (premises (4) to (28)), since the probability in (32) must even more closely approximate zero than the probability in (4) or (31). Also, we are faced with either rejecting N or rejecting L ∈ Q, yet both options confirm theism. If we reject N, then, by default, this confirms theistic causal explanations of the origin of L, as no other reasonable option remains. If we reject L $\in$ Q, then this also confirms theistic causal explanations of L, since no other reasonable alternative remains. Thus, the universe is life-friendly in the sense that conditions that are necessary for L $\in$ Q exist, yet the fine-tuning argument in premises (4) through (28) shows that this fact may be used to confirm theism. Also, the universe is not life-friendly in the sense that C $\in$ Q is not only exceedingly improbable on N, but is also insufficient for L $\in$ Q, and the fine-tuning argument in premises (29) through (38) shows that these facts may be used to confirm theism even more strongly.

This is not the end of problems for atheists, as theists may exploit the implications of (4) from another angle. Consider the following argument:

(39) $P((C \in Q)|N) \approx 0$

(40) $P(((L \in Q) \text{ and } (C \in Q))|N) < P((C \in Q)|N)$

(41) $P(((L \in Q) \text{ and } (C \in Q))|N) \approx 0$

(42) $P((\sim(L \in Q) \text{ or } \sim(C \in Q))| N) \approx 1$

Premise (39) is from (4). Premise (40) is another way to express the fact that, given N, C $\in$ Q is not a sufficient condition of L $\in$ Q. Premise (41) follows from substitution of (39) into (40). Premise (42) is the conditional disjunction that follows from the conditional conjunction in (41). Here, atheists embracing N are faced with the difficult choice of either rejecting L $\in$ Q or rejecting C $\in$ Q, yet either choice will leave unexplained what theism justifiably explains as the effect of the causal powers of God. Theism has greater explanatory power (this is especially true given the AFTLOP).

Atheists sometimes resist the implications of compelling theistic evidence by exhibiting an adamant blind faith in the future discovery of presently unknown non-theistic explanations of that evidence. This faith surely rivals, if not exceeds, that of even the most ardent adherents to religious belief systems. However, even if we blindly assume that such future discoveries will be made, then this assumption, along with the presently scientifically established improbability of naturalistic explanations of C and L, nevertheless disconfirms N:

(43) $P(((L \in Q) \text{ and } (C \in Q))|N) \approx 0$

(44) $P((L \in Q) \text{ and } (C \in Q)) \approx 1$

(45) $P(N|((L \in Q) \text{ and } (C \in Q))) \approx 0$

(46) $P(N) \approx 0$

Premise (43) is from (41). Premise (44) is the "blind faith" assumption we grant atheists who, despite presently established scientific evidence to the contrary, withhold from theistic belief on the (unjustified) grounds that C and L will be known at some future time to be members of Q. Premise (45) follows from (43) and (44), using the inference from $[P(X|Y) \approx k]$ to $[P(Y|X) \approx k]$, when $k \approx 0$, and when $P(X) \approx 1$ (this inference form has been previously justified, and is generalized from the details shown earlier in premises (5) through (23)). Premise (46) follows from (44) and (45), and is an instance of the well known *modus ponens* inference.

Thus we have shown that the "blind faith" atheistic assumption actually leads to a disconfirmation of the naturalism to which atheists so desperately cling. Now, it might be objected that the "blind faith" assumption has been misconstrued, since the assumption that (44) is true at future time T entails that (43) is false at T, rendering (45) and (46) both unjustified at T. This objection, however, may be rejected at once, since (43) is *now* presently scientifically established, regardless of whether it will be scientifically disconfirmed at T. We must not reject what is presently scientifically established on the basis of what may conceivably be scientifically discovered in the future. Furthermore, the smallness of the probability in (43) is the reason why (44) is labeled the "blind faith" assumption, since its smallness entails that it is highly unlikely that (43) will ever be scientifically disconfirmed. The "blind faith" assumption is, therefore, seen to be an implicit claim that science is false. If an atheist must reject, on blind faith, what is scientifically established so as to justify the atheistic worldview, then the arguments of that atheist surely ought to be rejected. Therefore, contra Smith (p. 104:1-11), anyone who claims "science is false and atheism is true" ought to be placed beyond the pale of academic respectability and be dismissed as an "anti-religious kook". It is time for atheists to "come out of the closet" regarding the implications of atheism.

The objection may be raised that the argument above is not conditioned upon L. In response, first note that (43) is derived from premises and conditions grounded in the assumption that conditions C exist, and members of C are selected based on knowledge of the laws of physics and of existing *life*. Also, note that if N is replaced with "N and L" in the argument above, then the conclusion becomes $P(N \text{ and } L) \approx 0$. Then, since L is true, and since N is assumed by virtue of the "blind faith" assumption, it follows that "blind faith atheists" hold to the high improbability of (N and L), while also assuming both N and L are true. This does not entail that blind faith atheists believe a contradictory state of affairs actually obtains, but it does show that they embrace a highly improbable alternative to theistic design of L or C, where theistic design of L or C is likely, given the implications of (28), (38), (42) and (46), and given the further confirming implications of the AFTLOP.

In other words, in the face of compelling evidence to the contrary, blind faith atheists embrace a highly improbable naturalistic explanation, where an alternative theistic explanation is far more likely. Granted, improbable events do sometimes occur, and the best explanation may sometimes be that an improbable possibility was in fact actualized.[12] This does not, however, give us license to favor whatever improbable explanation may suit our fancy. For even if it is the case that we know that the best explanation BE is that an improbable possibility was in fact actualized, this knowledge may be acquired and sustained through reflection upon the fact that BE is the most probable good explanation, even though BE entails the occurrence of an improbable event. So, given a set of possible and mutually exclusive explanations, inference to the best explanation does not occur if a probable explanation is rejected in favor of an improbable explanation. Thus, blind faith atheists do not opt for the best explanation when embracing a position that is highly improbable and strongly disconfirmed by justified contrary theistic explanations.

Finally, our entire discussion of the fine-tuning argument has been in the context of consideration of the laws M of physics, which are taken to be the impersonal causal explanation of the set Q of physical events. However, as shown in the AFTLOP (chapter 1), impersonal causes doubtfully exist, and the laws of physics generally describe God-caused physical event patterns. So, my fine-tuning arguments show the inadequacy of naturalistic explanations of certain anthropic coincidences, and they also show the superiority of justified theistic explanations of those coincidences. In addition, my AFTLOP substantially broadens the scope of justified theistic explanations to subsume virtually all physical events.

Therefore, probabilistic fine-tuning arguments derived from anthropic principle considerations confirm theism, and theistic design of physical events relevant to anthropic coincidences is only a small subset of the set of all physical events known to have a justified theistic causal explanation. Ikeda and Jefferys are not correct in their assessment.

Now consider the poker analogy used by Ikeda and Jefferys (p. 153:23-29). In this analogy, A (p. 153:24) is analogous to C, where C is defined as in my fine-tuning arguments above, and B (p. 153:25) is analogous to N (as defined by Ikeda and Jefferys). Recall that we may make the inference from $[P(X|Y) \approx k]$ to $[P(Y|X) \approx k]$ when $k \approx 0$, and when $P(X) \approx 1$ (this inference form has been previously justified, and is generalized from the details shown earlier in premises (5) through (23)). So, in my fine-tuning argument, the inference from (6) to eventually (23) is shown in detail and is facilitated by the critical fact (5), whereas, in the poker case, the inference from $[P(A|B) \approx 0]$ to $[P(B|A) \approx 0]$ is not permitted, since $P(A)$ is not nearly one. In fact, the probability in (5) is close to one, yet $P(A)$ is much less than one, and it is in this important sense that the poker analogy is not good. Therefore, the fact that $P(B|A)$ is not close to zero does not entail, by analogy, that $P(N|C)$ is also not close to zero.

The main thrust of my fine-tuning arguments is that (4) may be used to show that theism is very likely, not that F is false (p. 155:18-21). It is possible that my fine-tuning argument could be interpreted as an argument that God exists and causes certain physical events (e.g., C and L) in the universe, while still allowing for the possibility that other physical events described by laws of physics may be fully explained exclusively in terms of naturalistic causes. The AFTLOP (chapter 1), however, establishes that even these other physical events described by laws of physics are God-caused. The point, here, is that my fine-tuning argument is not used to establish that the life-friendly physical conditions represented by F do not exist. Indeed, those life-friendly conditions do exist, and the extreme improbability on N of those conditions suggests the conditions do not have a naturalistic cause, as I have previously argued. So, although I do not argue that the conditions represented by F do not exist, the hypothesis F is, itself, not reasonable, given that F presupposes naturalistic causes of those conditions exist, whereas my fine-tuning arguments and the AFTLOP together establish that such causes doubtfully exist. This result suggests that the physical conditions represented by F are unlikely to have a naturalistic cause, and this contradicts the unjustified assertion that F is known (p. 154:2-4) and that F is an observation (e.g., p. 155:12-14, 16-17). Furthermore, since F is likely false, and since Ikeda and Jefferys believe ~F "manifestly supports supernaturalism by refuting naturalism" (p. 166:12-17), it follows that they should recognize that it is likely that supernaturalism (theism) is supported and naturalism is refuted by the fact that F is unlikely.

Therefore, Ikeda and Jefferys misunderstand F, its degree of justification, and its role in assessing the probability of N (p. 156:14-19), and they are mistaken in supposing the fine-tuning argument does not undermine N (p. 156:17-18). Proponents of fine-tuning arguments, while rejecting F, may argue along the lines outlined in my fine-tuning arguments above. Also, the main theorem presented by Ikeda and Jefferys (p. 155:3-5) is used to argue that such proponents can not claim that F undermines N (p. 155: 27-28), but this completely misses the point that those proponents need not make such a claim when presenting fine-tuning arguments. In addition, they argue that these proponents sometimes claim that ~F undermines N (p. 155:22-26), but this claim also need not be a component of a fine-tuning argument. So, the "main theorem" (p. 155:3-5) is not even relevant to the fine-tuning arguments I have presented.

It is not the case that proponents of fine-tuning arguments must argue that each of F and ~F disconfirms N (p. 156:14-17). Rather, as mentioned earlier, they may be viewed as understanding that the universe is life-friendly in the sense that conditions that are necessary for L ϵ Q exist, yet the fine-tuning argument in premises (4) through (28) shows that this fact may be used to confirm theism. Also, they may be viewed as perceiving that the universe is not life-friendly in the sense that C ϵ Q is not only exceedingly improbable on N, but C ϵ Q is also insufficient for L ϵ Q, and the fine-tuning argument in premises (29) through (38) shows that these facts may be used to confirm theism even more strongly. In other words, C ϵ Q is necessary for a naturalistic explanation of life-friendly conditions C, yet (4) entails that C ϵ Q is very unlikely (given N), and this fact may be used to confirm theism, whereas the improbability of C ϵ Q (given N) entails that conditions C are not life-friendly in the sense that although C ϵ Q and L ϵ Q are necessary conditions for a naturalistic explanation of C and L, C ϵ Q is not a sufficient condition of L ϵ Q, implying that even if C ϵ Q were true, the improbability of L ϵ Q would persist. My fine-tuning arguments, therefore, have multiple "prongs" (p. 156:14-19), and there is no contradiction in the assertion that each prong is true.

Ikeda and Jefferys acknowledge the possibility of the existence of other life-filled universes (p. 156:25-30). The fact that unknown forms of life in unknown universes with unknown physical conditions might conceivably exist is indeed an interesting fact. I sometimes wonder what mysterious and unimaginably creative expressions of divine activity may exist in worlds (John 14:1-4) presently unknown to us. Perhaps the afterlife (Hebrew 9:27-28) will, among other things, consist of the joyous and endless discovery of the beauty of God's creativity (Revelation 21:1-8) which is to be ever more fully revealed to those who, while on Earth, lived a life in which genuine willingness to appropriately and positively respond to revealed truth was exhibited (John 10:27), even though this required denial of one's natural tendency to maximize the degree to which carnal self-gratification was achieved. Although such denial is a necessary condition of following Yeshua (Luke 9:18-27), who is the personal embodiment of truth (John 14:6), the alternative option of losing one's soul is hardly preferable, especially given the eternal consequences of our earthly actions (Matthew 24:36-25:46). Incidentally, a sufficient condition of following Yeshua evidently consists of all that is entailed by believing in him (John 3:16-21) who was raised from the dead (1 Corinthians 15:1-8). *Interested readers should not hesitate to fully pursue this way of life*, as the unenlightened natural state of man is sinful (Romans 3:21-26) and deserving of death (Romans 6:15-23), implying not only that one's personal need for receiving salvation (Romans 10:9-13) by grace through faith (Ephesians 2:1-10) is urgent, but also that our participation in the achievement of the loving goal of global evangelization and discipleship (Matthew 28:16-20) ought to be our foundational life principle as informed members of the conservative Evangelical community of believers who are unified in devotion to the supremely loving God who commands us to seek Him (Isaiah 55:6-9), love Him (Deuteronomy 6:4-9), and love others (John 13:34-35) as the outward expression of the love given us by the Holy Spirit (Romans 5:5) who indwells us and imparts the knowledge of God (1 John 3:24) with whom we are spiritually united (1 Corinthians 6:12-20), and in whose presence we are filled with immeasurable joy and eternal pleasures (Psalm 16:11).

Despite the possibility of other life-filled universes, however, (4) is true nonetheless. Proposition (4) is the claim that the physical conditions necessary for the naturalistic explanation of physical life are exceedingly improbable (given naturalistic explanations in terms of presently known laws of physics), and these conditions are known to be so improbable based on known laws of physics, not based on ignorance of physics (p. 156:26-30). Of course, every knowledge claim made by non-omniscient person J is based, in part, on J's ignorance of knowledge unknown to J, but this fact in no way necessitates that J's knowledge claims are unjustified. In fact, if J's knowledge claim is unjustified due to J's ignorance of knowledge unknown to J, then so too are the claims of Ikeda and Jefferys unjustified due to their ignorance of knowledge unknown to them. Of course, this result may be generalized to the self-refuting claim that J knows that J's knowledge claims are unjustified, but this only supports the fact already stated: every knowledge claim made by non-omniscient person J is based, in part, on J's ignorance of knowledge unknown to J, but this fact in no way necessitates that J's knowledge claim is unjustified. So, if Ikeda and Jefferys wish to object to science-based fine-tuning arguments, they must do better than object that such arguments are necessarily ignorant of presently unknown scientific knowledge.

Ikeda and Jefferys claim that Hugh Ross claims that $P(F|N)$ is small (p. 156:30-157:1; p. 157:36). However, F entails that there exist naturalistic causal explanations for at least some physical events, and I doubt Ross accepts that such explanations exist. No reason is given for supposing that fine-tuning arguments require the assumption that $P(F|N)$ is small. Since N entails F (as discussed earlier), $P(F|N)$ is, in fact, not small at all. Note, however, that the fact that $P(F|N)$ is not small does not entail that F is likely. Indeed, F is unlikely, given the results of my fine-tuning arguments and the AFTLOP, and $P(F|N)$ is not small for the simple reason that N entails F is likely. Proponents of fine-tuning arguments need not claim $P(F|N)$ is small, but may rather claim that (4) is true. (To further clarify the distinction between my fine-tuning arguments and those criticized by Ikeda and Jefferys, recall that the definition of N in their $P(F|N)$ is distinct from the definition of N in (4)).

Ikeda and Jefferys discuss the relative likelihood of a single-universe hypothesis versus a multiple-universe hypothesis (p. 157:3-158:11). In this discussion, reference is made to the possibility of the existence of an infinite number of universes (p. 157:3-9; p. 157:38-158:1). Later, reference is made to the possibility of the existence of an infinite set of deities (p. 161:31-32). The assertion that there could exist an actually infinite quantity, however, is controversial and in need of support, yet no compelling support is given. The arguments against the possibility of the existence of actually infinite quantities are neither addressed nor even acknowledged to exist.

Ikeda and Jefferys evidently believe that the fine-tuning arguments presented by Hugh Ross amount to the claim that a very small proportion of possible naturalistic universes could support life (p. 157:10-12; p. 161:4-7). It should be evident from my fine-tuning arguments presented earlier, however, that such a claim is not a necessary component of a fine-tuning argument. In fact, it has not even been established that the possibility of the existence of multiple universes (whether naturalistic or not) is even plausible. So, proponents of my fine-tuning arguments need not make unjustified speculative assertions about properties of possibly existing presently unknown naturalistic explanations of possibly existing multiple universes. The nonexistence of a justified naturalistic explanation of multiple existing universes entails not that my fine-tuning arguments consist of unjustified speculation, but that naturalistic multiple-universe theories are presently unjustified. My fine-tuning arguments consist of an emphasis on the possibility that naturalistic explanations of our universe exist in terms of presently known physical laws, not the possibility that naturalistic explanations of unknown multiple universes exist in terms of presently unknown physical laws. So, Ross need not claim that a very small proportion of possible naturalistic universes could support life, but he may rather claim that theistic implications result from the fact that (4) entails that a naturalistic explanation of C or L is very unlikely in terms of physical laws describing the only universe presently known to exist.

Additionally, proponents of fine-tuning arguments need not claim that observing F decreases the probability of N (p. 157:17-19), especially since F is arguably not even an observation. The AFTLOP, in particular, establishes that naturalistic explanations are unlikely, and this, in turn, entails that F (which entails that life can exist naturalistically) is unlikely. To be sure, there exist physical conditions C whose existence is a necessary prerequisite of identifying a naturalistic explanation of life, and if these conditions are represented by F, then this aspect of F is indeed an observation. However, the hypothesis F also includes the claim that these conditions "permit or are compatible with life existing naturalistically" (p. 151:1-3), and this claim entails that naturalistic explanations exist, yet no reason is given for supposing that such explanations ought to be either assumed or considered observed. So, even if it were true that observing F "cannot decrease the probability that N is true, and may increase it" (p. 157:17-19), we have no reason to suppose F is observed, and we have reason (the AFTLOP) to suppose F is not observed.

The conclusion that a multiple-universe hypothesis may be more likely than a single-universe hypothesis is, in part, grounded in the assumption that "the universe is governed by naturalistic laws" (p. 157:22-26). Since the AFTLOP and my fine-tuning arguments establish that naturalistic laws do not govern (cause) any physical events, we may reject the conclusion that a multiple-universe hypothesis may be more likely than a single-universe hypothesis. Given that Ikeda and Jefferys offer no reason to suppose that any universe is governed by naturalistic laws, this rejection is further justified. Also, the single-universe hypothesis is favored by the fact that our physical universe is the only physical universe we have observed. In fact, to the extent that it is true that other physical universes are not even observable (the space-time manifolds of distinct universes can not overlap), the single-universe hypothesis is favored. Even if it will be forthcoming that observations within our universe lead to confirmation of testable predictions of multiple-universe theories, this will not justify the assertion that such theories are consequently best, since the AFTLOP entails that those observations could be better interpreted as confirmation of the existence and causal activity of the theistic designer-creator-sustainer of the only universe known to exist. The appeal to the existence of multiple (nay, a potentially infinite number of) unobservable universes, each with supposedly different physical conditions, surely appears to be an *ad hoc* attempt to favor the multiple-universe theory. Additionally, if the multiple-universe theory is favored only if the above-quoted naturalistic presupposition (p. 157:22-26) is brought to the table, then that theory is hardly evidence for the existence of naturalistic explanations of physical events, unless we wish to embrace circular reasoning!

Even if a multiple-universe hypothesis were eventually established, it would not necessarily follow that there exist multiple-universe laws of physics that entail that life would probably exist in at least one of those universes. Also, even if there exist multiple-universe laws of physics that entail that life probably exists in at least one of those universes, it does not necessarily follow that such laws would render likely the existence of life in a universe such as ours. Furthermore, even if there exist multiple-universe laws of physics that entail that life probably exists in at least one universe such as ours, it does not follow that there exists a naturalistic explanation for the physical events described by those laws. This is especially true given the AFTLOP, which entails that physical events described by multiple-universe laws of physics would be caused by God. So, although multiple-universe physical laws, if ever identified, could conceivably provide a description of the existence of life in terms of a known law of physics (thereby refuting proposition (4), the foundation of my fine-tuning arguments), the AFTLOP would nevertheless entail that such laws are caused by God. All of the considerations above, and in particular, the fact that the single-universe hypothesis is in better accordance with the number of universes known to be observed, combined with the fact that a multiple-universe hypothesis would not be better justified unless we made the unjustified assumption that naturalistic laws govern (cause) all existing universes, entail that my fine-tuning arguments stand, further confirming the results of the AFTLOP.

Ikeda and Jefferys discuss the degree to which N is confirmed (or ~N is disconfirmed) by the observation F, given the possible existence of various hypothetical deities (p. 158:12-163:32). This discussion is built on the assumption that F is an observation, but it has been previously shown that no good reason has been provided to suppose F is observed. Since there is no good reason to suppose F is observed, and since the AFTLOP suggests F is unlikely, the discussion by Ikeda and Jefferys turns out to be an interesting detailed analysis of the implications of an unlikely state of affairs. In fact, it is conceded that theistic arguments not grounded in F are not undermined by that analysis (p. 159:32-36). So, since my fine-tuning arguments are not grounded in F, that analysis does not undermine my fine-tuning arguments.

It is suggested that Ockham's Razor may be used to slash the God hypothesis "if the predictions we get are indistinguishable from those of naturalistic law" (p. 161:12-14). There is a key distinction here between theism and naturalism, however. On naturalism (as defined by Ikeda and Jefferys, p. 152:30-32), given physical event E, and given that $P(E)$ is the probability that E has a naturalistic explanation in terms of a law of physics, it follows that $P(E) \approx 1$. On theism, however, a sufficiently powerful deity may cause E to occur, where it is known that E is unlikely to ever be described by any law of physics, in which case $P(E) << 1$. Since naturalism predicts $P(E) \approx 1$, yet theism does not so predict, the observation of proposition (4) is a case in which naturalism is disconfirmed, thus confirming theism by default. Furthermore, in response to the question raised by Ikeda and Jefferys (p. 161:12-14), we may ask: What would be the point of rejecting the God hypothesis in favor of causal explanations in terms of naturalistic laws, when the AFTLOP establishes that naturalistic laws are not even causal explanations at all, but are merely descriptions of physical event patterns caused by God?

Ikeda and Jefferys have evidently formulated a rejection of theistic fine-tuning arguments (p. 163:9-14) on the grounds that F is an observation (p. 162:23-24). Since F is not observed (as shown previously), we may reject their rejection of theistic fine-tuning arguments on the grounds that it is derived from a naturalism-of-the-gaps assumption (i.e., F). My rejection of their rejection is further strengthened by both the AFTLOP and my fine-tuning arguments which together entail that naturalistic explanations (including those entailed by F) likely do not exist. Thus, we may reject the final comments (p. 163:33-164:32), as they simply highlight key issues already addressed above.

In chapter 4 of part 2 of IPRG, Wesley C. Salmon argues that Bayes's theorem may be used to establish that the probability is very small that there exists an intelligent designer (God) of the universe. Salmon's analysis is evidently based on the assumption that mechanical impersonal causes are not improbable. However, the AFTLOP establishes that mechanical impersonal causes are, in fact, improbable. Since Salmon's argument is uninformed by this consideration, his argument is thus seen to abruptly crumble.

Salmon asserts that the number of known instances of mechanical causation in the universe is very large (p. 174:18-35). He presumably considers mechanical causes to be cases in which physical events cause physical events, where laws of physics provide generalized descriptions of physical event patterns in which subsequent physical events are caused by prior physical events, and where no action by an intelligent being is a component of this causal process. Salmon, however, does not explain why we should assume that the causal activity of an intelligent being is not the source of the physical events labeled "mechanically caused". In fact, the AFTLOP establishes that such events are caused by a person. So, the claim that P(A, B) is low (p. 174:34-35) is refuted, and the conclusion that P(A · C, B) is low (p. 175:25-37) does not follow. Neither does the conclusion follow that the intelligent design hypothesis is on a par with the mechanical hypothesis (p. 178:1-12), particularly since all cases in which the cause of a physical event is known are cases in which the cause is a person, and since no physical event is known to be caused by a physical event.

Salmon considers that very large projects intelligently designed by humans are likely designed by a group of humans, not a single human (p. 176:24-37). In an analogy to the universe as a whole, this observation might be used to attempt to disconfirm the theistic hypothesis that a single God designed the universe, since large intelligently designed projects are likely designed by a group, not an individual. In response, a Trinitarian theistic designer would be a composite unity of three persons, which is, in a sense, a group. More importantly, the analogy does not establish that a single God is unlikely to be the designer of the universe, but establishes that a single human is unlikely to be the designer of the universe. Since no reason is provided for supposing that a hypothetical designer of the universe must have creative capacities identical to humans, we need not suppose that a designer of the universe must be a large group of persons. Furthermore, the AFTLOP establishes that the creative capacities of God are most assuredly greater than human capacities, so the analogy to large projects intelligently designed by humans does not disconfirm theism.

Salmon considers that if God is considered to be a disembodied intelligence, then the nonexistence of observations of intelligent design (causation) by disembodied intelligent beings entails $P(A, B) = 0$ for such beings (p. 176:38-177:5). In response, some versions of theism do not require that the creator-God be disembodied. For example, one conceivable version of theism includes the belief that Jesus has a body (John 20:1-31) and that Jesus is the creator-sustainer of the universe (Colossians 1:16-17). More importantly, no reason is provided for the assumption that the laws of physics do not describe regular physical event patterns caused by God (disembodied or not). The AFTLOP, furthermore, establishes that God (disembodied or not) is the cause of the physical events described by the laws of physics, so the question of whether God is disembodied need not be answered prior to establishing that God is the cause of such events.

Salmon considers the idea that physical life is not caused by an intelligent designer, but by biological generation via genetic principles (p. 177:6-14). However, no evidence is provided for the assumption that genetic principles possess causal power. No justification is provided for the assumption that genetic principles do not describe the effects of the creative causal sustaining power of an intelligent designer (God). The AFTLOP, furthermore, establishes that God is the cause of the physical events described by laws of physics. Therefore, it is improbable that physical life is not caused by an intelligent designer, if physical life is explained by laws of physics. Incidentally, physical life is not fully explained by the laws of physics, and my fine-tuning arguments presented earlier use this information to establish that there exists an intelligent designer of physical life.

Salmon examines the claim that when moral attributes are conjoined to the theistic hypothesis, the likelihood of theism is decreased (p. 178:13-179:10), given that there are many conceivable ways God could diminish the quantity of evil in the world if God so desired (p. 179:11-32), and given the alleged consequent lack of justification for the inference to theism from physical observations of supposedly intelligently designed features of the physical world. First, in response, the term "evil" is not clearly defined in the discussion, so it is not even clear precisely what is meant by that term. "Evil" could conceivably be defined in many ways, and depending on the particular definition in use, certain alleged instances of evil may not be evil at all. In fact, it is possible to define "evil" such that evil does not even exist. So, the analysis is incomplete and inconclusive, especially given its failure to defend the fundamental claim that there exist instances of evil. Second, theistic hypotheses often include omniscience as a member of the set of attributes of God, and given that omniscience entails that God's knowledge of the complex nature of reality is exceedingly greater than that of man, it should be clear that man is in no position to assume he knows what actions would be antecedently expected of God to perform (p. 179:33-38). So, it has not been established that the world "might have been vastly improved" (p. 179:33-35). In fact, Hume's architect analogy (p. 180:1-15) does not establish that it is reasonable to believe that the world could have been vastly improved if God so desired, since God's supremely greater knowledge than that of man could include knowledge of good reasons unknown to man which entail that the world could not be so improved. Therefore, Salmon is wrong to infer $P(A \cdot B, C)$ is low, since his claim remains unjustified that he knows what to expect of a deity who may be inscrutable (p. 180:16-24).

Regarding the cause(s) of the universe, Salmon assumes that impersonal mechanical causes are on a par with causes by intelligence (p. 180:16-19). However, as discussed earlier and in the AFTLOP, there exist no known instances of impersonal mechanical causation, and all instances in which the source of causation is known are instances in which the source is a person. The AFTLOP also establishes that physical events not caused by man are caused by God, so Salmon's assumption may be rejected.

Salmon considers the idea that apparently gratuitous evil may disconfirm the hypothesis that God designed the physical world (p. 180:25-39). In response, the terms "evil", "gratuitous evil", and "apparently gratuitous evil" have not been defined, so it is not even clear what events or properties are the object of discussion. If "gratuitous evil" refers to evil events that God would not permit, then the existence of such evil would disconfirm the hypothesis that God exists. However, given that God may know reasons unknown to man which establish that God would not prevent the occurrence of any member of the set V of all evil events, it does not necessarily follow that God's existence is disconfirmed by the existence of apparently gratuitous evil, since each member of V that appears to man to be gratuitous may actually not be gratuitous for reasons known by God but not by man. The existence of apparently gratuitous evil might disconfirm theistic hypotheses in which God is scrutable, but it does not disconfirm theistic hypotheses in which God is inscrutable, since non-omniscient humans are generally in no position to evaluate the likelihood that an omniscient inscrutable God would perform any particular set of actions. Theists can know God exists, even if they do not fully understand the nature and extent of God's actions. One can know the sun shines brightly, even if one does not understand how or why it so shines.

Salmon's belief that proponents of design arguments must consider moral attributes (p. 180:40-181:2) is questionable. My fine-tuning arguments, for example, do not consist of consideration of moral attributes possibly possessed by God, yet they establish that God exists.

Salmon assumes that intelligent design arguments are grounded in the assumption that alleged evidence of intelligent design is known to be actual evidence of intelligent design by virtue of "the adjustment of means to ends" in the physical world (p. 181:2-4). However, the structure of my fine-tuning arguments does not rest on ambiguous or question-begging notions of adjustment of means to ends. So, Salmon's analysis is uninformed by the structure of fine-tuning arguments such as mine.

Salmon frequently assumes (or considers the assumption) that there exist impersonal causes of physical events. For example, he considers the assumption that "order exhibited by living organisms comes from biological generation" (p. 181:20-21). However, no evidence is provided for the assumption that there exists a physically ordered system that is not caused by a person. As noted in the AFTLOP, all cases in which the cause of a physical event is known are cases in which the cause is a person. No reason is provided for supposing that biological generation causes physically ordered systems. No reason is given for believing that biological generation is not simply a description of a category of physical events caused by a person. The claim is unjustified that biological generation causes order in living organisms, since "biological generation" may be interpreted as the subset of the laws of physics that pertains to physical events associated with physical life, and since physical laws, by definition, describe physical event patterns. No justification is provided for the claim that the physical laws of biological generation somehow cause the physical event patterns they describe.

For the reasons described above, a number of related claims may now be seen to be erroneous. For example, Salmon (Philo) is again mistaken when effectively claiming that order can arise out of biological generation (p. 182:23-25). Also, Salmon (Philo) is wrong to claim that all known instances of intelligent design "issue from biological organisms—

biological generation always lies behind intelligence" (p. 182:25-27). No evidence is given for the assumption that it is essential that biological generation always lies behind intelligence. Furthermore, the AFTLOP establishes that God is the cause of the biological generation physical laws, which implies that we need not assume that biological generation lies behind God's intelligent causation of physical events. Additionally, the claim that we have no experience of intelligent creation as a prior source of biological generation (p. 182:27-28) is not only flatly refuted by the results of my fine-tuning arguments, but also appears to be a case of begging the question. Why should we assume, for example, that atoms, stars and galaxies are not physical events caused by a God who is not biologically generated? The claim that we have no experience of God causing such events may result merely from one's failure to appreciate the implications of the nature of physical event causation as outlined in my theistic arguments which entail that intelligent design, consistent with our experience, lies behind the operation of all physical causal principles (p. 182:28-30). So, Salmon is simply wrong when claiming the order in the universe can not be shown by experience to be evidence of intelligent design (p. 183:8-10).

Salmon claims that Darwin showed that "chance mutations and natural selection could lead to the evolution of the species" (p. 183:16-20). In response, observe that it is simply assumed that mutation and natural selection laws of physics cause the evolution of the species. Even if the mutation and natural selection laws described by Darwin are correct, it does not follow that those laws somehow cause the evolution of the species they describe. In fact, we have no evidence that any physical law causes any physical event. Also, as established in the AFTLOP, all physical events not caused by man are caused by God. So, even if Darwin's mutation/selection theory of evolution is a correct description of biological physical events, God is the cause of that theory's obtaining. Likewise, molecular biology does not show how biological order is reproduced by mechanical principles, and neither do Kepler's laws show how order in the solar system is produced by mechanical principles. In fact, since all such physical laws describe regular physical event patterns, and since those physical event patterns are caused by a non-human person (see the AFTLOP), it reasonably follows that events described by Kepler's laws or by molecular biological laws are caused by God (p. 183:22-32). So, the reason physical order entails intelligent design is not because it is merely assumed as an a priori principle, but because it is in our experience that the nature of physical order is such that physical order is intelligently designed.

Salmon recasts the concept of order in terms of the entropy of a physical system (p. 183:33-186:35). Salmon concludes that the vast majority of physical systems which come into being in low entropy states do not result from the purpose or design of a conscious agent (p. 186:28-34). However, no evidence is provided to support the assumption that there exists a physical system not caused by a person. In fact, the AFTLOP establishes that Salmon's assumption is very much mistaken. So, regardless of the amount of entropy of a caused physical system, we may conclude that the system is caused by a person, since causation is, by virtue of its observed nature, known to be personal. It reasonably follows that a being (God) who is much more powerful than man is the cause of the physical universe (regardless of the degree of entropy it possesses), since the physical universe is a caused system, and since the power of man is clearly insufficient as a cause of that system.

Salmon claims that there exist orders of magnitude more instances of evidently impersonal mechanical causation of low entropy systems in comparison to the relatively much smaller number of known instances of low entropy systems created by humans (p. 186:36-187:22). In response, the claim remains unsubstantiated that physical events such as atomic processes within stars and galaxies are instances of low entropy systems not caused by a person. The mere fact that no human is observed to cause such atomic processes hardly entails that those processes are not caused by any person. Furthermore, the AFTLOP establishes that such processes are caused by a non-human person (God), flatly contradicting Salmon's unjustified claim to the contrary. Additionally, the sum total of all free human physical actions integrated over all human history is not obviously significantly less than the number of atomic processes in the history of the universe. For example, merely a single human person could freely cause his physical body to assume a particular low entropy position at each moment throughout a day, and the sum of all atomic processes integrated throughout each moment of a day, throughout each day of one's life, and throughout each human life, leads to a considerably large number which is not obviously significantly less than the number of atomic processes in the history of the universe alleged to have no personal cause. Furthermore, this immense number of instances of physical events known to be caused comprises a set of physical events, where each member of that set is known to be caused by person, whereas the atomic processes referenced by Salmon comprise a set of physical events whose cause is not directly observed. So, as shown in the AFTLOP, the known (personally caused) nature of all events whose cause is known is such that physical events whose cause is not directly observed are reasonably assumed to be personally caused, though not necessarily by a human. This inference is acceptable even if the ratio of "known personally caused physical events" to "physical events whose cause is not directly observed" is small, as the inference is grounded in the application of reasonable and accepted principles used to extrapolate from observed properties of events to properties of events not directly observed. Again, see the AFTLOP for details.

Salmon's claim that atomic formation processes within stars are somewhat understood (p. 187:16-17) arguably reveals underlying naturalistic presuppositions. In particular, Salmon presumably means that identification of physical laws that describe physical events justifies the assumption that the events described by those laws are not caused by a person. After all, physical laws of stellar evolution describe physical event changes, not the formative causes of those changes. So, Salmon's claim that stellar laws of physics describe *formation* processes is inaccurate. The laws do nothing in the way of identifying the possible formative causes of the processes. Rather, the laws simply describe the regular physical event patterns which occur. Furthermore, the inference from "physical laws describe it" to "no person caused it" is a classic naturalistic presupposition that is both unjustified and widespread throughout the scientific community. Note that I do not object to the fact that stellar physics, as developed in modern science, accurately describes physical event changes within stars, but I do disagree with the unjustified assertion that identification of such physical laws somehow entails that the events described by those laws may be somehow mysteriously explained away as "caused by nature". Physical laws describe physical event patterns. The AFTLOP establishes that those patterns not caused by man are caused by God. There is no good reason to suppose "nature" causes or forms anything at all.

Given the above analysis of Salmon's position, his conclusion that God is probably not the intelligent designer of the universe (p. 187:36-188:36) is, needless to say, unjustified. My contention remains that physical events not caused by man are caused (designed) by God. Salmon's misuse of Bayes's theorem is grounded in inaccurate assessment of probabilities, and his inaccuracy stems from a misunderstanding of the implications of the nature of physical event causation.

Finally, lest my argument that all causation is personal be construed as unscientific by virtue of being unfalsifiable (p. 190:10-13), it should be noted that I would readily acknowledge the existence of impersonal mechanical causes if a supremely knowledgeable and reliable person (i.e., God) assured me that it is God who is assuring me of the existence of such impersonal causal entities, but in that case, I would not be concerned that my theistic arguments might crumble, since God's assurance would, itself, entail that God exists. So, although my interpretation of the nature of physical event causation is used to show God exists, the possibility of that interpretation being falsified is plausible only on the condition that God enables me to know that it is God who is giving me the knowledge that my interpretation is inaccurate. Thus, if my interpretation is correct, then God probably exists, and the only way I could plausibly come to know that it is incorrect is if I come to know that it is God who is enabling me to know that it is incorrect, in which case God probably exists. Either way, God probably exists.

In chapter 5 of part 2 of IPRG, Wesley C. Salmon argues in defense of his critique contained in chapter 4 of part 2 of IPRG, and he argues against an objection raised by Nancy Cartwright. Salmon, however, persists in his misunderstanding of the implications of the nature of physical event causation. For example, he continues with his unsubstantiated claim that the universe is full of objects "whose existence can be adequately explained without recourse to intelligent design on the part of a creator" (p. 196:25-28). Salmon must not merely assume what is a fundamental point of dispute between theists and atheists. Rather, Salmon must adduce evidence which may be used to establish that physical entities such as atoms, molecules, stars and galaxies represent instances of impersonal mechanical causation. To be sure, Salmon has cited substantial quantities of scientific information, but this information represents cases in which the physical events in question are caused in such a way that the cause is not directly observed. For example, the observation of stellar evolution in nebulas is not the observation of the cause of the evolution, but is the observation of the effect of the cause of the evolution. The cause of the evolution is not directly observed, but only the effect is observed. The assumption remains entirely unsubstantiated that physical events in nebulas are effects caused by prior physical events. There is no good reason to suppose that any physical event is caused by a physical event. So, since Salmon's observation of star formation in nebulas represents the observation of the creation of an ordered structure, and since there is no reason to suppose that that creation is the effect of a prior physical cause, and since the nature of physical event causation is observed to be personal (see the AFTLOP), it follows that Salmon's observation of star formation represents creation by a person (God) who is assuredly immensely greater in power and knowledge than man. The psalmist was right: "The heavens declare God's glory" (Psalm: 19:1).

In chapter 6 of part 2 of IPRG, Michael Martin expands ideas formulated in Salmon's arguments and develops a set of atheistic teleological arguments. First, Martin defends Salmon's argument, ultimately concluding that it "gives good grounds for supposing that God did not create the universe" (p. 202:8-9). However, as noted earlier, Salmon's argument rests on a number of unsubstantiated claims. For example, Salmon assumes (without proof) that entities such as galaxies, planets, atoms and molecules are not the result of intelligence (p. 199:31-33; p. 201:2-4). Also, Salmon asserts (without proof) that "biological generation and mechanical causation often produce order" (p. 199:35-37). In addition, the creator (God) is regarded as a spiritual disembodied intelligence (p. 200:10-12), but orthodox Christian theology asserts that Jesus has a body and is the creator. It is claimed that we have no experience of a disembodied intelligence that produces order (p. 200:11-12), but the personal nature of all experiences of produced order implies that the universe (an ordered system) is produced by a person, regardless of whether that person happens to be embodied in some way. In fact, the personal cause of the physical universe was doubtfully embodied by a physical body at the time of creation of the physical universe, so we may infer that the creator of the universe was probably physically disembodied at the time of creation. This evidence flatly contradicts Martin's assertion that "Experience surely teaches that there are no disembodied beings" (p. 201:31-32). Assuming the creator/sustainer of the universe is presently physically disembodied, it follows that virtually every physical event in the history of the universe is an instance in which a disembodied being causes a physical event, again contradicting Martin's assertion that we have no experience with disembodied beings. Additional evidence of physically disembodied beings includes spiritual experiences such as out-of-body experiences, near-death experiences, heaven/hell experiences, and angelic/demonic experiences (I personally know of individuals who have had experiences such as these). This evidence also disconfirms Martin's assertion. So, Salmon and Martin are mistaken in supposing that "disembodied intelligence has never operated in any fashion" (p. 201:34-36). Also, Martin assumes our experience is such that a single being does not produce extremely large ordered objects (p. 202:1-2), but the fact that individual humans do not produce extremely large ordered objects does not entail that the non-human personal cause of the existence/sustenance of the physical universe is not the action of a single individual. Therefore, Martin's defense of Salmon's argument may be rejected.

Martin restates and expands Salmon's argument (p. 202:10-203:6) and considers several instantiations of it. The first instantiation he considers is the argument from embodiedness (p. 203:7-205:30), in which he considers God to be a disembodied person who created the universe (p. 203:7-8). In response, it is worth first noting that orthodox Christian theology consists of the belief that Jesus is both the divine creator and a being with a body, so it is not clear whether the argument from embodiedness aims at striking down this widespread version of theism.

In Martin's discussion of premise (1) of the argument from embodiedness, he assumes that in all uncontroversial cases of created objects, "we know of no cases where an entity is created by one or more beings without bodies" (p. 204:7-10). If Martin's term "created" is taken to be synonymous with "caused", and if Martin's term "body" is assumed to be a physical body, then Martin is seen to be claiming that all uncontroversial cases in which physical objects are known to be caused are cases in which the objects are caused by one or more beings with physical bodies. Now, as established in the AFTLOP, uncaused physical events are implausible, and this fact, in conjunction with Martin's assumption that caused physical events are probably caused by one or more beings with physical bodies, entails that all physical events in the universe are probably caused by one or more beings with physical bodies. (It is unclear whether Martin is aware of this noteworthy implication.) However, physical bodies are exceedingly implausible at early stages of the evolution of the universe (indeed, my fine-tuning arguments entail that physical bodies are exceedingly implausible on naturalism at any past or present stage of the evolution of the universe), and this, in turn, entails that it must be false that all physical events in the universe are probably caused by one or more beings with physical bodies, and this, in turn, consequently implies either that it is incorrect that uncaused physical events are implausible, or that Martin's assumption is incorrect that caused physical events are probably caused by one or more beings with physical bodies. Since it is established in the AFTLOP that it is true that uncaused physical events are implausible, we may reject Martin's assumption that caused physical events are probably caused by one or more beings with physical bodies. Therefore, we may reject premise (1) of the argument from embodiedness.

In other words, the observed nature of physical event causation is that physical events are caused by persons. Since most physical events are evidently not caused by human persons, it follows that most physical events are caused by one or more non-human persons. This inference is reasonably established even prior to consideration of the more controversial question of whether the personal cause of most physical events happens to be one or more embodied beings. The beings in premise (1), therefore, are seen to have been restricted, without justification, to be embodied beings, when the personal nature of physical event causation may be used to establish the existence of an immensely vast set of physical events caused by one or more beings with no physical body. Thus, Martin is mistaken in his claim that no created (caused) entity is known to be created (caused) by a disembodied entity (p. 204:40-41).

Consonant with Martin's desire to minimize controversial assumptions (p. 204:7-9; p. 205:13-15), the observation of the nature of physical event causation in the world may begin with the observation that all instances in which physical events are known to be caused are instances in which the cause is a person (the question of whether the person is always physically embodied may remain open at this point in the reasoning). In other words, the wrongly restrictive phrase "with bodies" should be removed from premise (1). Now, these observations, in conjunction with the implausibility of uncaused physical events, entail that all physical events in the universe are likely caused by one or more persons. Since the power and knowledge required to cause these events clearly exceeds by many orders of magnitude the power and knowledge possessed by human persons, it follows that the personal cause of most physical events in the physical universe is a being(s) with immensely greater power and knowledge than that of man. Therefore, God exists, where God is simply the name used to identify the being(s) whose likely existence has already been established. In other words, when premise (3) is modified such that the wrongly restrictive phrase "with bodies" is removed, premise (3) entails that God exists, where God is the name used to identify the being(s) whose existence as creator of the universe is established in that premise. Now, even if premise (4) is accepted by theists, premise (5) does not follow, since removal of the "with bodies" phrase in premise (3) results in the inapplicability of the *modus tollens* inference. Thus, Martin has unwittingly provided a workable framework for establishing the existence of God. The removal of the phrase "with bodies" from premises (1) and (3), in conjunction with the understanding that all physical events have a personal cause, is the key to identifying the theistic implications of the nature of physical event causation in the world. For further discussion of the implications of inclusion or removal of phrases such as "with bodies" in premises such as (1) and (3), see my discussion of premise (9) in my AFTLOP (chapter 1).

If Martin accepts the argument from embodiedness, then premise (3) of that argument entails that the universe does, indeed, have a personal creator or creators. It is strange that Martin does not emphasize this truly remarkable conclusion! Premise (3) is surely a creation hypothesis, and one could define "God" as the creative being or beings who are responsible for creating the universe. So, if Martin accepts his own argument from embodiedness, then Martin is a creationist! I hope he joins me in encouraging and promoting the acceptance of creationist theory. As we work together to further investigate the nature of the creator as revealed through the creation, we also ought to investigate the world religions so as to determine whether the creator has revealed through them the divine will for our lives and for the world. This is a reasonable, intellectually honest response, and I hope Martin joins me in pursuing these avenues of research.

If Martin rejects the argument from embodiedness, presumably due to rejection of the supposition that the universe is a created entity, then Martin's analysis ought to include justification for the rejection of that supposition. Since Martin has not provided such justification, his analysis remains incomplete.

The second instantiation of Martin's atheistic teleological argument form is his argument from multiple creators (p. 205:31-206:38). In response, it is worth first noting that orthodox Christian theology consists of the belief that God's nature is triune in the sense that God is a composite unity of three persons: God the Father, God the Son (Jesus), and God the Holy Spirit. So, the argument from multiple creators is not obviously aimed at striking down this widespread version of theism.

Martin claims that our experience is such that "all large and complex entities are created by a group of beings working together" (p. 205:32-33). In response, Trinitarian theism consists of the belief that God created the universe, where God is, in a sense, a "group" of three beings or personalities who coexist within the Godhead. So, even if Martin's above-quoted experience were accurate, it would not clearly be a problem for Trinitarian theists. Furthermore, as shown above in my discussion of the argument from embodiedness and also in the AFTLOP, the nature of physical event causation in the world is such that all physical events not caused by man are caused by God. So, since man's power and knowledge is clearly insufficient as a cause of most physical events, and since God may be a single being (as even premise (3) of the argument from embodiedness allows), God must be the cause of atoms, stars, galaxies, physical event patterns described by the laws of physics, etc., which, if God is a single being, contradicts Martin's consequently disconfirmed claim that all large and complex entities are created by a group of beings working together. Therefore, it is far from established that our experience is such that only groups of beings working together create large and complex entities. We may, thus, reject premise (1) of the argument from multiple creators.

Martin's claim (p. 205:32-33) is further disconfirmed by the fact that the immensely powerful and knowledgeable nature of the creator(s) of the universe is such that it is far from clear that a large group of creators is likely required to create the universe. After all, once we acknowledge the existence of one or more beings who created the universe (recall, even Martin acknowledges this in premise (3) of his argument from embodiedness), it becomes readily apparent that the magnitude of the causal powers of the creator(s) is profoundly greater than that of man. A super-powerful creator can perform super-powerful actions. The creation of the universe is a super-powerful action. So, it is surely possible that a single super-powerful creator could create the universe, and this fact renders dubious Martin's assertion that multiple creators are probably required to create the universe. The creator(s) of the universe should not be assumed to possess causal powers very similar to that of man, especially since the causal powers of the creator(s) have been shown to be very dissimilar in magnitude to that of man. Thus, premise (1) is further disconfirmed.

We may also conclude that Martin has not justified the claim that "if the universe is a created entity, it was created by a group of beings" (p. 205:33-36), all of Martin's examination of the nature of complex humanly-created entities notwithstanding (p. 206:20-35). Sure, the degree of complexity of humanly-created entities is generally directly proportional to the number of human entities involved in the creation, but the vastly greater power possessed by the creator(s) of the universe is such that the assumption is unsubstantiated that all features of the nature of humanly-created entities are closely analogous to all features of the nature of entities created by the creator(s) of the universe. Martin has not justified the assumption that the magnitude of human power and the number of humans required to create entities of complexity C is such that the creator(s) of the universe probably possess a similar magnitude of power and probably require a similar number of creators to create entities of complexity C. In fact, that assumption not only enjoys no compelling positive evidential support, but also is strongly disconfirmed by the immensely greater power which the creator(s) are known to possess by virtue of an examination of the nature of physical event causation in the world as briefly examined above and closely examined in detail in the AFTLOP. Therefore, both premise (1) and premise (2a) may be rejected.

If Martin accepts the argument from multiple creators, then premise (3) of that argument entails that the universe is indeed created by a group of beings. It is strange that Martin does not emphasize this quite remarkable conclusion! Premise (3) is surely a creation hypothesis, and one could define "God" as the group of beings responsible for working together to create the universe. So, if Martin accepts his own argument from multiple creators, then Martin is a creationist! I hope he joins me in encouraging and promoting the acceptance of creationist theory. As we work together to further investigate the nature of the creator(s) as revealed through the creation, we also ought to investigate the world religions so as to determine whether the creator(s) has revealed through them the divine will for our lives and for the world. This is a reasonable, intellectually honest response, and I hope Martin joins me in pursuing these avenues of research.

If Martin rejects the argument from multiple creators, presumably due to rejection of the supposition that the universe is a created entity, then Martin's analysis ought to include justification for the rejection of that supposition. Since Martin has not provided such justification, his analysis remains incomplete.

The third instantiation of Martin's atheistic teleological argument form is his argument from apparent fallibility (p. 207:1-209:5). Martin's term "fallibility" is evidently interpreted as "mistakes and errors", but the concept of "mistakes and errors" remains ambiguous, and until this concept is explicated in detail, it will remain unclear what entities are the object of analysis in the argument from apparent fallibility. Martin does not offer a clear definition, but only explains the concept with a few examples. He even asserts that the universe often "appears to theists to contain mistakes and errors of creation" (p. 208:37-38), but this assertion is far from established, especially since the terms "mistakes" and "errors" have not even been defined. Therefore, we may reject the argument from infallibility on the grounds that it appeals to a vague and inadequately defined concept which renders the argument ambiguous and inconclusive.

Martin's argument from apparent fallibility can not succeed unless it is established that the universe is likely created by a creator(s) who created it with mistakes or errors. Assuming, for the sake of argument, that the concept of mistakes/errors has been clarified, Martin must establish that the universe contains apparent mistakes or errors. The examples provided by Martin consist only of alleged apparent inefficiencies in the process of evolution (p. 208:18-20) and alleged apparent errors in genetics (p. 208:20-22). In response, Martin has not clearly identified what he means by "the process of evolution". Martin's analysis is incomplete, since he has not responded to arguments offered by theistic evolutionists in defense of a theistic evolutionary interpretation of biological events. It is also incomplete due to failure to respond to critiques of biological evolutionary thought. Furthermore, as discussed earlier and in the AFTLOP, the power and knowledge possessed by the creator(s) of the universe far exceeds that of man, so there is consequently no clear reason to suppose man should think he is in a position to know why the creator(s) would act in any particular way. Our inability to understand how a physical process may be considered efficient by the creator(s) in no way renders likely the assumption that the creator(s) do not consider the process efficient. So, since Martin has not even established that certain features of the process of evolution appear to be greatly inefficient, he can not infer that such allegedly apparent inefficiencies are probably actual inefficiencies. Additionally, Martin evidently assumes that biological evolutionary processes must be maximally efficient, if they are created by God. This assumption also remains unjustified. Regarding genetics, our inability to understand why the creator(s) of the universe permit/cause the known laws of genetics does not entail that certain features of those laws constitute "genetic deficiencies". Given God's immensely greater knowledge than that of man, we are evidently in no position to evaluate why God may act in any particular way. So, Martin has not even established that his alleged example of an apparent genetic error is actually an apparent genetic error, since what Martin may erroneously claim to be an apparent genetic error may actually be part of the creator(s) grand design not fully understood by Martin. Even if it is true that apparent human mistakes and errors in created objects are usually actual human mistakes and errors, it does not follow that apparent mistakes and errors in the objects created by the creator(s) are probably also actual mistakes and errors, since the creator(s) immensely greater knowledge than that of man entails that man is doubtfully in a position to knowledgeably critique the quality of those objects created by the creator(s). Thus, Martin's argument from apparent infallibility fails to account for the profound difference between the knowledge of man and the knowledge of the creator(s). In addition, the AFTLOP establishes that the laws of physics describe physical event patterns caused by God, so it follows that any genetic or biological evolutionary physical laws that may exist are caused by God, regardless of whether the detailed nature of those physical event patterns is understood by man to be free of errors or mistakes.

Martin assumes that appearances to theistic believers are irrelevant (p. 208:35-36), but premise (2) is the believer's supposition that the universe is a created entity, so the argument from apparent fallibility is built on a view of the universe as perceived by believers. If we accept premise (2), then it stands to reason that the creator(s) of the universe possess much greater knowledge and power than that of man. Therefore, it follows that man is doubtfully in a position to determine whether any alleged instance of apparent infallibility on the part of the creator(s) is actually an instance of apparent infallibility on the part of the creator(s), since the creator(s) may well have access to knowledge unavailable to man. In particular, the creator(s) may well know reasons which establish that the creation is not infallible, even though some created men may claim (without justification) that instances of apparent infallibility exist. Furthermore, my revision of Martin's atheistic teleological argument from embodiedness discussed earlier, in conjunction with my fine-tuning arguments and the AFTLOP, together entail that God exists, regardless of the existence of any alleged instances of God's apparent infallibility. So, the argument from apparent infallibility might conceivably be restructured to establish the existence of actions performed by God, where it is unknown why God performed such actions. Our lack of knowledge of detailed reasons for which God performed action A, however, entails neither that God did not perform A, nor that God does not exist.

If Martin accepts the argument from infallibility, then his acceptance of premise (2) entails that Martin is a creationist. Presumably Martin, in fact, rejects premise (2), yet his analysis of the argument from infallibility includes no justification for that rejection. Thus, either Martin is a creationist or his analysis is incomplete due to failure to justify rejection of premise (2), and neither of these disjuncts entails that God does not exist.

The fourth instantiation of Martin's atheistic teleological argument form is his argument from finiteness. This argument rests fully on the assumption that unlimited power is not finite power (p. 209:9-13). This assumption may be flatly rejected. If God's power is both unlimited and finite, then there is truly no limit to the magnitude of power God could exercise, with the exception of "limitations" due to logical impossibilities. For example, God's inability to make a square circle might be considered by some to be a limit on God's power, but this limit is merely due to the logical impossibility of a square circle, and is not due to God's power actually being anything less than the maximum possible power a being could possess. Furthermore, J.P. Moreland and William Lane Craig have drawn a distinction between potentially infinite quantities and actually infinite quantities,[13] and if God's power is potentially infinite, then it may be understood as being both unlimited and finite, but not actually infinite. The restriction of God's power to the status of "unlimited and finite" is not really a substantive restriction, however, since the logical impossibility of actually infinite quantities is no more a restriction on God's power than is God's inability to make a square circle. Indeed, power that is both unlimited and finite is the maximum conceivable power that a being could possess, and this power may be labeled "infinite" so long as it is understood to be potentially infinite, not actually infinite. Thus, we may reject premise (4) of the argument from finiteness, since the infinite power traditionally attributed to the theistic God may be interpreted as being potentially infinite power which is finite and unlimited. The conclusion (5), therefore, does not follow, and the argument from finiteness fails to disconfirm the existence of God.

Martin speculates that if the universe has a creator(s), then the power of the creator(s) might be "greatly enhanced through superadvanced technology" (p. 210:20-22). In response, the creator(s) might possess power that is not so enhanced. Furthermore, a theistic interpretation of physical events provided by the AFTLOP provides a justified causal explanation for the operation of technology, whereas, on atheism, no clear causal explanation is evident. So, theism has greater explanatory power. Furthermore, God's immensely greater power than that of man (as established in the AFTLOP, in my fine-tuning arguments, and even in the above discussion of my revision to the argument from embodiedness) is such that the assumption remains unjustified that we must appeal to superadvanced technology to explain the source of the power of the creator(s). Rather, God's immensely great power is such that God may well be a single person with potentially infinite power, given our considerations here.

If Martin accepts the argument from finiteness, then his acceptance of premise (2) entails that Martin is a creationist. Presumably Martin, in fact, rejects premise (2), yet his analysis of the argument from finiteness includes no justification for that rejection. Thus, either Martin is a creationist or his analysis is incomplete due to failure to justify rejection of premise (2), and neither of these disjuncts entails that God does not exist.

The fifth instantiation of Martin's atheistic teleological argument form is his argument from preexisting material. Premise (4) may be immediately called into question. First, perhaps our universe is at the end of a long chain of multiple universes which the Christian God has caused to evolve, in which case our physical universe may have been created from preexisting material in an ontologically prior universe. In this case, premise (4) is false, and the argument from preexisting material may be rejected. Second, perhaps the Christian God created our universe from a timelessly preexisting material, in which case premise (4) is false, and the argument from preexisting material may be rejected. Since orthodox Christian theology does not reject either of these two possibilities so far as I am aware, we have reason to reject premise (4).

Examination of a recent defense[14] of premise (4) is recommended for the interested reader, but the evidence offered in support of *creatio ex nihilo* appears to me to be ambiguous. Even if premise (4) is accepted, however, premise (2a) may be rejected on the grounds that since the nature of the creative capacities of the creator(s) of the universe differs substantially from that of man, it is not established that the nature of the entities created by the creator(s) is identical to the nature of the entities created by humans. In fact, premise (2a) seems reasonable only if we suppose the universe is created by a human, but since the universe is doubtfully created by a human, it is doubtful that premise (2a) is true.

If Martin accepts the argument from preexisting material, then his acceptance of premise (2) entails that Martin is a creationist. Presumably Martin, in fact, rejects premise (2), yet his analysis of the argument from preexisting material includes no justification for that rejection. Thus, either Martin is a creationist or his analysis is incomplete due to failure to justify rejection of premise (2), and neither of these disjuncts entails that God does not exist.

Martin's consideration of the universe as a created object (p. 211:14-213:24) fails to justify rejection of the claim that the universe is a created object. Martin develops an argument from the tests of artifice (p. 212:23-30) in which test T is taken to be evidence of creation such as "machining, materials that do not exist in nature, regular markings, and the like" (p. 212:17-18). In response, test T is clearly a test for evidence of creation by man, so the phrase "it is not created" in premise (1) should be replaced by "it is not created by man". It follows that premise (3) should read "The universe is not created by man". Consequently, we may reject premise (5), as *modus tollens* does not apply.

Test T includes identification of materials that do not exist in nature. However, on atheism, all materials exist in nature, since all events are taken to be natural events. So, if atheism is true, then test T can never be used to identify a material that does not exist in nature. Since atheists such as Matson and Martin evidently agree that test T can be used to identify a material that does not exist in nature, it follows that Matson and Martin reject atheism!

If Test T is defined as evidence that a physical event P exists, where no known law of physics explains the existence of P, then Martin is seen to have defined "created object" such that most physical events are, by definition, uncreated. Needless to say, this is a case of begging the question of whether most physical events are created. Given this unacceptable version of test T, we may reject premise (1).

If Test T is interpreted as evidence E of a person's causal activity, where evidence such as E does not occur independent of a person's causal activity in the world, then since the AFTLOP provides evidence that all physical events are caused by persons, all physical events satisfy test T. Since the physical universe comprises all physical events, the physical universe satisfies test T. Thus, we may reject premise (2).

In conclusion, Martin's atheistic teleological arguments thoroughly fail to disconfirm the existence of the theistic God. We may, therefore, rightly reject Martin's concluding comments (p. 213:25-29).

In chapter 7 of part 2 of IPRG, Bruce and Frances Martin cite cases which, in their opinion, are inconsistent with Intelligent Design, which they define as "the purposeful fashioning of each species by an Intelligent Designer—by implication God" (p. 215:1-216:17). In response, each of the cases cited by Bruce and Frances Martin are cases in which physical processes are taken to be evidence against the existence of an Intelligent Designer (God). However, the AFTLOP establishes that God is the cause of those physical processes, regardless of whether man understands God's reasons for causing those processes. Theism provides a justified causal explanation of physical processes, yet Bruce and Frances Martin provide no justification for the existence or continuing evolution of the physical world in accordance with the laws of physics. Theism has greater explanatory power, and atheism may be rightly rejected, especially given the results of both the AFTLOP and my fine-tuning arguments.

Stephen Jay Gould's quote (p. 216:23-26) reveals that Gould thinks he knows the actions God would perform. However, given that God's knowledge is immensely greater than that of man, the assumption remains unjustified that Gould knows that God does not have sensible reasons for performing any particular action. After all, in each case in which Gould thinks a sensible God would not perform action A, God may have good sensible reasons for performing action A, where Gould does not know those reasons.

It is claimed that vestigial elements are accounted for by evolution, but not by Intelligent Design (p. 217:15-17). In response, evolution provides no justified causal explanation of any physical event. Biological evolutionary laws are attempted human descriptions of changes in biological events, but these descriptions, even if true, do not provide causal explanations of the events they describe. More generally, physical laws describe (not cause) physical events. We must not assume, without proof, that physical laws somehow cause the physical event patterns they describe. Bruce and Frances Martin provide no justification for the belief that biological evolutionary laws cause the physical event patterns they describe. Therefore, they have not justified the claim that evolution provides an account (i.e., a causal explanation) of vestigial elements. Furthermore, my fine-tuning arguments and the AFTLOP disconfirm atheism and confirm theism, so Intelligent Design stands justified.

Since evolutionary laws are merely descriptive, and not causal, the theoretical possibility exists that God may be the cause of the obtaining of those laws. Bruce and Frances Martin do not even consider the theistic evolution position, so their analysis is surely incomplete.

Anatomical inefficiency is taken to be evidence not of Intelligent Design, but of natural selection (p. 217:18-20). In response, natural selection is merely descriptive, not causal. No justification is given for the assumption that natural selection laws somehow cause the biological evolution they describe. Since theism offers a justified causal explanation of physical events, yet atheism does not, we may favor theistic causal explanations of biological events, regardless of which biological evolutionary theory (if any) eventually proves to be true, and regardless of whether we understand why God may have caused any particular vestigial or anatomical features.

Instances of alleged anatomical inefficiency amount merely to the objection that the anatomy of a biological structure should be expected to be different if it were designed by God. However, given that God's knowledge is immensely greater than that of man, the assumption remains unjustified that man should suppose he is in a position to know why God would perform any particular action. Since, therefore, God may have good reasons for God's actions, where those actions may forever remain unknown to man, it follows that man should not assume he knows what anatomical design God should create, if God exists.

Eyes are confidently claimed to have evolved many times in the animal kingdom, yet the evidence offered in support of this claim is merely a speculative presumption (p. 218:20-22). Needless to say, justification has not been provided for the claim.

Again, evolution is claimed to offer an explanation of some biological facts (p. 218:33-35). However, the evolutionary explanation is descriptive, not causal. No justification is provided for the assumption that evolutionary explanations somehow cause the events they allegedly describe. Once again, we see an example of a non-theist who provides a description of an observation, while erroneously supposing that the description also causes the observation. Descriptions do not cause observations! This myth must be aggressively exposed and refuted! Causal explanations are in order, yet no such explanation has been provided by the Martins.

The Martins resort to unanswered questioning tactics (e.g., p. 218:29-30; p. 218:35-37), but little if anything substantive is established by such questions. The mere fact that a question is unanswered does not, in and of itself, entail that the answer favors a non-theistic interpretation. If the correct answer to a raised question confirms a particular theory, then it would be helpful to provide justification.

The claim is made that biological features of physical life lend support, at face value, for polytheism, not monotheism (p. 218:38-41). However, this claim is not squared with the consideration that Ockham's Razor might be interpreted to favor monotheism over polytheism, even given those biological features.

Bruce and Frances Martin are aware of the fact that an inscrutable God may have reasons unknown to man for choosing to cause the actions God causes (p. 219:1-3). Since the AFTLOP and my fine-tuning arguments establish that God exists and is the cause of physical life, it follows that biological facts discussed by Bruce and Frances Martin are caused by God. They may not know why God has so acted, and this may result from the possibility that God's ways are largely inscrutable. Nevertheless, the existence of God as Sustainer and Designer is inferred from an analysis of the nature of physical event causation and an understanding of the limits of explanations in terms of physical laws, and these inferences are grounded in observations solidly established in the physical sciences. As such, the case for the existence of God is both scientific and religious. The supposition that science can be divorced from religion is pure silliness (p. 219:5-6), and the science classroom deserves intelligent examination of all evidence and arguments, not merely an examination restricted to biological evolutionary religious dogma.

The claim is made that nature selects favorable variations (p. 219:9-11). In response, there is no good reason to suppose "nature" selects (causes) anything at all. If "nature" refers to physical events described by known laws of physics, then nature causes events only if physical events can cause physical events. Since we have no evidence that any physical event is caused by a physical event (see the AFTLOP for details), the suggestion that nature possesses causal powers is unjustified.

It is claimed that "mutation occurs randomly" (p. 219:11-13), yet no justification is provided for the claim that any random physical event exists. In fact, the AFTLOP and my fine-tuning arguments together entail that physical events not caused by man are caused by God. Since man is not the cause of mutations, it follows that God causes mutations, and if God causes mutations in accordance with a grand design and intentional plan, then mutations are not random, but are events intentionally caused by God for reasons that may not be known by man.

Thus, mutations may be random in the sense that man knows no physical law which enables man to provide accurate mutation predictions, but the assumption remains unjustified that mutations are truly random in the sense that they are not even intentionally caused by God in accordance with a grand purpose and design.

It is claimed that "Neither intelligence nor design seems at work in producing such cruel mutations..." (p. 219:22-24). In response, Bruce and Frances Martin do not explain why they are likely to be in a position to know why God would inform them regarding God's reasons for causing the mutations God causes, if God exists and causes mutations. Given God's immensely greater knowledge than that of man, God's reasons may simply be inscrutable. Furthermore, given the AFTLOP and my fine-tuning arguments, we have reason to believe God exists, regardless of whether we understand why God may perform any particular action. Therefore, the claim that there is an appearance of absence of intelligence or design might be justified simply because God has chosen not to make such appearances evident to those who make that claim. This, in no way, entails either that God does not exist or that God is not the cause of mutations. These considerations do suggest, though, that God may withhold the knowledge of God from some people for reasons we may not understand. Perhaps God will use the AFTLOP and my fine-tuning arguments to help the Martins come to understand good reasons for believing intelligence and design appear to be at work in the physical world.

The reference to "cruel mutations" carries the implication that if God causes mutations, then God's act of causing mutations is not good. However, God may have good reasons unknown to man which establish that it is good that God causes/permits the mutations God causes/permits. Furthermore, the satan-demon hypothesis may actually be another possible explanation of the causal origin of "cruel mutations", in which case it is not even God who is the cause of the mutations. Granted, cruel mutations might be able to come into existence through a satanic-demonic explanation only if God actually permitted such action, assuming God is sufficiently powerful and willing to fully control such permits, but this does not imply God is somehow culpable for having originated an evil action, since God's permission of God-regulated satanic-demonic activity might serve God's ideal purpose and grand design for maximizing ultimate good in ways that may be partially or largely inscrutable. The theist can know God exists without fully understanding why God causes or permits any particular event. Given

God's immeasurably great knowledge, it may well take a few thousand years of further development of my relationship with God in the afterlife to even begin to partially grasp the immensity of the complexity of the nature of God's thoughts and actions, but that's ok! I do not now need to be omniscient prior to knowing God, although I do now eagerly anticipate future revelation as one of the many benefits of being a graciously forgiven and redeemed child of an unspeakably loving Father!

Another possible explanation of the origin of "cruel mutations" is the idea that God's foreknowledge of man's eventual free choice to cause sinful rebellion to frustrate God's ideal purposes is the basis upon which God justly built a curse into the nature of physical event patterns such that the laws of physics do not serve or reflect God's ideal plan for man, but reflect God's best possible response to man's frustration of that ideal. Justification for the belief that this scenario is true would require that many issues and concepts be fleshed out in considerable detail, and this project surely lies outside the scope of the present analysis. Suffice to say, the inference from the existence of allegedly cruel mutations to the favoring of biological evolutionary theories over intelligent design hypotheses (p. 219:22-24) is profoundly overly simplistic and unwarranted, given the considerations in the present critique.

The Martins favor evolutionary theory over Intelligent Design (p. 220:5-8). Implicit in the reasoning is the assumption that both theories provide causal explanations of physical observations, and also implicit is the assumption that evolutionary theory is in better accordance with the observations. In response, evolutionary theory is not even a causal explanation! Evolutionary theory may be understood as a subset of the laws of physics which pertain to biological event patterns. Since physical laws are, by definition, descriptive, evolutionary theory is thus seen to be merely an allegedly accurate description of biological events. There is no reason to suppose that descriptions of physical events somehow cause the described events. If the Martins assume that explanations in terms of physical laws are not merely descriptive, but are also causal, then justification for this critical assumption must be provided. Since no such justification is provided, and since an Intelligent Design hypothesis is strongly confirmed by the AFTLOP and my fine-tuning arguments, we may reject evolutionary theory in favor of Intelligent Design, especially since Intelligent Design is so far superior in that it does provide a (justified) causal explanation of biological events. The Martins may have difficulty identifying the intelligently designed features of the physical world (p. 220:22-25), but their difficulty is evidently not due to a lack of evidence. Even if physical laws of biological evolution accurately describe biological event changes (and I remain skeptical), the fundamental question of the causal origin of the obtaining of those laws remains justifiably answerable only in terms that render theism probable, as detailed in the AFTLOP and my fine-tuning arguments. So, the fact that the Martins favor evolutionary laws of physics reveals their underlying acceptance of operative physical laws which, themselves, imply the existence of a Physical Law Designer.

The Martins claim that an "Intelligent Designer would create only successful species" (p. 220:36-37). In response, the Martins have not justified the claim that they are in a position to know what an Intelligent Designer would create, if an Intelligent Designer exists. There is no obvious reason why we should suppose it is not possible that an inscrutable Intelligent Designer exists. Given the AFTLOP and my fine-tuning arguments, God's evidently immensely greater knowledge than that of man suggests that God's ways may well be largely inscrutable, apart from divine revelation. So, the Martins are thoroughly unwarranted in claiming to have acquired the remarkably extensive knowledge of the specific kinds of species an Intelligent Designer would create, regardless of the degree to which the Designer's knowledge exceeds their own, and regardless of the potentially marvelously complex nature of the Designer's reasoning.

Evolutionary theory does not account for the causal origin of the existence of allegedly unsuccessful species (p. 220:36-37). As mentioned earlier, evolutionary theory is an attempted description of biological events, and this description must not be endowed with creative-sustaining powers unless that endowment is justified. At most, evolutionary theory may accurately describe biological event patterns, but even if this were true (and, as mentioned above, I remain skeptical), it leaves open the possibility that those events may actually be caused by a Designer. Therefore, all this fuss about whether biological evolutionary theories accurately describe biological event patterns misses the point! The question of the causal origin of the continuing existence/sustenance of the physical universe in accordance with the laws of physics is the critical question in need of examination, and the AFTLOP and my fine-tuning arguments together provide a justified (p. 221:1-2) theistic answer, regardless of whether any particular biological evolutionary theory eventually wins the day in the court of scientific opinion. Therefore, Intelligent Design does not fail to meet "fundamental elements of rational inquiry" (p. 221:24-25), but is the established result of rational inquiry.

The Martins conclude with a comment that reveals an erroneous conception of Intelligent Design (ID) theory. They claim that ID theory is able to "account for everything by divine edict" (p. 221:25-26). In response, ID proponents need not insist that "everything" may be causally explained by the Designer. Theists may claim that some events are caused by other free creatures, and theists may also claim that some entities are abstract and uncaused. If the Martins mean that all ID proponents claim that every *physical* entity is causally explained by the Designer, then this is, likewise, doubtful, since no such claim is essential to ID theory. So, the Martins misconstrue ID theory. Furthermore, they go on to assert, unintelligibly, that by explaining everything "by divine edict, Intelligent Design explains nothing" (p. 221:25-26). Needless to say, this idea is unintelligible! If theory H explains everything, then necessarily, H does not explain nothing. Rather, if H explains everything by some means, then it is necessarily the case that H explains something, not nothing. I could speculate ad infinitum (potentially ad infinitum, that is) as to what the Martins may actually be attempting to communicate, but I refrain. A note of clarification from an informed party would be appreciated on the question of what the Martins actually mean here. Pending receipt of such notification, I maintain the objections raised in this critique.

In chapter 8 of part 2 of IPRG, Richard Dawkins, in the opening paragraph, claims there is not only absence of evidence for the existence of God, but also evidence for the nonexistence of God (p. 223:10-11). Dawkins does not justify these claims, but presumably considers the remainder of his article to provide the justification. The analysis that follows shows that Dawkins has failed to establish his claims are true.

Dawkins claims that order and apparent purposefulness of biological life has come about through a process that is a consequence of evolution by natural selection (p. 224:13-22). In response, if "come about" means "cause", then Dawkins is claiming that evolution by natural selection causes the diversity of life on Earth. However, evolution by natural selection has not been shown to *cause* anything at all. Even if evolution by natural selection were the correct description of changing biological events on Earth, it would only be the description of biological event patterns, not the cause of those patterns. Descriptions are not necessarily causes. If Dawkins believes evolution by natural selection somehow causes the event patterns it describes, then justification must be provided for this belief. No justification is provided. Given the AFTLOP and my fine-tuning arguments, we have good reason to believe that persons (not physical laws) cause events described by physical laws. Therefore, we have reason to reject the claim that causal powers may be attributed to evolutionary descriptions, and we have reason to believe that God is the cause of the event patterns which evolutionary descriptions are designed to describe, regardless of whether any evolutionary biological description happens to be true. In short, even if evolutionary laws were true (I have my doubts), Dawkins has failed to identify the causal origin of the obtaining of those laws.

Dawkins proceeds to further embrace the naturalistic fallacy, which I identify as the supposition that there exist physical events not caused by a person. He claims "laws of physics are capable of achieving this result" (p. 224:24-27), yet fails to justify his belief that physical laws can *achieve* (rather than merely describe) anything at all. He also claims that random genetic mutations cause chance physical events (p. 225:21-36), yet fails to justify the claim that any physical event is caused by anything other than a person's free exercise of power. In addition, he claims that the modern eye could spring from a less elaborate eye (p. 226:5-7), but does not justify the belief that any physical event can have sprung forth from (i.e., can have been caused by) a prior physical event. Dawkins also speculates that DNA is a later product of a more primitive form of natural selection that is no longer in operation (p. 228:22-36), but he does not establish that any form of natural selection can actually *produce* (rather than merely describe) any physical entity. Additionally, Dawkins mistakenly assumes that the big bang "initiated the universe" (p. 228:34-36), implying that a physical event can cause a subsequent physical event, whereas the AFTLOP establishes that the big bang is God's action of initiating the universe. Also, Dawkins makes an incomplete reference to a book by Peter Atkins in which it is allegedly shown that God, as creator, would not actually need to do anything at all (p. 228:41-229:6) to initiate everything, yet Dawkins gives no support for the assumption that God is neither the fully active creator (initiator) of the universe nor the sustainer of the continuing existence of the universe as described by physical laws. An incomplete reference to an idea in a book is hardly sufficient to confirm the atheistic interpretation of physical events offered by Dawkins, when the AFTLOP and my fine-tuning arguments provide strong confirmation of a theistic interpretation. Therefore, we may conclude that Dawkins has failed to shoulder the burden of proof in regards to his acceptance of the naturalistic fallacy.

Even if evolution were at least theoretically capable of doing the job Dawkins claims it does, he has not established that it has actually done the job. For example, it is generally not controversial that evolution requires, in theory, very long time periods to lead to significant diversification of life, yet the time during which diversifying life has appeared on Earth is not clearly established to be sufficient for theoretical evolutionary explanations to actually obtain. Dawkins treats three billion years as if that is a sufficiently long time period (p. 226:14-31), but such assumptions ought to be quantified and justified with technicality and precision. Broad sweeping of a multitude of unjustified and unstated assumptions under the carpet of three billion years fails to demonstrate that it is "easy to believe that an eye could have evolved from no eye by small degrees" (p. 226:30-31). After all, if 985 trillion years were shown to be the approximate expected time required for evolution by natural selection to lead to diversification of life as has appeared on Earth, then the fact of the quick appearance of diversified life on Earth in only a few billion years could, itself, form the raw data upon which an evolutionary design argument could be structured. If Dawkins can argue against this conceivable line of argumentation, then it would be helpful for him to do so. Until he does, the possibility of such evolutionary design arguments will render his analysis inconclusive. More importantly, even if three billion years were shown to be sufficient for evolutionary laws to plausibly describe the appearance of diversified life on Earth, it remains to be proven that those laws actually cause the events they describe. Theism, therefore, reigns supreme over atheism, since theism (as justified by the AFTLOP and my fine-tuning arguments) identifies the person (God) who causes the physical universe to continue to exist and evolve in accordance with physical laws, regardless of whether any biological evolutionary theory is true.

Dawkins recognizes his need to establish that each of the intermediates on the evolutionary path would have been favored by natural selection and would have survived (p. 226:32-228:12). His acknowledgment that half an eye may not be useless (p. 227:1-7) hardly entails that all necessary intermediates on the evolutionary path to an eye would have been favored by natural selection and would have survived. Likewise, the theoretical possibility that wings could gradually evolve (p. 227:8-19) hardly establishes that it is plausible that such a possibility has ever been actualized, given the time constraints and other conditions on Earth which are known to have existed. In other words, Dawkins appears to be arguing "If evolution is conceivable, then it is probable", but this argument form is sound only if appropriate justification is provided, and Dawkins has failed to provide that justification.

Granted, Dawkins does offer the fossil record and genetic codes (p. 227:30-228:4) as evidence that theoretically possible evolutionary explanations such as those mentioned above are actually correct explanations. However, his fossil argument amounts to the claim that the fossil record is consistent with what would be expected if evolution actually had happened. The problem with this reasoning is that "observation A is consistent with theory B" does not entail "B is the best explanation of A". Consistency between observation and theory does not guarantee inference to the best explanatory theory has been made. Furthermore, the fossil record is consistent with various theistic theories of creation, and Dawkins has failed to justify the claim that the fossil record confirms his atheistic evolution better than theistic creation, and the need for him to provide such justification is very much in order, especially given theistic arguments (e.g., the AFTLOP and my fine-tuning arguments) which entail that his atheistic evolutionary interpretations of biological event patterns are incorrect. Likewise, his genetic code argument amounts to the claim that the similarity in genetic material amongst all living creatures implies descent from a common ancestor. Here again, the reasoning is unsound. After all, the similarity in genetic material amongst all living creatures is also consistent with God having created each creature to be as it is. Dawkins has not shown that his atheistic evolutionary interpretation of biological event patterns is better than any theistic interpretation. Furthermore, the atheistic fossil argument and atheistic genetic argument assume the existence and continuing sustenance of the physical world in accordance with the laws of physics, yet on atheism there is no justified explanation of the continuing existence of the world as described by those laws. Theism, however, provides a justified explanation of both the existence and continued sustenance of the physical world in accordance with the laws of physics, as it rightly identifies God as the cause of the obtaining of the laws of physics, regardless of whether any evolutionary law is ever established.

Dawkins characterizes the debate as a choice between either his atheistic evolutionary interpretation or a theistic interpretation in which God deceptively causes evolutionary interpretations to appear correct even though they are not (p. 228:4-12). In response, characterization of the debate in this manner is, itself, deceptive, as theists may argue either that evolutionary interpretations do not appear correct, or that God would be properly identified as the cause of the obtaining of any evolutionary law that appears to obtain. Therefore, Dawkins mischaracterizes the debate, and since the AFTLOP and my fine-tuning arguments strongly confirm theism, we may conclude that the Argument from Design and other theistic arguments stand firm, despite the misguided allegation to the contrary (p. 228:13-21). Sadly, the measly response to the question (p. 228:14) of whether there exist arguments (other than the Argument from Design) for the existence of God suggests Dawkins may not have done his homework. In fact, I even doubt Dawkins genuinely believes that atheistic intellectuals would concur that he has "destroyed" the Argument from Design (p. 228:13-14) in just the few short pages of his article, especially given that Dawkins is presumably aware of the extensive literature on this centuries old topic.

The concluding paragraph (p. 229:7-15) is loaded with many assumptions that deserve a response. First, explanations built on simple premises are not necessarily more preferable than those built on more complex premises. Rather, the most preferable explanation is the simplest explanation that best explains all available evidence. Dawkins may provide an explanation for ultimate origins that begins with a simpler premise than the causal action of God, but this does not entail that the explanation provided by Dawkins is preferable, since it has not been shown that the explanation given by Dawkins explains all available evidence. Specifically, the AFTLOP and my fine-tuning arguments together imply physical events are caused by persons, and the atheistic explanation provided by Dawkins does not account for this evidence, but merely assumes (despite evidence to the contrary) that a physical event can cause a subsequent physical event. Therefore, the theistic identification of the action of a person (God) as the causal origin of the universe is a better explanation than that given by Dawkins, since Dawkins provides no justification for his interpretation of the nature of physical events, whereas the creation/design hypothesis is consistent with the observed nature of physical events. Specifically, since physical events are caused by persons, and since the irreducible minimum initial physical state of the universe is a physical event, it follows that the initial physical state is caused by a person (God). Second, God is not statistically improbable (p. 229:12-15), but is inferred from the nature of physical event causation (see the AFTLOP) and from the scientifically established limits to explanations in terms of physical laws (see my fine-tuning arguments). Granted, God is statistically improbable if we assume God is an evolved biological life form, but this assumption is not essential to theism.

Sure, no human knows everything, but I would expect an educated scientist such as Dawkins to seriously invest in the project of evaluating arguments for the existence of God in contemporary philosophy of religion literature. Intellectual honesty demands that theism be given a fair hearing before writing it off as "a gigantic waste of time and a waste of life" (p. 223:11-12). Evidently Dawkins has not yet fulfilled this duty.[15] I would be pleased to see him continue his journey toward truth by providing a thorough and detailed response to the arguments I make in this book. I am awaiting his reply, and eagerly anticipate what new truths we may both discover through a constructive and charitable dialogue.

NOTES

1. See http://www.asa3.org for details.
2. Ross, Hugh (2001). *The Creator and the Cosmos: How the Greatest Scientific Discoveries of the Century Reveal God*. Colorado Springs, CO: Navpress, 3rd rev. ed., pp. 195-198.
3. Tegmark, Max (1998). *Is "the Theory of Everything" Merely the Ultimate Ensemble Theory?* Annals of Physics, v. 270, p. 1.
4. Ibid., p. 46.
5. Ross (2001), pp. 150-153.

6. Shanks, Niall (2006). *God, the Devil, and Darwin: A Critique of Intelligent Design Theory.* Oxford: Oxford University Press, p. 222. See also Young, Matt (2001). *No Sense of Obligation: Science and Religion in an Impersonal Universe.* Bloomington, IN: 1ˢᵗ Books Library, p. 221.

7. Ross (2001), pp. 195-198.

8. Shanks (2006), p. 215.

9. Ross, Hugh (2006). *Creation as Science: A Testable Model Approach to End the Creation/Evolution Wars.* Colorado Springs, CO: Navpress, p. 179.

10. Shanks (2006), p. 213.

11. Ibid., pp. 212-213.

12. This point is emphasized by Shanks (Ibid., pp. 214-215). His analysis, however, fails to account for the version of fine-tuning argument presented here.

13. Craig, William Lane and Moreland, J. P. (2003). *Philosophical Foundations for a Christian Worldview.* Downers Grove, IL: InterVarsity Press, chapter 23.

14. Beckwith, Francis J., Mosser, Carl, and Owen, Paul eds. (2002). *The New Mormon Challenge: Responding to the Latest Defenses of a Fast-Growing Movement.* Grand Rapids, MI: Zondervan, chapter 3.

15. See Dawkins, Richard (2006), *The God Delusion.* Boston: Houghton Mifflin Company. This book is a good first step for Dawkins in the direction of meeting his obligation to examine theistic arguments, but my arguments in this present book render Dawkins (2006) incomplete and in need of revision. Also, see my critique of Dawkins in chapter 7 of this book. I await his reply.

CHAPTER 5

Atheistic Inductive Evil Arguments Refuted

I now examine the inductive evil arguments for atheism found in the book "The Improbability of God" edited by Michael Martin and Ricki Monnier, and published by Prometheus Books in 2006, ISBN: 1-59102-381-5. I urge you to purchase a copy of "The Improbability of God" (IPRG) so that you may fully understand the context of the critical remarks below.

In chapter 1 of part 3 of IPRG, Quentin Smith argues for the nonexistence of God using a probabilistic argument (p. 236:3-9) which hinges significantly upon the claim that ultimately evil natural laws exist. In response, Smith does not define the terms "evil" and "good", and so it is wholly unclear what properties are the object of Smith's analysis. If a definition of these terms is not provided, then Smith's argument can not even get off the ground. Thus, I don't even know what Smith is talking about when he uses these terms (see, for example, p. 237:12-25), for I can not agree that some particular event is good or evil, when I don't even know what definition is assumed. These terms do not have self-evident or universally accepted definitions, and it may be possible to establish that the process of defining "evil" and identifying its objective existence leads to the revelation of a moral reality much better explained by theism than atheism. Any atheistic inductive evil argument, it appears, must include consideration of this critical and fundamental issue that is overlooked in Smith's argument.

I have shown in the AFTLOP that the nature of physical event causation is such that the causal origin of physical events described by physical laws is the free action of a person. Therefore, if a definition of "evil" were provided, and if ultimately evil natural laws were subsequently shown to exist on that definition, it would follow that those laws are caused by a person who, evidently, is much more powerful than man. It follows that a super-powerful person (God) exists, regardless of whether we understand why God would permit/enable such a law to obtain. In other words, Smith does not square his claim that ultimately evil natural laws disconfirm the existence of God with the results of the AFTLOP which entail that God is the cause of physical laws (e.g., allegedly ultimately evil natural laws) not caused by man.

The theist may accept that Smith's argument disconfirms the hypothesis that God exists, while maintaining that the positive evidence for the existence of God (e.g., the AFTLOP and my fine-tuning arguments) considerably counter-balances that disconfirmation such that belief in God is still rationally required. However, the theist may make the even stronger claim that Smith's argument does not even disconfirm the hypothesis that God exists, since Smith's argument goes through only if premise (3) is accepted (p. 236:6), and acceptance of premise (3) assumes acceptance of the unstated (and unjustified) assumption that we are in a position to determine what is ultimately evil (or not evil). Given Smith's understanding of God (p. 236:3), it is evident that if God exists, then God's knowledge is immensely greater than that of man, and this knowledge may include the understanding of reasons unknown to man which establish that although God has good reasons for having prevented the obtaining of any ultimately evil natural law, God also has good reasons for presently preventing the set H of humans from acquiring the knowledge K that God has good reasons for having prevented the obtaining of any ultimately evil natural law. Thus, Smith, being a human with finite knowledge, has not established that he is in a position to know that if God exists, then it is not the case that Smith is a member of H.

Smith might conceivably respond to the above discussion by claiming that his knowledge of the absence of positive evidence for the existence of God, where God has good reasons for preventing him from acquiring knowledge K, entails that he has justified belief in the nonexistence of God, given P. J. McGrath's principle discussed in the 1987 article "Atheism or Agnosticism" in volume 47 of *Analysis*.[1] In response, even if one accepts McGrath's epistemic principle (p. 247:3-5), the theist may emphasize that since it is not the case that there is an absence of positive evidence for the existence of God (see, for example, my AFTLOP and fine-tuning arguments in chapters 1 and 2), it is reasonable to infer that Smith is a member of H. Thus, Smith's argument from evil natural laws fails.

In chapter 2 of part 3 of IPRG, William L. Rowe presents an argument (p. 251:28-34) for the nonexistence of God based on the existence of evil that is evidenced by human and animal suffering. In response, as in the case of Smith's article in chapter 1 of part 3, Rowe does not define the terms "good" and "evil", and so it is wholly unclear what properties are the object of Rowe's analysis. If a definition of these terms is not provided, then Rowe's argument can not even get off the ground. Thus, I don't even know what Rowe is talking about when he uses these terms (see, for example, p. 251:10-24), for I can not agree that some particular case is good or evil, when I don't even know what definition is assumed. These terms do not have self-evident or universally accepted definitions, and it may be possible to establish that the process of defining "evil" and identifying its objective existence leads to the revelation of a moral reality much better explained by theism than atheism. Any atheistic inductive evil argument, it appears, must include consideration of this critical and fundamental issue that is overlooked in Rowe's argument.

Assuming the terms "evil" and "good" are defined as I suspect Rowe might define, Premise (1) may be rejected via "the G. E. Moore shift", as Rowe rightly notes (p. 256:12-257:30), and my AFTLOP and fine-tuning arguments could comprise much of the rational basis for this strategy, although additional argumentation would likely be required to establish that God is omnibenevolent (wholly good). (Reasons for accepting that God is omnibenevolent arguably exist, but analysis of such reasons lies beyond the scope of the present analysis.) However, the theist may also attack premise (1) by noting that it has not been established that we are in a position to know (apart from divine revelation) what action an omnipotent, omniscient, omnibenevolent God could perform in any particular case, since it is likely far beyond our ken to determine the results of God's decision procedures which could consist of the evaluation of factors relevant to divine desires such as the following:

(a)   The maximization of the number of people in the set S of people who freely choose to positively respond to revealed truth such that they become well oriented in their relationship to God.

(b)   The maximization of the degree to which each person in S receives his just eternal reward for freely performing each of the members of the set of good works he performs.

(c)   The minimization of the number of people not in S.

(d)   The minimization of the degree to which each person not in S receives his just eternal punishment for freely performing each of the members of the set of evil works he performs.

(e)   The achievement of good divine purposes unfathomed (or unfathomable) by man.

Since the set of all free human actions consists of a tremendously complex array of interdependent relationships, and given that just a single person's free decision to perform or not perform some seemingly trivial action in response to an awareness of an allegedly apparent instance of pointless evil could influence the subsequent course of human history in ways which are wholly unpredictable by man, it is quite evidently far beyond our ken as humans to trace out the decision procedures God may employ. Therefore, premise (1) of Rowe's argument may be rejected, as the atheist's claim that (1) is true entails that the atheist knows the results of likely exceedingly complex decision procedures, whereas no justification has been provided for the assumption that the atheist actually possesses such knowledge. Since God's immeasurably greater knowledge than that of man entails that we have no reason to suppose that the atheist is in a position to evaluate what action God is likely to be able to perform in any particular case, it follows that the atheist does not know premise (1).

If God exists, then God knows *much* more than we do, so we are in no position (apart from divine revelation) to say what God could or would do in any particular case, since God's actions are likely a function of numerous variables, including variables representing God's inscrutable beliefs and knowledge. Thus, we are not in a position to claim that there exists any instance of apparently pointless suffering. The claim "X appears to person J to be Y" means that J believes that X seems to be Y. However, X can seem to J to be Y only if J is in a position to determine whether X is likely Y. If J knows that J is in no position to determine whether X is likely Y, then J surely does not know whether X seems to be Y. Given God's immeasurably greater knowledge than that of man, we humans know that we are in no position to determine whether allegedly apparently pointless evil is actually apparently pointless evil. Since we do not know that allegedly apparently pointless evil is actually apparently pointless evil, it follows that we do not know that apparently pointless evil exists. Therefore, the fawn's suffering (p. 253:16-33) is not known to be apparently pointless, and what seems to Rowe to be likely regarding instances of intense suffering (p. 254:31-41) is not known to be complete or accurate, given the non-omniscient and limited nature of his human reasoning relative to God's omniscience.

Absent the existence of apparently pointless suffering, Rowe's atheistic argument crumbles, since all evil may occur in conjunction with God's good and grand divine plan, and since atheists are in no position to adduce evidence to the contrary. Rowe is not justified in claiming that "the fawn's intense suffering was preventable and, so far as we can see, pointless" (p. 253:29-30). Rather, Rowe may only make the claim that he does not know the point (if one exists) of the fawn's intense suffering, and from this claim it does not follow either that the suffering was preventable by God or that it is pointless so far as we can see, since God may have reasons unknown to us which establish that God is justified in permitting the suffering. "So far as we can see" is not very far at all in comparison to God's "sight", so human judgment of God's actions is wholly unjustified. Shall the pot say to the potter (Isaiah 29:16), "You have not made me!" Surely not!

Now that it has been shown that Rowe has not provided rational support (p. 255:3-10) for premise (1) of his argument, it may be observed that theists know Rowe is wrong, although Rowe may not so know. In fact, as a theist, I would acknowledge that Rowe might even possibly be an example of an atheist who is justified in his atheism (even though I know atheism is false), in which case Rowe might consider theists such as myself to be *friendly theists*. I do submit, however, that the implications of the critical remarks in this present book, in conjunction with my AFTLOP and fine-tuning arguments, render the friendliness of my theism to be such that it removes from the atheist the epistemic right to embrace atheism, and as such, my theism is not so friendly after all, given that although it allows for the possibility of the existence of atheists who are justified in embracing atheism, it also compels all who understand my theism to reject their atheism.

In chapter 3 of part 3 of IPRG, William L. Rowe begins with the presentation of an argument for the nonexistence of God based on an inference from P (p. 263:30-31) to Q (p. 264:11-12). He considers three possible theistic responses (p. 264:13-265:12), and examines more closely only the first and third of those, eventually concluding that "unless we have good reasons to think that O exists (or some other reason to reject Q), we are justified in believing that O does not exist" (p. 269:4-6).

In response, if the AFTLOP and fine-tuning arguments are good reasons for the belief that O exists, then Q may be rejected on that basis, even if one accepts that P tends to support Q. This response is of type B (p. 264:25-34). The objection may be raised that the AFTLOP and my fine-tuning arguments do not actually establish that God is omnipotent, omniscient, and omnibenevolent. Although this is true, the arguments for the existence of God in my AFTLOP and fine-tuning arguments may be considered more compelling than the possible disconfirmation of that God by virtue of consideration of P's tendency to support Q. Therefore, this type B response to Rowe's argument is sufficient to confirm theism and disconfirm atheism.

A stronger response of type A (p. 264:15-24), however, is available to the theist, since P may be rejected on the grounds that O's immensely greater knowledge than that of man is such that no man is capable of determining what action O is likely to perform in any particular case. Since knowledge of the moral status of O's actions likely requires considerations far beyond our ken, we are likely incapable of judging the moral quality of O's behavior and, thus, we do not know P. In fact, generally speaking, an individual could know P only if that individual could know particular properties of conceivably good states of affairs, yet the complex nature of reality is such that conceivably good states of affairs may not actually be likely to be good metaphysically possible states of affairs. In fact, Rowe has not established the existence of an objective basis for proclaiming that any particular (conceivable or actual) state of affairs is actually good. There is no objective basis for grounding the moral status of a state of affairs unless that basis is a ground of objective moral facts. Rowe has not justified his assumption that the good states of affairs in P are known to be good by virtue of being in compliance with an objective basis for determining goodness. Therefore, it is not established that the allegedly good states of affairs in P are actually good.

In short, Rowe has not defined "good", he has not shown that the allegedly good states of affairs in P satisfy that definition, he has not shown that theists are committed to accepting either his definition or the means by which he may attempt to show that the allegedly good states of affairs in P satisfy that definition, he has not addressed the problematic consideration that there could exist a person who does not know that good states of affairs known by the person do not lack J, and he has not shown that, given these considerations, one is not consequently justified in rejecting P.

Given the above discussion, it is far from obvious whether any particular allegedly good state of affairs lacks J (p. 266:12-13). Also, Rowe assumes the existence of some unstated methodology whereby the degree of value/disvalue of goods/evils may be determined (p. 266:13-16), yet provides justification for neither the claim that this methodology may be implemented so as to accurately identify degrees of value/disvalue, nor the claim that the methodology has been appropriately implemented to estimate the value/disvalue of the particular goods/evils he considers. Rowe also misses the point in his claim that an omnipotent, omniscient being could obtain particular goods without permitting E1 or E2 (p. 266:16-18), as our interest is rather in what O could obtain. If Rowe meant to claim that O could obtain particular goods without permitting E1 or E2, then this claim may be rejected for the reasons already discussed. In addition, even if one grants that some goods are not known to posses J, it does not follow that those goods are known to lack J, and it does not follow that those goods lack J. Therefore, Rowe's claim that P is true remains unsubstantiated. So, since P is not known, the inference from P to Q is, of course, not justified.

Rowe considers that if one accepts P, then the inference to Q may be justified on the basis of a principle that may be used to infer from knowns to unknowns (p. 266:20-31). Let KU represent this principle. KU may be interpreted as follows: If many observed entities of type A have property B, then all unobserved entities of type A also have property B (p. 266:28-29). Rowe understands that KU may generate unjustified inferences in some cases, but he evidently assumes that KU may be accepted and applied in any case in which there is no good reason to not do so. Thus, if one accepts P, then KU may be used to make the inference from "the goods we know about lack J" to "the goods we do not know about lack J", so long as there is no good reason to not apply KU in this case. Rowe considers the argument that KU does not apply in this case due to the existence of a defeater (p. 266:40-268:30), but concludes that in the absence of a defeater, KU does apply and, thus, P tends to support Q (p. 268:29-30).

In response to the preceding discussion, first recall that I have already argued that P is not known. Nevertheless, assuming that P is known, the inference from P to Q may be made through application of KU unless there is a good reason to not apply KU. In this case, however, there is a good reason to not apply KU. As mentioned earlier this chapter, if O exists, then it has not been established that we are in a position to know (apart from divine revelation) what action O could perform in any particular case, since it is likely far beyond our ken to determine the results of O's decision procedures which could consist of the evaluation of factors relevant to divine desires such as the following:

(a)   The maximization of the number of people in the set S of people who freely choose to positively respond to revealed truth such that they become well oriented in their relationship to O.

(b)   The maximization of the degree to which each person in S receives his just eternal reward for freely performing each of the members of the set of good works he performs.

(c)   The minimization of the number of people not in S.

(d)   The minimization of the degree to which each person not in S receives his just eternal punishment for freely performing each of the members of the set of evil works he performs.

(e)   The achievement of good divine purposes unfathomed (or unfathomable) by man.

Since the set of all free human actions consists of a tremendously complex array of interdependent relationships, and given that just a single person's free decision to perform or not perform some seemingly trivial action in response to an awareness of an allegedly apparent instance of pointless evil could influence the subsequent course of human history in ways which are wholly unpredictable by man, it is quite evidently far beyond our ken as humans to trace out the decision procedures O may employ. So, if O exists, then the nature of the knowledge possessed by O is clearly beyond our ken, and as such, we are simply in no position to make the inference from P to Q, since KU does not apply. In other words, if not-Q, then P could be likely anyway, and this fact defeats the inference from P to Q.

Rowe objects that "we do know of very significant goods" (p. 268:20), implying that it is not necessarily the case that significant goods that do not lack J can not be known. The theist may agree with this objection, emphasizing that although we humans have the capacity to conceive of possibly significantly good states of affairs in general terms, we do not actually possess the ability to even remotely begin to achieve the overwhelming objective of calculating the value of all of the particular conceivable variations in the unthinkably immense set of genuine metaphysical possibilities one must consider when evaluating decision procedures which must account for such divine desires as those mentioned above. Thus, Rowe's example, described in vague and general terms, of an allegedly significant good (p. 268:20-22) thoroughly fails to successfully challenge my claim that if not-Q, then P is likely anyway. After all, knowledge of this allegedly good state of affairs is consistent with my claim "P is likely, given not-Q, since KU does not apply". In addition, even if Rowe's vague and general example of an allegedly significant good is a genuinely good theoretically conceived state of affairs, it remains to be shown that a particular actualization of this theoretical conception is a real metaphysically live option. In fact, Rowe has not even established that his hypothetical example of an allegedly significant good is actually a hypothetical example of an actual significant good, since he has not shown how the hypothetical state of affairs coheres with possible divine desires such as those mentioned above such that the state of affairs is actually known to be good. Furthermore, Rowe has not even given an objective basis for determining goodness in general.

Another problem for Rowe is that KU is a principle which may be used to draw theistic conclusions. For example, one could argue that given the observation that every known instance of causation is a case in which the cause is a person (see the AFTLOP), every unknown instance of causation is a case in which the cause is a person. From this point, it is not difficult to show that the instances of causation not caused by man are caused by a person(s) with knowledge and power immensely greater than that of man, and this person(s) has properties such that the appropriate identification of the name of that person(s) is God. So, Rowe is not justified in using KU to infer that P entails Q is likely, and KU turns out to be an inference form that resembles reasoning employed in the AFTLOP which establishes that God exists.

Rowe ends his article with a discussion of Hick's "soul-making" theodicy (p. 269:7-273:30), and he concludes that the theodicy "does little or nothing to diminish the force of the strongest arguments from evil" (p. 273:28-30). My critique of Rowe, however, shows that his argument from evil is not strong at all.

In chapter 4 of part 3 of IPRG, William L. Rowe examines his argument for the nonexistence of God based on an inference from P (275:14-16) to Q (P. 275:17-18) to not-G (p. 276:2). His discussion of a variety of issues relevant to the argument is provided in the context of $Pr(G/k) = 0.5$. Rowe's discussion may be quite helpful for those who perceive that $Pr(G/k) = 0.5$ represents their epistemic state. However, given the AFTLOP and my fine-tuning arguments, I find that $Pr(G/k) = 0.5$ does not represent my epistemic state, since my theistic arguments are an essential component of my background knowledge. So, for example, I could grant that P does make it likely that ~G if $Pr(G/k) = 0.5$, yet claim that since $Pr(G/k)$ is actually much greater than 0.5, it does not follow that P makes it likely that ~G (p.285:19-21). Also, I may grant that even if $Pr(P/G\&k)$ is very high, then $Pr(G/P\&k) < 0.5$ (given $Pr(G/k) = 0.5$), yet claim that since $Pr(G/k)$ is actually much higher than 0.5, the high value of $Pr(P/G\&k)$ renders $Pr(G/P\&k)$ much higher than 0.5 (p. 288:28-32).

Rowe examines Wykstra's parent analogy (p. 289:1-291:13) and concludes that it fails to show that "if God exists the goods that justify him in permitting much human and animal suffering are quite likely to be beyond our ken" (p. 291:12-13). In response, the parent analogy arguably has its strengths and weaknesses. The theist may reject the parent analogy on the basis of the "significant disanalogies" Rowe cites (p. 290:14-26), yet maintain that if God exists, then the goods that justify his permission of any particular evil are quite likely beyond our ken. I have repeated this point twice already, but it is worth repeating once more that if God exists, then it has not been established that we are in a position to know (apart from divine revelation) what action God could perform in any particular case, since it is likely far beyond our ken to determine the results of God's decision procedures which could consist of the evaluation of factors relevant to divine desires such as the following:

(a) The maximization of the number of people in the set S of people who freely choose to positively respond to revealed truth such that they become well oriented in their relationship to God.

(b) The maximization of the degree to which each person in S receives his just eternal reward for freely performing each of the members of the set of good works he performs.

(c) The minimization of the number of people not in S.

(d)   The minimization of the degree to which each person not in S receives his just eternal punishment for freely performing each of the members of the set of evil works he performs.

(e)   The achievement of good divine purposes unfathomed (or unfathomable) by man.

The "butterfly effect" in atmospheric dynamics refers to the fact that potential physical events of seemingly negligible consequence, such as a minuscule deviation from the actual flight path of a butterfly in Australia, could interact with subsequent physical event evolution in accordance with physical laws such that eventually a tornado path in Kansas could be altered.   Limited observational capability in conjunction with chaotic nonlinear atmospheric dynamics renders specific, detailed prediction of such effects far beyond our ken.   Likewise, there exists a "suffering butterfly effect", a term I have coined to describe phenomena in the realm of free human actions, which refers to the fact that it is entirely beyond our ken, for example, to state precisely the net effect on human history of God's permitting a person 3287 years ago to have observed an allegedly apparent evil that was agonizing, unnecessary, and preventable (e.g., the suffering and death of a beautiful butterfly, or E1 or E2), assuming God exists. Since the set of all free human actions consists of a tremendously complex array of interdependent relationships, and given that just a single person's free decision to perform or not perform some seemingly trivial action in response to an awareness of an allegedly apparent instance of pointless evil could influence the subsequent course of human history in ways which are wholly unpredictable by man, it is quite evidently far beyond our ken as humans to trace out the outrageously complex decision procedures God may employ. So, if God exists, then the nature of the knowledge possessed by God is clearly beyond our ken, and as such, we are simply in no position to say what action God would perform in any particular instance.

Therefore, even if Rowe happens to be correct in his speculation about what God might always desire to do when God permits suffering for the sake of some good beyond our ken (p. 291:1-6), it does not follow that there are not often instances in which that divine desire is overridden by other competing desires to achieve other divine objectives, where the decision procedures used to implement those objectives are likely far beyond our ken, and where the practical implementation of those objectives consists of results in which some humans are left wondering why God has so acted, if God exists.   If Rowe objects that his speculation about what God might do is, itself, based on the questionably relevant parent analogy, then he may simply reject that analogy in favor of the suffering butterfly effect which establishes that if God exists, then it is unlikely that we are in a position to know why God would permit any particular evil. In light of the considerations above, it follows, more generally, that we are in a position to know neither what action God would ever likely perform in any particular case, nor why God would (or would not) ever perform such action, unless divine revelation were made available to us such that we could evaluate the likelihood of a particular divine action, given conditions representing the state of affairs in question. We can know God acts, while not knowing why God so acts. Given the issues discussed here, Rowe's conclusion (p. 291:11-13) is not justified.

The objection may be raised that my view is inconsistent in that I claim we are not in a position to evaluate the likelihood that God would perform any particular action in any case, yet the AFTLOP implies that we do know some events God will likely cause in the future, namely, physical event patterns consistent with known physical laws. In response, this objection misses the critical qualification that I claim we are in a position to know neither what action God would ever likely perform in any particular case, nor why God would (or would not) ever perform such action, *unless divine revelation were made available to us such that we could evaluate the likelihood of a particular divine action, given conditions representing the state of affairs in question.* So, my position is not inconsistent if our knowledge of future physical event patterns described by laws of physics is viewed as a form of divine revelation. On this interpretation, God enables us to acquire the knowledge that the AFTLOP implies God's existence and probable future activity in the physical world in terms of known physical laws, whereas we have no such divine revelation regarding the basis upon which we may determine whether God's actions are morally justified. We may know some of what God does, yet not know why.

My claim that we have no basis upon which to determine whether God's actions are morally justified might be viewed as being grounded in the supposition that we have no basis whatever to determine the moral status of any action, divine or human. Such a position would tend to undercut theistic moral arguments grounded in the claim that some moral truths are either self-evident or cognitively accessible to those who engage in appropriate reflection upon such matters. In response, a complete examination of moral theistic arguments lies beyond the scope of the present analysis, but it is sufficient to note that our inability to pass moral judgment on God's actions (unless divine revelation enables us to do so) may be the result not of our inability to perceive any distinction between objectively good and objectively evil states of affairs, but may result from our ability to neither identify the fullness of God's decision procedures, nor implement those procedures so as to determine the moral status M of any particular state of affairs, even though it may be true that the objective degree of good/evil of M would be readily apparent to us if we could actually perceive the results of that implementation. Therefore, my position need not be viewed as undercutting theistic moral arguments. The person uninformed by divine revelation may be morally in the dark on many issues, but we need not suppose that person is hopelessly morally ignorant, as that person may perceive objective moral reality to some degree, yet be unable to perceive the moral status of some of God's actions, even if that person knows those actions are caused by God.

Since we have now established that we are not in a position to evaluate the likelihood that God would perform any particular action in any particular case (unless divine revelation enables us to make such judgments), Rowe's "likely, if not certain" reflection (p. 291:15-20) is seen to be most assuredly unlikely and uncertain. Furthermore, Rowe has not even defined "good". Rowe has not shown that some good he allegedly knows satisfies that definition. Rowe has not shown that theists are committed to accepting either his definition or the means by which he might attempt to show that some good he allegedly knows satisfies that definition. Assuming God exists, Rowe has identified neither the decision procedures God is likely to employ, nor the means by which we may determine that the results of God's implementation of those procedures is such that we would not be left wondering why God has so acted. Therefore, Rowe's wild speculation (p. 291:14-292:22; p. 294:4-6) about what God either could or would do in particular situations is simply that: wild speculation. We should not accept premises grounded in wild speculation. Rowe encourages acceptance of P on the basis of wild speculation. Therefore, we should not accept P on the basis of that wild speculation.

One of Rowe's reasons for believing P is his belief B1 that he knows that "many goods we know of are insufficient to justify God in permitting E1 or E2" (p. 297:9-10). In response, Rowe has not justified his claim that he knows the objective moral status of those allegedly "many goods". Rowe also fails to identify the decision procedures God is likely to employ (assuming God exists), nor the means by which we may determine that the results of God's implementation of those procedures is such that we would not be left wondering why God permits E1 or E2. Sure, Rowe's belief B1 may disconfirm the existence of a God whose existence would entail it is likely that Rowe would not have belief B1, but it does not disconfirm the existence of a God whose existence would not entail it is likely that Rowe would not have belief B1. Rowe's ignorance of divine decision procedures beyond our ken renders Rowe's atheistic conclusion unjustified, since there may exist a God who has reasons unknown to Rowe which establish that it is good for God to permit Rowe to have belief B1. Rejection of B1 is in order.

Another of Rowe's reasons for believing P is his belief B2 that God could realize goods "without having to permit E1 and E2 (or something just as bad)" (p. 297:10-13). As mentioned earlier, Rowe's wild speculation about what God could or would do in any particular circumstance is unjustified, as he has neither identified God's decision procedures, nor shown how we can know that God's implementation of those procedures would be such that Rowe's belief B2 would be true and justified, assuming God exists. God may have reasons beyond our ken for permitting E1 and E2, and we are in no position to dispute this. We may, thus, reject belief B2.

Rowe states that another reason for his believing P is his belief that theodicists have failed to show that any known goods are a morally sufficient reason for God's permitting E1 or E2 (p. 297:13-15). In response, even if we grant that known theodicists have failed to show the moral justification of the ways of God, known attempts to show that the ways of God are morally unjustified have also failed. Our inability to pass moral judgment upon God's actions (assuming God exists) flows from our ignorance of divine decision procedures likely far beyond our ken. We should not be surprised (and might as well expect) to discover no known theodicy accomplishes the objective of providing the detailed morally sufficient reasons for God's actions, since no action is an island (i.e., all actions are interfaced with God's decision procedures, if God exists), and those procedures are consequently beyond our ken, given the human inability to synthesize such an unspeakably immense quantity of information.

Thus, Rowe has given us no good reason for believing that P is true. What many of us may have is knowledge that many apparent goods are not known to be morally sufficient reasons for God's permission of some evils, but this entails neither that those apparent goods are known to be morally insufficient reasons, nor that those apparent goods are even ultimately good. This knowledge does not support P, and divine decision procedures beyond our ken (assuming God exists) imply P will doubtfully ever be known. We have no justification for the assumption that the goods we know of are representative of the goods there are, and there is no good reason to suppose we should know that goods we know of are likely to morally justify God's actions. Finally, even if we grant P (despite the good reasons for rejecting it), Rowe concedes the argument from evil may be counterbalanced such that it could be rational to believe in theism, given strong evidence for theism (p. 297:29-32). Since the AFTLOP and my fine-tuning arguments provide strong evidence for theism, we may reject atheism in favor of theism. The evidential argument from evil is dead.

In chapter 5 of part 3 of IPRG, William L. Rowe responds to some objections to his argument from evil raised by Alvin Plantinga (p. 302:1-309:3). I am sympathetic toward a number of points made by Rowe. However, although I am not inclined to raise the objections raised by Plantinga, the objections to Rowe's argument from evil that I made earlier in this present chapter stand firm, even given the details of Rowe's reply to Plantinga. Therefore, I continue to maintain that Rowe's argument from evil is dead.

In chapter 6 of part 3 of IPRG, William L. Rowe responds to some objections to his argument from evil raised by Michael Bergmann (p. 311:1-317:20). Rowe interprets Bergmann's position as the claim that the only way one can justify (1) (p. 313:21-25) is by rejecting a skeptical thesis such as ST1 (p. 311:5-6). Rowe's response is that Bergmann has failed to show "that there is no way of justifying (1) that doesn't involve a rejection of ST1" (p. 315:21-23). In response, how might Rowe justify (1) without rejecting ST1? Rowe considers the good parent analogy as one possible response (p. 313:38-314:2). However, there are significant disanalogies between God and a loving parent, as noted by Rowe (p. 290:17-26), and these disanalogies are grounds for rejecting the good parent analogy. Therefore, we may reject the claim that the good parent analogy is a plausible means by which (1) may be justified, where that justification does not consist of rejection of ST1. In fact, given the disanalogies, we may reject the suggestion (p. 313:34-36) that the good parent analogy is a good analogy.

Rowe considers a way of justifying (1) by attempting to meet Bergmann's challenge to show that (2a) is more likely than (2b) (p. 315:25-31). Rowe lists four conditions (p. 315:31-316:28); let C represent those conditions. Rowe claims that C "is an *inherently* implausible idea not dependent for its implausibility on a *prior rejection* of one or more skeptical theses" (p. 317:8-11). Although Rowe evidently grants that one might argue that C is implausible by assuming the falsity of a plausible skeptical thesis (p. 317:7-8), he claims that his knowledge of the implausibility of C is grounded in the fact that that implausibility is inherent, and not ultimately derived from rejection of a thesis such as ST1. In response, since Rowe's position hinges so heavily on the notion of an "inherently implausible idea", it would be helpful to define that term. Unfortunately, Rowe provides neither a definition, nor an identification of the sufficient conditions of an idea being properly identified as inherently implausible, nor the evidence that there exist sufficient conditions of C being properly identified as inherently implausible. He simply asserts that C is inherently implausible. Rowe's proof by assertion is inadequate and hardly compelling, and it fails to meet the intended challenge.

Perhaps Rowe means that an idea J, given background knowledge k, is inherently implausible if and only if knowledge that P(J/k) is low is derived from consideration of the nature of J in and of itself, where that consideration is independent of any knowledge in k that may otherwise influence our perception of the likelihood of J. The problem with this definition is that "consideration of the nature of J in and of itself" occurs in the context of one's knowledge of the nature of the consideration of entities in and of themselves, and the knowledge of the nature of such considerations is itself an element of k. Thus, an inherently implausible idea, by definition, must be identified as such by virtue of being known to be unlikely given only consideration of the nature of that idea in and of itself, yet that consideration necessarily entails that consideration of information external to the nature of that idea also occurs. It follows that the concept of an inherently implausible idea is, itself, implausible, which entails that it is unlikely that Rowe knows C is inherently implausible. (If Rowe would like to provide a better definition of "inherently implausible", then I'm all ears!)

So, Rowe wants to believe that C is improbable, and he wants to believe that that belief is not derived from a prior rejection of a skeptical thesis, but is rather derived from the perception that C is inherently implausible, yet, to my knowledge, he has not met my challenge to provide a definition of the concept of an inherently implausible idea, where that definition includes the sufficient conditions for the proper identification of an idea as being inherently implausible, nor has he shown that C satisfies that definition. Pending our discovery that my challenge has been met, we may conclude that it is plausible that Rowe's belief that C is implausible is ultimately grounded in rejection of a skeptical thesis such as ST1, since the only known way of justifying (1) is by rejecting ST1, and since Rowe has provided no means (other than proof by appeal to the poor "good parent" analogy, or proof of inherent implausibility by mere assertion) of grounding his belief that C is implausible. (Incidentally, our entire discussion has contained the assumption that evil exists, yet no definition of evil has been provided. The problem of evil is hardly a problem if it has not even been established to exist. Also, it has not been shown that theists are committed to the definition of evil that Rowe may have in mind.)

Furthermore, and more importantly, Rowe acknowledges that strong evidence for the existence of God may justify the claim that C is plausible (p. 317:12-14). Since the AFTLOP and my fine-tuning arguments provide strong evidence for the existence of God, it follows that C is plausible. The objection may be raised that the AFTLOP and my fine-tuning arguments establish the existence not of an omnipotent, omniscient, omnibenevolent God, but of a super-powerful super-knowledgeable person whose moral status is undetermined. This objection, however, only helps the case for God's existence, where God is defined simply as a super-powerful and super-knowledgeable person, since such a God is immune to objections directed at God's moral status, his status being undetermined by our present epistemic state. I do not intend to suggest that there are not good reasons for supposing God is omnibenevolent, but since God's existence may be established by the AFTLOP and my fine-tuning arguments independent of consideration of the problem of evil, it follows that atheists may convert to theism on this basis, independent of their having resolved whether God is likely to be benevolent, given the nature of God, good, and evil in the world. Atheists might not necessarily convert in one giant leap to full-blown omnibenevolent theism grounded in, say, Biblical divine revelation. The smaller hop to a restricted version of theism in which God is merely established to be the super-powerful super-knowledgeable person established by my AFTLOP and fine-tuning arguments might be a smaller first step.

Then again, given the horror of hell,[2] it is much safer to submit to the Gospel of Jesus Christ at once, reserving time for the resolution of fine points of theology and philosophy for post-conversion contemplation. The objection might be raised that the idea of horrendous evils, such as the appalling agony of the eternal conscious human suffering and torment of the damned in hell, renders unlikely the existence of the Christian God (p. 312:17-24). In response, it has not been established that we are in a position to believe that evil that God permits in this world (and in hell) is not a consequence of God's effectively accomplishing morally justified purposes unknown to us. Furthermore, the question of the probability of the existence of the Christian God is, itself, a question deserving book-length analysis and, as such, lies beyond the scope of the present analysis.

The cursory consideration of these issues, here, serves primarily as a reminder of the potentially eternal significance of our free response to the results of such analysis. It is not as if we are some 180 pages deep into a theoretical exploration of technicalities of interest only to specialists in theology or philosophy, but rather, we are well on our way toward establishing not only that God exists, but that the latest statement of modern atheism is fully inadequate as an alternative to the theistic worldview. This result is of unspeakably profound significance, and is most assuredly relevant to us all, for if God exists, then what does He require of you?

In chapter 7 of part 3 of IPRG, Michael Martin presents an inductive argument from evil based on the failure of known theodicies (p. 319:1-327:6).[3] Martin's argument (p. 320:13-26) is grounded in the rational belief principle in premise (1) (p. 320:13-18). This principle consists of three components, but a fourth component is missing: (iv) if P is true, then we are in a position to determine the likelihood that there exists a good reason for believing A. After all, even if there exists no evidence for P, and even if known evidence E disconfirms P, it is true that if P likely entails the existence of reasons beyond our ken for believing A, then our lack of knowledge of any reason to believe A is not evidence against P, regardless of the number of failed attempts to give reasons for believing A. Rather, the lack of knowledge of any reason to believe A, given a large number of failed attempts to give reasons for believing A, is to be expected even if P is true. So, in cases in which this fourth component of the rational belief principle is not satisfied, it is not rational to believe that P is false, since the assumption is not justified that one is in the position to determine the likelihood of the existence of reasons for believing A or, consequently, P. Therefore, since Martin's premise (1) may be rejected, so too may we reject his conclusion (p. 320:26).

Martin's argument is also built on the assumption that premise (2) is true (p. 320:19). In response, the AFTLOP and my fine-tuning arguments constitute good positive reasons that God exists. Thus, premise (2) may be rejected, and so too may we reject the conclusion (p. 320:26). The objection may be raised that the AFTLOP and my fine-tuning arguments establish the existence of a super-knowledgeable, super-powerful person G2, not the existence of an omniscient, omnipotent, omnibenevelont person G1. In response, this objection serves to assist the atheist in her conversion to theism, since arguments from evil do not disconfirm the existence of G2, as the moral status of G2 is undetermined. Atheists may come to accept the existence of G2, even if the question of the existence of G1 remains unresolved in their minds. Remember: atheism and G1-theism are not the only available options, as is often erroneously assumed. (Incidentally, I believe there exist good reasons for believing G1-theism, but analysis of such issues lies beyond the scope of the present analysis.)

Martin restates his argument (p. 320:33-36) in inductive form. Premise (c) is incorrect, and should be replaced by: (c') We have no known evidence that H. Premise (c) does not follow from (c'), as the possibility exists that there is unknown positive evidence that H, given (c'). Unless it is reasonable to believe that H entails that we are likely in a position to possess positive evidence that A, we may reject (c), since the possibility exists that unknown evidence for A provides positive evidence that H. Therefore, conclusion (d) does not follow, since it has not been established that H entails that we are likely in a position to possess positive evidence that A, and consequently, it has not been established that we are in a position to evaluate the probability of ~H.

Martin uses an analogy B to illustrate his mode of inference (p. 322:29-323:3). In response, the analogy does not apply to our consideration of the possibility that God has a sufficient moral reason R for permitting the evil that exists, since if God exists, God likely has reasons beyond our ken for performing the actions he performs. In particular, if God exists, then God may interact with the world and its inhabitants such that the following divine desires are satisfied:

(a)   The maximization of the number of people in the set S of people who freely choose to positively respond to revealed truth such that they become well oriented in their relationship to God.

(b)   The maximization of the degree to which each person in S receives his just eternal reward for freely performing each of the members of the set of good works he performs.

(c)   The minimization of the number of people not in S.

(d)   The minimization of the degree to which each person not in S receives his just eternal punishment for freely performing each of the members of the set of evil works he performs.

(e)   The achievement of good divine purposes unfathomed (or unfathomable) by man.

Since it is likely far beyond our ken to determine the results of God's decision procedures which could consist of the evaluation of factors relevant to divine desires such as those mentioned above, it has not been established that we are in a position to know (apart from divine revelation) what action God could or would perform in any particular case. It would be good for God to interact with the immensely complex interrelationship between all human (and any possible angelic or demonic) actions and their subsequent effects on human history so as to achieve the above divine desires. Since we are clearly in no position to trace the implementation of divine decision procedures required to accomplish such objectives, we are surely in no position to determine how God would or could likely act in any particular case, assuming God exists.

So, in the analogy B, Jones's friends are evidently likely to be in a position to possess some evidence of any foul play that may have possibly occurred, yet we humans are evidently not likely to be in a position to possess any possibly existing evidence of God's morally sufficient reasons for permitting existing evil, unless we either acquire knowledge of specific reasons by means of divine revelation, or we acquire knowledge which entails that although such specific reasons exist, we do not know those reasons in detail. In short, Jones's friends are likely to know of any cover-up, but we are unlikely to know any of God's morally sufficient reasons for permitting evil. The existence of a cover-up does not entail the existence of reasons for believing the cover-up occurred, where those reasons are likely beyond our ken. The existence of God, however, does entail the existence of reasons for which God permits evil, where those reasons are likely beyond our ken. Jones's friends, therefore, may be justified in concluding a cover-up probably did not occur, whereas we are not justified in concluding that God does not have morally sufficient reasons for permitting existing evil, if God exists. Granted, it would be ad hoc and arbitrary for Jones's friends to suppose there exists a good unknown reason for believing a cover-up existed (p. 323:40-41). It would also be ad hoc and arbitrary for us to suppose that good unknown reasons exist for believing God has morally sufficient reasons for permitting evil, unless we have positive evidence (e.g., the AFTLOP and my fine-tuning arguments) for the existence of God. However, unlike analogy B, in which it is not ad hoc and arbitrary for Jones's friends to conclude a cover-up likely doesn't exist, it is ad hoc and arbitrary to conclude that God doesn't exist, since absence of evidence of God's morally sufficient reasons for permitting evil is not evidence of absence of such reasons, as we are not in the position to determine the likelihood of the existence of such reasons. As noted above, the AFTLOP and my fine-tuning arguments establish the existence of G2, not G1. Therefore, it would be better to say that my positive evidence for the existence of God establishes the existence of G2, and since the existence of G2 is consistent with the existence of apparently pointless evil, Martin's argument from failed theodicies, even if it were sound, would not disconfirm the existence of G2.

In light of the above discussion, Martin is mistaken in supposing that there is no evidence that God's reasons for permitting evil are likely beyond human comprehension (p. 323:29-30). The fact that many theists might think they know, at least in part, why God permits evil does not contradict my claim that God's reasons for permitting evil are likely beyond human comprehension (p. 323:30-35), but rather entails that theists (apart from divine revelation) do not fully understand why God permits existing evil, even though they may believe they have identified key factors which may play a significant role in God's decision procedures. We can know God acts, yet not fully understand why God so acts.

Martin wonders why theists suppose that his rational belief principle in premise (1) should be treated differently in the context of religion than in other contexts (p. 323:7-9). My answer is that Martin's rational belief principle is inadequate, in general. As discussed above, I have supplied a fourth component (iv) to his principle which alleviates the problem of using different principles in different contexts. In the context of analogy B, Jones's friends may use my rational belief principle to conclude that a cover-up probably does not exist. In the context of our consideration that God may have reasons (unknown to us) for permitting evil, the rational belief principle may not be used to conclude that God probably does not exist, since component (iv) of that principle is not satisfied. Specifically, the condition is not satisfied that if God exists, then we are in a position to determine the likelihood that there exists a good reason for believing the assumption that God has good unknown reasons for permitting existing evil. In both contexts the same four-component rational belief principle is applied, but only in analogy B does that principle yield the result that the belief in question should be believed to be false, since all four components are satisfied in the context of analogy B, whereas the fourth component is not satisfied in the context of consideration of the belief that God exists and has good unknown reasons for permitting evil.

To his credit, Martin does appear to perceive that God's existence renders probable the existence of knowledge unknown by humans (p. 324:1-4). It is not difficult, as shown above, to subsequently infer that God's existence entails the likely existence of reasons for permitting evil, where those reasons are unknown by man. Martin seeks to avoid this inference by drawing results from an unpublished paper by Paul Draper (p. 324:13-19). Martin does not explain why Draper's perspective should be accepted. I have no access to this mysterious unpublished paper, so I have no way of evaluating the arguments contained therein. Needless to say, Martin has failed to justify his claim.

Incidentally, our entire discussion has contained the assumption that evil exists, yet no definition of evil has been provided. The problem of evil is hardly a problem if it has not even been established to exist. Also, it has not been shown that theists are committed to the definition of evil that Martin may have in mind. For example, if Martin defines moral evil in terms of subjective psychological/sociological theories (p. 324:39-40), then since objective evil arguably doesn't even exist in this case, neither does there objectively exist the "problem of evil". We can not object that God has no morally sufficient reason for permitting the objective existence of evil, if evil does not objectively exist. Martin's argument is, therefore, incomplete and in need of serious revision. Since the revisions for which I have argued do not lead to the atheistic conclusion Martin desires, his argument does not disconfirm theism.

Even if theists are committed to belief in the existence of evil (however Martin may define it), it remains to be shown that apparently pointless evil exists. After all, if God exists, then God knows *much* more than we do, so we are in no position (apart from divine revelation) to say what God could or would do in any particular case, since God's actions are likely a function of numerous variables, including variables representing God's inscrutable beliefs and knowledge. Thus, we are not in a position to claim that there exists any instance of apparently pointless suffering. The claim "X appears to person J to be Y" means that J believes that X seems to be Y. However, X can seem to J to be Y only if J is in a position to determine whether X is likely Y. If J knows that J is in no position to determine whether X is likely Y, then J surely does not know whether X seems to be Y. Given God's immeasurably greater knowledge than that of man, we humans know that we are in no position to determine whether allegedly apparently pointless evil is actually apparently pointless evil. Since we do not know that allegedly apparently pointless evil is actually apparently pointless evil, it follows that we do not know that apparently pointless evil exists. Therefore, the result Martin quotes from Paul Draper may be rejected (p. 324:13-19), pending proof that apparently pointless evil exists. Furthermore, Martin's premises (3) and (4) (p. 320:20-25) assume the existence of apparently pointless evil, and we may therefore reject these premises, pending proof that apparently pointless evil exists. We are not justified in supposing that apparently pointless evil exists, given the non-omniscient and limited nature of our human reasoning relative to God's omniscience. Sure, we may observe that we have no known reason for which God (if God exists) permits some evil E, but we may not subsequently infer that E is apparently pointless. Rather, we may simply infer that we do not know whether E is pointless, since we are in no position to determine whether a possibly existing God has appropriately implemented divine decision procedures beyond our ken such that E either is or is not pointless, given God's divine purposes. From "I don't know whether E is pointless" it does not follow that "E is apparently pointless." Thus, we have reason to reject premises (3) and (4), and consequently another reason to reject the conclusion Martin seeks (p. 320:26).

We are in no position to determine the likelihood that God (if God exists) has good reasons for permitting existing evil. It follows that the failure of any past theodicies does not disconfirm the existence of God (p. 324:20-30).

Martin claims that successful naturalistic explanations of apparently pointless natural evil can be provided in terms of natural laws (p. 324:35-39). But from whence the natural laws? God! My AFTLOP establishes that God is the cause of physical events described by laws of physics. Here Martin is seen to embrace the classic naturalistic fallacy: explanations in terms of laws of physics are caused by those laws. Clearly, physical laws are, themselves, mere descriptions of regular physical events patterns, so physical laws do not cause natural evil, but rather, physical laws describe regular physical event patterns caused by God. The atheistic appeal to natural laws as a causal explanation of natural evil fails, since the existence of natural laws entails the existence of God (see my AFTLOP for details).

The objection may be raised that if God is the cause of physical event patterns described by physical laws, and if those patterns describe physical events which are sometimes evil, then it follows that God is sometimes the cause of evil physical events, contradicting the assumption that God is omnibenevolent. In response, unless the terms "evil" and "omnibenevolent" are clearly defined, there is no clear contradiction. Also, there may exist good unknown reasons for believing that at least some events we label as "natural evil" are not actually evil, since we are not clearly in a position to determine what is evil in any particular case unless we are enlightened by divine revelation. Even if some physical events described by physical laws are evil, it may be that God is not actually the cause of those evil events, as those events may be caused by evil spiritual beings (e.g., demons). Given these considerations, therefore, we may conclude that the casting of natural evil in terms of physical laws has been established neither to confirm atheism, nor disconfirm theism. Also, as discussed above, Martin's casting of moral evil in terms of psychological/sociological theories (p. 324:39-325:1) is inadequate.

Martin describes a procedure for identifying successful theoretical perspectives (p. 325:4-12). He then provides an illustration of that procedure (p. 325:13-23). The theist may gainfully employ this procedure when T1 represents the theoretical perspective in which a theodicy known by man is taken to explain, in all detail, the morally sufficient reasons for God's permission of existing evil, and when T2 represents the theoretical perspective in which a theodicy unknown by man is taken to explain, in all detail, the morally sufficient reasons for God's permission of existing evil. Since explanations from perspective T1 are (and continue to be) unsuccessful, and since explanations from perspective T2 are successful, and since available evidence disconfirms T1 and confirms T2, we may favor T2 over T1. The objection may be raised that Martin has in mind his atheistic theoretical perspective T3 which he takes to be more successful than T2. In response, T3 is not to be favored over T2, since T2 is not unsuccessful, since T3 is unsuccessful, and since there is positive evidence for T2.

Martin quotes a point made by Hare and Madden (p. 325:24-32), and then provides an illustration (p. 325:33-326:17). It is assumed that "there is no independent reason for the existence" of God (p. 326:7-9), yet my AFTLOP and fine-tuning arguments constitute independent reasons for the existence of God. The objection may be raised that my theistic arguments, as discussed earlier, establish the existence of G2, not G1. In response, the existence of G2 is consistent with the existence of apparently pointless evil, so G2 is immune to arguments from evil. The atheist may, therefore, reject atheism in favor of G2.

Martin rejects the claim that the meaning of the terms in his indirect argument from evil is not very similar to arguments in ordinary life (p. 326:18-24). In response, the nature of God is clearly different from the nature of man.

In Martin's conclusion he reiterates that his argument assumes there is no positive evidence for the existence of God, and he quotes his book[4] to support that claim. Given my AFTLOP and fine-tuning arguments, and given the lengthy critique of atheism in this present book, Martin's book is now clearly outdated and in need of revision.

In chapter 8 of part 3 of IPRG, Thomas Metcalf presents an atheistic argument from non-gratuitous evil (p. 328:1-335:41). Metcalf begins with a statement that implies that at least some intense suffering and premature death is evil (p. 328:1-4). In response, the term "evil" is not explicitly defined, and without a definition it is not clear what properties are the object of investigation. Metcalf's essay is therefore ambiguous and inconclusive, as theists are not obviously committed either to the definition he may have in mind, or the means by which he may demonstrate that at least some instances of intense suffering and premature death are evil. For example, if an instance of premature death of a young orphan girl achieves, among other good objectives, the goal of both preventing significant future earthly suffering and escorting the girl to a place of eternal bliss in heaven, then it is far from clear (and arguably false) that the premature death is an instance of evil. Furthermore, theists could argue that all deaths occur at the good time appointed by God, implying that premature death doesn't even exist. Therefore, Metcalf needs to provide a clear definition of evil, and he must show how theists are committed to his demonstration that particular events or event-types are evil.

Assuming Metcalf defines evil in a way that I suspect he may, I tend to agree that theists are committed to the belief that gratuitous evil is incompatible with God's existence (p. 328:9-330:19). Metcalf then argues that God's existence is disconfirmed by the nonexistence of hypothetical situation (S) (p. 330:34-35). He then claims that the Principle of Assurance (PA) (p. 331:7-9) may be used to argue that either "God does not exist, or God has some good reason not to bring about (S) that outweighs the force of (PA)" (p. 331:14-15). Metcalf's atheistic argument succeeds only if he can show that if God exists, then God does not have some good reason not to bring about (S) that outweighs the force of (PA).

In response, we are not in the position to know whether God (if God exists) does or does not have some good reason not to bring about (S) that outweighs the force of (PA). Metcalf anticipates this objection (p. 335:11-14) and responds that he has "adduced some evidence that God would bring about (S) if he existed" (p. 335:14-16). Metcalf's response, however, completely misses the point. The skeptical theist may argue that since we are not in a position (apart from divine revelation) to know in detail why God performs the actions God performs, there is no evidence available to us that confirms the hypothesis that God would bring about (S) if he exists. Let E represent the evidence that Metcalf has adduced that allegedly confirms the hypothesis H that God (if he exists) would bring about (S). The skeptical theist maintains that it is not reasonable to believe that E confirms H. It is reasonable to believe E confirms H only if we make the assumption A that we are in a position to determine whether evidence of type E is likely to confirm or disconfirm H. Metcalf does not provide support for assumption A, but merely asserts that E is likely to disconfirm H. What Metcalf must do is show that he has justification for the belief that A. Merely asserting that E disconfirms H fails to provide such justification, and pending support for A, we may reject the claim that "the balance of evidence favors" Metcalf's position (p. 335:16-18).

Metcalf's speculation regarding what evil may be necessary to sacrifice greater good (p. 335:18-24) is just that: speculation. We have no good reason to suppose Metcalf is capable of identifying hypothetical divine decision procedures of a possibly existing super-knowledgeable, super-powerful God and tracing out the full implementation of those procedures (given all relevant evidence) such that he can determine whether the results of that implementation would likely be confirmed by available evidence. In short, Metcalf's "adduced evidence" assumes he is in a position to know both what action God could do in any particular case, and why God would perform that action in that case. Since Metcalf has not provided justification for these critical assumptions, his argument may be rejected.

Metcalf considers a prima facie reason for thinking God would actualize (S) (p. 335:25-33). In response, prima facie reasons are inferior to reasons grounded in more complete and thorough examination of relevant considerations. Even if Metcalf thinks he has a prima facie reason for assuming that he knows what God would do, Metcalf ought to reject that assumption upon deeper contemplation of the nature of the knowledge and decision procedures beyond our ken that God (if God exists) would likely use to determine what action is best. We may, therefore, be skeptical of any suggestion or implication that good prima facie reasons to think God would actualize (S) are actually good reasons to think God would actualize (S). Good prima facie reasons are not necessarily good reasons.

Therefore, we may conclude that Metcalf has not shown that reason R is not a good reason for believing that we are not in a position to determine whether there is a good reason for God not to actualize (S), where R is the consideration that since God's decision procedures (if God exists) are likely beyond our ken, we are likely not in a position to determine why

God would perform any particular action in any particular case. It follows that Metcalf's argument from non-gratuitous evil fails to confirm atheism.

NOTES

1. McGrath, P. J. (1987). *Atheism or Agnosticism*. Analysis, v. 47, pp. 54-57.
2. Wiese, Bill (2006). *23 Minutes in Hell*. Lake Mary, FL: Charisma House.
3. This is an edited version of his argument in Martin, Michael (1990). *Atheism: A Philosophical Justification*. Philadelphia: Temple University Press, pp. 341-49, 361.
4. Ibid.

CHAPTER 6

Atheistic Arguments From Nonbelief Refuted

I now examine the nonbelief arguments for atheism found in the book "The Improbability of God" edited by Michael Martin and Ricki Monnier, and published by Prometheus Books in 2006, ISBN: 1-59102-381-5. I urge you to purchase a copy of "The Improbability of God" (IPRG) so that you may fully understand the context of the critical remarks below.

In chapter 1 of part 4 of IPRG, Theodore M. Drange presents an argument for the nonexistence of the Evangelical Biblical Christian God (p. 341:1-356:9). Drange structures his argument on p. 342:7-33. In response, premise (A3) is a crucial weakness in the argument. Drange considers Argument (6) as a possible means of supporting (A3), but ultimately regards it as a failure (p. 345:13-31).

Drange's only support for (A3) is Argument (7) (p. 345:32-346:25). In response, God's desire that people obey his forceful command that people believe in his son does not suggest that God's desire for situation S is not overridden by any other desire (p. 345:33-37). "Person J desires that the set Q of people obey J's forceful command C" does not entail "No conditions M exist such that given M, J has an overriding desire that the members of Q not obey C". Therefore, Drange's claim that the force of Argument (1) supports (A3) remains unsubstantiated. Likewise, God's greatest command (i.e., that people love God maximally) does not suggest that God's desire for situation S is not overridden by any other desire (p. 345:37-41). "Person J desires that the set Q of people obey J's greatest command C" does not entail "No conditions M exist such that given M, J has an overriding desire that the members of Q not obey C". Thus, Drange's claim that the force of Argument (2) supports (A3) also remains unsubstantiated. In Drange's third argument in support of Argument (7), he claims that the force of Argument (3) suggests that S is a maximum priority in God's mind, and that achieving S is not overridden by any other desire (p. 345:41-346:5). In response, the fact that priority R is a very high priority in one's mind does not entail that no conditions M exist such that given M, priority R is overridden by some other priority. Drange makes the unjustified inference from "Priority R is a high priority" to "R is never overridden by any other priority".

Nothing in the Biblical passages cited by Drange supports that inference. Therefore, Argument (7) fails to support (A3). Given the failure of Argument (6) and Argument (7) as support for (A3), (A3) is now seen to stand unsupported. On this basis, we may reject (A3) and, consequently, we may reject the conclusion (E) (p. 342:33).

Drange considers the Future-Kingdom Defense (p. 348:1-349:41). Although I am not inclined to pursue this line of defense, I did find some of Drange's comments objectionable. In particular, Drange claims "there are conceptual problems with the idea of a general resurrection" (p. 348:29-34). In response, there is no conceptual problem at all. It is easy to conceive of the concept of a resurrection in one's mind. Furthermore, a sufficiently powerful God should have no difficulty performing a resurrection, if that God strongly desired such an event.

Additional objections of mine include the following: that today is the day of salvation (2 Corinthians 6:2) does not necessarily entail that no post-death salvation events will ever occur. (Incidentally, I don't recommend postponing acceptance of salvation through the Gospel of Jesus Christ to test this theory! Better safe than eternally sorry....) Also, that men are judged after physical death (Hebrews 9:27) does not necessarily entail no salvation events ever occur between the time of physical death and the time of the judgment. (Again, don't test this theory by waiting until after physical death to see if this is possible! Obey the Gospel of Jesus Christ now! Repent and live!)

Drange assumes virtually all people in a post-death state who are given an opportunity for salvation would positively respond to that opportunity so as to become rightly related to God (p. 349:7-13). In response, man's sinful nature is such that there is evidently no guarantee that he will choose rightly, in general. Adam sinned in Eden (Genesis 3). Others sin, despite their knowledge that their actions are sinful (Romans 1:32). Paul identifies with his own struggle against the sinful nature (Romans 7:19). Judas agreed to betray Jesus, even having accompanied Jesus throughout his miraculous ministry (Matthew 26:14-16). Still others sin despite God's clear judgment against that sin (Revelation 16:9, 11, 21). So, given a standard conservative Evangelical interpretation of the nature of reality as described in the Biblical data, we have reason to doubt post-death sinners are likely to repent, even if given an opportunity to do so.

Drange also wonders what purposes God may have, given certain conditions (p. 349:14-33). In response, why should we suppose that we are in a position to know what actions God would likely perform in any particular situation? Or, for that matter, even if we think we know what actions God may likely perform in some situation, why should we suppose we are in a position to know, in detail, why God would likely perform those actions? In other words, the thoughts and ways of a super-powerful, super-knowledgeable God are likely to be largely inscrutable, and there is no reason to suppose we are in a position to know why the future-kingdom explanation is true (if it is true), even given the assumption that the Evangelical Christian Biblical God exists.

Drange also considers the Free-Will Defense (p. 350:1-352:32). I am not inclined to favor the Free-Will Defense, but I do find some of Drange's comments in this section to be dubious. Drange assumes "People *want* to know the truth. They *want* to be shown how the world is really set up" (p. 350:15-16; p. 350:31-32; italics his). In response, the Biblical passages I cited earlier establish that man is inclined towards a sinful nature which rejects truth (see also Romans 1:18 and 3:23). Thus, sin is, in a sense, irrational, and man is inclined towards irrationality in that sense, implying that "normal" people are, to some degree, truth-suppressing and irrational, contra Drange's supposition to the contrary (p. 351:17-19; 351:22-23).

I do tend to agree with Drange that it may be possible that God could reveal to more people that P (p. 342:9-13) is true without interfering with their free will (p. 351:24-25). However, it does not follow that it would be good of God to reveal to more people that P is true, as Drange would seem to assume. Let W represent the set of people, where:

(1) Each member of W does not know P;

(2) Each member of W is a human on Earth with the cognitive capacity to understand truths such as P;

(3) Each member of W would, given knowledge of P, freely choose to remain in sin, acting so as to reject the free gift of salvation.

Drange would appear to suppose that if more people in the world acquired knowledge of P, then all (or nearly all) of those people would positively respond to that knowledge such that they would freely choose to act so as to become forgiven of their sins, receiving the free gift of salvation. This supposition is far from clear, however, given man's sinful and irrational tendencies as previously outlined. If it is true that many of those who presently do not know P are members of W, then it is far from clear that it would be good of God to enable them to know P. Given that a person's punishment in hell is proportioned to the degree to which revealed truth is rejected, it may be good of God to prevent the members of W from acquiring knowledge of P, since their knowledge of P would only serve to increase the quantity of revealed truth they reject, thereby increasing their eternal punishment in hell. The hiddenness of God evidenced by limited knowledge of P worldwide, therefore, may be viewed as being consistent with God's good desire D to minimize truth revealed to members of W. Since we are in no position to identify and trace out the implementation of divine decision procedures required to accomplish such divine objectives, we are incapable, as humans with such limited knowledge, of determining whether the present degree of belief in P worldwide happens to correspond to what would be expected, given God's desire D. Thus, the existence of the Evangelical Christian Biblical God is not disconfirmed by the fact that situation S does not obtain. God's desire D may be viewed as a possible desire that God would want more strongly than situation S. Absent evidence that God does not have desire D (if God exists), we may reject premise (A3) and, consequently, we may reject conclusion (E) (p. 342:33). This defense may be called the Justified Hiddenness Defense, since the nonexistence of situation S may result from God's morally justified decision to hide from those who would resist a good response to knowledge of P. My argument is not that every person on Earth who presently does not know P is a member of W, but rather my argument is that we are in no position to determine whether many (or most) on Earth who presently do not know P are members of W. My argument is a defense, not a theodicy.

The Justified Hiddenness Defense may be understood as being grounded in the Divine Revelation Principle (DRP): God desires to maximize truth revealed to those who would choose good actions in response to that revelation, and God desires to minimize truth revealed to those who would choose bad actions in response to that revelation. The DRP may be a significant factor in God's overall divine decision procedures used to determine God's actions in the world. Biblical support for a principle such as DRP includes, for example, Matthew 13:12, Matthew 25:29-30, and Luke 8:18. DRP also carries with it, to me, a sense of just being morally right. If I am capable of immediately perceiving morally right states of affairs independent of rigorous proof, then my direct perception that DRP carries the ring of truth may be viewed as evidence that it is true, absent evidence to the contrary.

Even if my Justified Hiddenness Defense fails, there remains the Unknown-Purpose Defense. Drange claims that Argument (7) supports (A3) more strongly than the Unknown-Purpose Defense argues against it (p. 353:9-25). In response, Argument (7) has been shown to not support

(A3) at all, as explained earlier in detail. Furthermore, if God's unknown purposes are viewed as the result of God's implementation of divine decision procedures beyond our ken, and if significant factors in those decision procedures are understood to include considerations such as those emphasized in the Justified Hiddenness Defense, then the nonexistence of support for (A3) consequently renders the Argument from Nonbelief weaker than my response to it. My response may be viewed as the claim that divine hiddenness (evidenced by the nonexistence of situation S) is justified for reasons not fully understood, but which likely include considerations cited in the Justified Hiddenness Defense as significant considerations in God's overall decision procedures. Thus, (A3) remains unsupported, and I have identified considerations which may likely play a significant role in divine decision procedures, where we are in no position to determine whether it is likely that the implementation of those decision procedures would result in a world different from what we presently observe.

Drange wonders why God has not revealed more regarding God's purposes for permitting nonbelief in P (p. 353:26-39). In response, we have no good reason to suppose that we are in a position to claim that we know what God could or should do in any particular situation, unless divine revelation enables us to acquire such knowledge. Furthermore, widespread nonbelief in P may be viewed as consistent with DRP, which is arguably a significant factor in God's decision procedures, given that Biblical data are understood to be a form of divine revelation. Therefore, the unsound Argument from Nonbelief is not an obstacle to my belief in P, and if the Argument from Nonbelief is an obstacle to other's belief in P, then God has good reasons for permitting them to persist in their unenlightened epistemic state, assuming God exists. God's revelation is sufficient to maximize appropriately accepted knowledge on the part of those who are willing to positively respond to it, and God's hiddenness is sufficient to minimize inappropriately rejected knowledge on the part of those who are unwilling to positively respond to it. God's love is thus manifested in the divine desire to maximize the eternal reward of the saved, and minimize the eternal punishment of the lost. It is far from established, therefore, that God's secrecy runs counter-productive to God's overriding desires established through implementation of God's decision procedures (p. 353:29-34; 354:11-16; 354:40-41). These possible considerations are consistent with the Biblical data, and we are in no position to claim that such possible considerations are not actually significant considerations in God's decision procedures, since those procedures are likely far beyond our ken, assuming God exists.

Drange considers the relative merits of W-N vs. W-U (p. 353:40-355:6). He claims that W-N is preferable to W-U, since W-N provides a less mysterious explanation of the nonexistence of situation S (p. 354:37-355:6). In response, less mysterious explanations are not necessarily better justified than more mysterious explanations. In particular, justified explanations with greater mystery are better than unjustified explanations with lesser mystery. Furthermore, my response to the Argument from Nonbelief is not grounded purely in appeal to unknown truths, but entails that we do know, to some extent, a possibly significant factor in God's decision procedures used to determine God's actions, assuming God exists. The real issue at stake, here, is the overall case for the existence of the Evangelical Christian Biblical God, and consideration of all evidence relevant to this issue lies beyond the scope of the present analysis. However, even if we grant that W-N is better supported than W-U, given considerations on pages 354-355, it does not follow that W-U is not better supported than W-N, given consideration of all evidence relevant to the case for the existence of the Evangelical Christian Biblical God. Therefore, Drange's considerations are inadequate as a basis for rejecting the existence of that God, as the full range of relevant evidence has not been properly examined. This inadequacy is especially evident, given not only the unfounded premise (A3), but also my successful meeting of Drange's challenge to identify a "purpose on God's part that would explain why he has not brought about situation S" (p. 355:7-9).

In chapter 2 of part 4 of IPRG, Theodore M. Drange responds to an essay written by Christopher McHugh (p. 357:1-360:34). Drange interprets McHugh's Expectations Defense as the claim that if the Evangelical Christian God exists, "then we *should* expect to find just as much evil and nonbelief as there actually is" (p. 357:11-13; italics his). Drange disputes this claim, and argues that if the Evangelical Christian God exists, "then it would be unreasonable to expect there to be as much nonbelief in the gospel message as there is" (p. 360:30-31).

In response, we are not in a position to determine the quantity of nonbelief or evil that the Evangelical Christian God (GC) is likely to permit, if GC exists. Drange asks how GC could permit 2/3 of the present world to be non-Christian (p. 359:3-4). Given that GC exists, we may answer this question by responding that we are simply in no position to determine what proportion of the world's population should be expected to be Christian. We have no good reason to suppose we should know what GC could or should permit, if GC's ways are inscrutable. However, since the ways of GC are not entirely inscrutable, being revealed to some degree in the Biblical data, we may be able to infer considerations which may likely play a significant role in GC's overall decision procedures used to determine GC's actions, but since the full details of those procedures are not revealed in the Biblical data, we are in no position to infer detailed expectations of, for example, the percentage P of the world that should be presently expected to be Christian, assuming GC exists. Consequently, we are in no position to infer the probability of God's nonexistence from P.

Assuming GC exists, P is likely an unfathomably complex function of a great many variables that measure, for example, such quantities as the value of conditions determined by all past human actions, the value of the subsequent future impact of all past human actions, the value of conditions determined by all past actions of demonic/satanic beings, the value of the subsequent future impact of all past actions of demonic/satanic beings, the value of the best overall path of human history in light of GC's largely inscrutable purposes. Many more variables could surely be added to this list, but the list is already sufficient to establish that we are simply in no position to identify the best divine decision procedure available to GC, nor are we in a position to determine the results of the implementation of that procedure, given the actually existing world. Passages such as 1 Timothy 2:4, and commands such as the Great Commission, presumably reveal divine desires that play a critical and dominant role in GC's decision procedures used to make value judgments needed for identifying and performing morally justified divine actions, but this consideration hardly entails that it is not the case that P should be 1/3, if GC exists. The value of P may, in fact, be due largely to man's sinful tendency to reject and suppress truth, rather than due to GC's inability to forcibly increase the value of P. Furthermore, as I discussed earlier in my Justified Hiddenness Defense, GC's careless and forceful increase of P would likely run counter-productive to GC's overriding desire to act consistent with the DRP. As a result, my attack on ANB is not "totally baseless and incomplete" (p. 359:6-11). Thus, it should be evident that since P is a function not only of divine desires and actions, but also a function of human and demonic desires and actions, and since the full knowledge of such desires and actions lies hopelessly beyond our ken, we mere humans of such finite knowledge are simply in no position to determine the probability that the present value of P is what would be expected, if GC exists. Therefore, given these considerations, no inference from the value of P to the likelihood of the existence of GC is justified. The ANB presumes we possess knowledge that we do not actually possess. Rejection of the ANB is in order.

Drange objects that the worldwide missionary effort will likely not succeed without divine assistance (p. 359:20-22). In response, this objection is grounded in the assumption that present missionary work is divinely unaided. Evangelical Biblical Christians would reject that assumption, viewing GC as intimately concerned with and involved in the details of each person's life experiences, including those of the Evangelical missionaries.

Drange also expresses concern about the eternal destiny of the unevangelized (p. 359:22-24), presumably because it is allegedly problematic that GC (whose ways are fair and just) would appear to be unfair by permitting many people to die in their sins and be eternally condemned without ever having conscious knowledge of the Gospel message essential for salvation. In response, we are in no position to claim that it appears unfair that GC (assuming GC exists) would permit the existence of the unevangelized. GC may have good reasons unknown to us which justify GC's permission of the existence of the unevangelized. Indeed, given good reasons for believing GC exists, it is reasonable to believe GC is fair and just in the permission of the existence of the unevangelized, even if we do not know the reasons for which GC permits the existence of the unevangelized. So, Evangelical Biblical Christians need not be concerned about the unfairness objection to God's permission of the existence of the unevangelized. Furthermore, the role of the DRP in the Justified Hiddenness Defense may be a significant factor in GC's divine decision procedures which, given the human tendency to reject and suppress truth, ultimately explain GC's permission of the existence of many unevangelized persons.

Drange claims the existence of "good biblical support for ANB's premise (A3)" (p. 359:29-31). In response, as shown in detail earlier, Drange has provided no Biblical support for (A3).

Drange claims that denial of premise (A3) entails that "GC, in the final analysis (taking into account all of his desires), does not want universal (or near-universal) belief in the gospel message" (p. 359:34-37). In response, Drange's claim is incorrect. Instead, denial of (A3) may be understood as entailing that GC, in the final analysis, does not want universal belief in the gospel message, given the existence of some persons who refuse to accept it. It does not follow, however, that GC, in the final analysis, does not want universal belief in the gospel message. Let GA represent the set of persons who, upon hearing the gospel message, would ultimately respond to it positively (GA represents the gospel acceptors). Let GR represent the set of persons who, upon hearing the gospel message, would ultimately respond to it negatively (GR represents the gospel rejectors). So, GC may possess the idealized desire that, given the existence only of persons who are members of GA, universal belief in the gospel occurs, whereas the actual existence of some persons who are members of GR entails that God's desires are such that not all members of GR acquire knowledge of the gospel message. Drange, therefore, misconstrues what is entailed by rejection of (A3).

Drange raises four questions (p. 359:38-360:13), and claims that those who reject (A3) "owe us answers" (p. 360:16-17) to those questions. In response, given good reasons for believing GC exists, (A3) may be justifiably rejected without having provided answers to the questions. One acceptable response to the four questions is to emphasize that since GC's ways are largely inscrutable (absent divine revelation), we are in no position to suppose that we should know why GC would perform any particular action in any particular case. Another response to the questions is the simple observation that the existence of GC's command to pursue the goal of global evangelization and discipleship entails neither that the goal will be universally achieved, nor that GC even expects the goal to be universally achieved. It can be good to pursue generalized broad-sweeping good ideals, even with the knowledge that the ideal may not be fully achieved in actuality, given the actual existence of entities which preclude the accomplishment of that ideal. Furthermore, the

Biblical data clearly suggest (A3) is false, given passages such as Matthew 7:13-14 and Revelation 20:15. Since GC knows not all persons are members of GA, we appear to have no guarantee that GC knows that the gospel will be accepted worldwide at any time prior to the time of the new Jerusalem (Revelation 21:1-5) or perhaps the time of the Millennial Reign (Revelation 20:1-6). I may not be certain why GC does what GC does, but this entails neither that (A3) is not justifiably rejected, nor that GC's existence is unlikely.

In chapter 3 of part 4 of IPRG, Victor Cosculluela seeks to strengthen Drange's ANB by arguing "for the claim that God does not have conflicting desires" (p. 364:35-36). In response, premise (1) (p. 364:37-39) contains the built-in assumption that all desires have the same properties. This is clearly an erroneous assumption. A distinction may be drawn between an idealized desire and a practical desire. An idealized desire DI is a desire for conditions C, where actual conditions A are such that conditions C are not attainable and, consequently, DI is not possibly satisfied in the real world. A practical desire DP is a desire for conditions C, where actual conditions A do not preclude the possibility that conditions C are attainable and, consequently, DP may possibly be satisfied in the real world. So, God could have an idealized desire that a state of affairs X obtain, while having a practical desire that a state of affairs not-X obtain. Such conflicting desires would manifest no moral defect or knowledge limitation on God's part, but would simply serve to emphasize the distinction between idealized and practical desires.

An idealized desire DI may conflict with a practical desire DP, but this entails neither that DI is better than DP, nor that DP is better than DI. "Desire D is best" is ambiguous, and should be replaced with "Desire D for conditions C is best, given actual conditions A" so as to avoid confusion between idealized desires and practical desires. The confusion may be avoided by simply checking to see whether it is known that conditions A are such that conditions C may possibly be satisfied in the real world. If it is known that conditions A are such that conditions C may possibly be satisfied in the real world, then the desire in question is known to be a practical desire. If it is known that conditions A are such that conditions C are not possibly satisfied in the real world, then it is known that the desire in question is an idealized desire. Given human knowledge limitations, a human person J may possess desire D, where J does not know whether D is an idealized desire or a practical desire. Also, in special circumstances, J may possess an idealized desire which is subsequently discovered to be a practical (and perhaps even a fulfilled practical) desire. In the case of God's desires, given God's possession of immeasurably great knowledge, God presumably knows both that none of God's idealized desires will ever be fulfilled, and also that all of God's practical desires will be fulfilled.

For reasons discussed by Cosculluela (p. 365:1-366:35), God may well have no conflicting desires within any particular category of desires. Thus, God may well have no conflicting idealized desires, and God may well have no conflicting practical desires, but it does not follow that God has no conflict between an idealized and a practical desire. So, if God's idealized desire DI for conditions C (given actual conditions A) conflicts with God's practical desire DP for conditions C (given actual conditions A), this entails that although DI may be God's best possible idealized desire (given conditions A), and although DP may be God's best possible practical desire (given conditions A), conditions C are such that DI is not possibly satisfied in the real world, whereas DP will be satisfied in the real world.

Given my clarification of the distinction between distinct desire categories, it follows that Cosculluela's argument fails to strengthen the ANB, since it fails to establish that God possesses no conflicting desires. Thus, Biblical evidence of God's desire for worldwide acceptance of the gospel message may not be used to argue that (A3) is true, as any such Biblical evidence may be viewed as evidence of God's idealized desire which, given the existence of persons who refuse to accept the gospel, is not actually possibly satisfied in the real world. Nevertheless, God's possession of that good idealized desire manifests God's loving desire for all of humanity, and we who desire to express our love for God may press on towards the goal of accomplishing God's idealized desires (Philippians 3:12-14), even though we know that we have fallen short of God's glorious divine ideal (Romans 3:23).

In chapter 4 of part 4 of IPRG, Theodore M. Drange presents two arguments for the nonexistence of the Evangelical Christian God: The Argument From Confusion (AC) and The Argument From Biblical Defects (ABD).

AC (p. 369:15-374:32) may be challenged in a number of ways. Premise (A2) (p. 370:7-9) is built on the assumption that G-beliefs are necessary for the kind of relationship that the Evangelical Biblical Christian God (GC) desires to have with Christians. In response, Evangelical Biblical Christians need accept this assumption only if a good reason is provided in its support. For example, Evangelical Biblical Christians would consider Biblical support for that assumption to be a good reason for accepting it. Drange does not provide Biblical support for that assumption. Furthermore, there is Biblical evidence that if GC exists, then it is not the case that GC desires that all Christians possess G-beliefs at all times in their earthly lives. For example, although one of the thieves on the cross (Luke 23:40-43) was apparently considered to be rightly related to GC, no good reason exists for assuming that the thief possessed G-beliefs, and the nonexistence of a complete Evangelical Christian Bible at that time entails that the thief did not possess G-beliefs. In addition, Matthew 11:25-27 entails that even little children can positively relate to GC, yet little children doubtfully possess much of what is identified by G-beliefs. Additionally, Biblical passages such as Acts 16:31 or Romans 10:9-13 identify sufficient conditions for receiving salvation, yet there is no reason to suppose these conditions include possession of G-beliefs. Thus, the Evangelical Christian interpretation of Biblical passages does not support the view that possession of all the detailed beliefs represented by G-beliefs is a prerequisite for relating to GC in accordance with GC's will, as premise (A2) claims. The favored Evangelical interpretation is, rather, one in which possibly highly limited initial beliefs and knowledge are developed and expanded through continuous spiritual growth (2 Peter 3:18; Philippians 1:6; Philippians 3:12-14).

Premise (B) of AC (p. 370:10-11) may also be challenged. Most Evangelical Biblical Christians would likely accept that information essential for one's receiving salvation (and, consequently, becoming rightly related to God) could be communicated to human person J even if J does not first acquire all true beliefs about, for example, GC's nature and GC's laws. Indeed, as humans with such limited knowledge, the full nature of GC and GC's laws is likely far beyond our ken. So, it is arguable that possession of all true beliefs represented by G-beliefs is not only unnecessary for J's becoming rightly related to God, but is also not possible, as the full extent of all such true beliefs surely lies far beyond J's ken. One can be saved from his sins, yet not fully possess G-beliefs. It must be emphasized that GC's knowledge is exceedingly greater than that of mere man (see, for example, Isaiah 40:28, Isaiah 55:8-9, Psalm 147:5, and Romans 11:33-34). Clearly, given GC's immeasurably greater knowledge than that of man, we humans are in no position (apart from divine revelation) to determine what action GC might perform in any particular situation, and we are in no position (apart from divine revelation) to determine why GC performs any particular action. Even given that the Biblical data are a divine revelation of GC's nature and laws, it does not follow that any earthly Christian has fully and perfectly identified and integrated every associated true belief into a maximally justified Evangelical Biblical worldview. The life of an Evangelical Christian is a "work in progress", and so, too, is the development of any person's worldview, whether Christian, atheist, or anything else. Thus, since the existence of GC does not entail that any Christian on earth possesses G-beliefs, the nonexistence of any Christian on earth in possession of G-beliefs does not disconfirm the existence of GC. Premise (B) may be rejected.

Even if premise (B) were true, it remains unclear whether GC's "want" would be an idealized desire or a practical desire (see discussion of this distinction earlier this chapter for details). In general, person J can possess an idealized desire that conflicts with J's practical desire. Thus, GC's "want" in premise (B) could be an idealized desire that is overridden by a conflicting practical desire to the contrary, which would render premise (C) unsubstantiated.

Premise (C) of AC (p. 370:12-14) may be rejected for a number of reasons. Even if dubious premises (A) and (B) were true, it would not follow that premise (C) is likely true, since premise (C) presumes specific knowledge of the will of GC, whereas it has not been established that we are in a position to determine the likelihood that GC (if GC exists) would possess any particular desire in any particular situation. Granted, Evangelical Christians presume that proper interpretation of the Biblical data reveals knowledge of factors relevant to GC's will, but no Biblical passage implies that a complete and thorough understanding of all details of GC's decision procedures has been revealed, and passages such as Romans 11:33-34 imply that such understanding is not available to us. Since the Bible does not reveal all the details of GC's decision procedures, Evangelical Biblical Christians (apart from some other special revelation) are incapable of either identifying those detailed procedures or tracing out the results of the proper implementation of those procedures. Consequently, our general lack of understanding of these procedures entails that we are generally unable to determine GC's specific and precisely outlined desires. We may infer from the Biblical data various idealized desires GC likely possesses in specific circumstances, but it is not evident that those data entail that GC can never possess conflicting practical desires to the contrary. Thus, even if GC would possess the idealized desire that Christians be prevented from becoming confused or conflicted about beliefs identified by G-beliefs, GC may possess a conflicting practical desire to the contrary in some unspecified cases X, where X represents the set of all such unspecified cases. Therefore, in any case that is a member of X, GC would not prevent confusion or conflictedness, and premise (C) would be false. Furthermore, Drange is in no position to claim that it is false that every instance of confusion or conflict he cites is a case that is a member of X, and, consequently, conclusion (G) does not follow from (C) and (F). Conclusion (G) may also be rejected for all of the other reasons mentioned above which entail that AC is invalid or unsound.

Drange evidently concedes that G-beliefs need not include true beliefs regarding all conceivable theological propositions (p. 372:10-12). But then, how are we to decide just what beliefs are of fundamental significance such that they are G-beliefs? Drange offers no clear methodology that may be employed to make such a determination, but merely asserts that some unspecified fundamental issues exist which comprise G-beliefs (p. 372:12-15). This position is unacceptable. Drange appears, here, to be pulling back from the claim that persons rightly related to God must possess every true belief identified by G-beliefs (as defined on p. 369:15-370:2), but this now raises the question of precisely what beliefs are G-beliefs. Until and unless we understand what definition Drange has in mind, in light of his concession, it remains unclear what beliefs are identified by G-beliefs, and AC is consequently rendered ambiguous and inconclusive. AC is, thus, quite the antithesis of a "most forceful argument" (p. 372:16-17).

My position is not that appropriately defined G-beliefs do not exist. Rather, my position is that such beliefs are person-relative, being likely determined by a multivariable function, the detailed knowledge of which is likely far beyond our ken as humans with such limited knowledge of factors relevant to a thoroughly detailed understanding of issues considered by GC to be maximally important and beneficial to the uniqueness of each person's life.

Belief in the existence of GC is not disconfirmed by the existence of confusion or conflict amongst Christians regarding the beliefs considered to be G-beliefs. AC has been shown to be unsound. Given good reasons for believing in the existence of GC, Evangelical Biblical Christians may know that GC has morally justified reasons for his permission of the existence of confusion/conflict amongst Christians regarding G-beliefs, even if those Christians do not fully understand the moral basis for GC's actions. Indeed, the Biblical data imply GC's judgments are unsearchable, so it is no surprise that human Christians with such limited understanding of GC's ways should not fully understand why GC acts in some particular way.

Drange wrongly uses the observation of confusion and conflict amongst Christians to infer GC's nonexistence. My response is that AC is unsound, and my explanation of the confusion and conflict is in terms of a form of the Unknown-Purpose Defense (UPD). Specifically, if GC exists, then we have no reason to suppose we are in a position to determine why GC permits existing confusion and conflict amongst Christians. Therefore, the existence of that confusion and conflict in conjunction with our lack of full understanding of why GC permits it (assuming GC exists) does not disconfirm the existence of GC, but is comfortably (though perhaps somewhat mysteriously) compatible with it. Recall the DRP (Divine Revelation Principle) introduced earlier, which states: God desires to maximize truth revealed to those who would choose good actions in response to that revelation, and God desires to minimize truth revealed to those who would choose bad actions in response to that revelation. GC arguably considers DRP to be a significant consideration in GC's overall decision procedures used to determine the best actions GC can perform in any situation. Biblical support for a principle such as DRP includes, for example, Matthew 13:10-17, Matthew 25:29-30, and Luke 8:18. So, since the DRP may play a significant role in the moral justification of GC's permission of Christian conflict and confusion, my defense is not entirely grounded in appeal to unknowns, as the DRP is a known factor. Therefore, God's hiddenness, evidenced by lack of unanimity amongst Evangelical Christians regarding G-beliefs, may be viewed as morally justified for reasons grounded in the DRP. My Unknown-Purpose Defense is, thus, better identified as a Justified Hiddenness Defense, where God's hiddenness is justified for reasons not completely unknown, but for reasons which include consideration of the DRP.

Drange objects that appeal to mystery explains nothing and is unenlightening (p. 373:25-27). In response, as mentioned above, my defense is not purely an appeal to merely logically possibly existing unknown purposes GC may possess, but is grounded in consideration of the DRP which may well play a significant role in GC's overall decision procedures, the complete knowledge of which is generally likely to be far beyond our ken. My defense, therefore, is a helpful explanation in that it sheds light on an important principle, and it emphasizes the consequences of our being in a state in which our knowledge is profoundly inferior to that of GC.

Drange objects that it "would make no sense" (p. 373:36) for GC to both permit the existence of confusion amongst GC's people and emphasize the value of GC's people acquiring knowledge of truth (p. 373:27-37). In response, the fact that this issue would make no sense to Drange does not entail that Drange's argument is correct, as Drange has not established why the existence of GC would entail that this issue would make sense to Drange. If Drange would not respond positively to a greater measure of revealed spiritual truth regarding this issue, then it could be good of GC to not reveal such truth to Drange, given the DRP. Furthermore, given both the DRP and our inability to fully understand GC's ways (assuming GC exists), we are in no position to claim the existence of GC is incompatible with the existence of confusion amongst GC's people. In addition, GC's idealized desire that GC's people acquire knowledge of spiritual truth would be consistent with GC's practical desire that such knowledge exist in conjunction with some confusion amongst GC's people. Also, conflicting beliefs amongst GC's people can help to focus their inquiry and research, and ultimately lead to new discovery of greater revelation, and it is far from clear that this benefit is undesirable. Indeed, one benefit of fellowship and community (Hebrews 10:24-25) is the "sharpening effect" (Proverbs 27:17), and if conflicted beliefs ultimately lead to a sharpened knowledge of greater revelation, then this may be viewed as consistent with GC's desire that GC's people acquire knowledge of truth through the sharpening influence of fellowship and community.

Drange does not understand why GC would command GC's people to pursue the goal of global evangelization, yet permit the existence of people who are never evangelized (p. 373:37-374:1). In response, the existence of GC does not entail that Drange should understand this issue.

Also, idealized divine desires may conflict with practical divine desires, and such conflict simply serves to emphasize the distinction between these distinct desire categories, and such conflict in no way renders improbable the existence of GC. So, GC may possess the idealized desire that GC's people pursue the goal of global evangelization, and GC may also possess the practical desire that only some subset of the global population be evangelized by GC's people. GC's purposes may not be fully understood by us mere humans with such finite knowledge of factors relevant to GC's decision procedures, but we may nevertheless identify significant principles such as the DRP which may play a key role in GC's overall decision-making process.

Drange also does not understand why GC would inspire the Biblical Scriptures for the purpose of instructing people, while permitting the existence of confused followers of GC (p. 374:1-17). To be sure, if GC's existence entails that GC's inspiration of the Biblical Scriptures is such that GC's only purpose in inspiring them was to ensure that all of GC's people would always be divinely enabled to have only and always mutually consistent beliefs and knowledge of elements of G-beliefs, then the existence of conflictedness in the beliefs and knowledge of followers of GC might be taken as evidence of the nonexistence of GC. However, Drange has not even come close to establishing such a conclusion, nor has he even established that we have good reason to suppose we are in a position to know all of GC's purposes in inspiring the Scriptures, assuming GC exists. Furthermore, my DRP is derived from the Biblical data, and is consistent with GC's permission of the existence of confusion regarding G-beliefs amongst fellow followers of GC. Therefore, in light of the considerations above, AC is no difficulty at all for those who follow GC.

Drange presents the Argument from Biblical Defects (ABD) (p. 374:33-378:2) and concludes that it constitutes "good objective evidence for the nonexistence" of GC (p. 377:38-39). In response, premise (A) (p. 374:33-34) stands unsupported, and may be rejected by followers of GC for a number of reasons. For example, GC's people believe that the Biblical books such as Jeremiah, Isaiah, Ezekiel, etc., contain a written record of God's revelation, yet GC's people have no good reason to suppose that every writing containing revelation through these prophets is included in the Biblical texts. Since lost writings not included in the Bible may have contained GC's written revelation at some time in the past, premise (A) may be false. Evangelical Biblical Christians need not be committed to acceptance of (A). Perhaps Ezekiel wrote a revelation from GC that was divinely designed for his friend, and perhaps that written revelation was permanently lost in some fire or earthquake three years after his friend read the revelation....who are we to say? More generally, we have no reason to suppose all written records of GC's revelation are in the Bible, since some records may have been lost.

The early church accepted the gift of prophecy as a spiritual gift through which GC brought revelation (e.g., Acts 11:27-30). Some of the prophets from Jerusalem (Acts 11:27) may have been instruments through whom GC brought revelation, and some of that revelation may well have been recorded in writings not included in the Bible, contradicting premise (A). Once again, we have evidence which Evangelicals may view as disconfirming premise (A). Given the lack of support for premise (A), we may dismiss the ABD at once.

Premise (B) (p. 374:35-375:2) is a speculative guess as to what properties GC would cause the Bible to possess. No good evidence is provided in support of (B). Furthermore, given our lack of knowledge of GC's divine decision procedures (assuming GC exists), we are in no position to suppose we know what properties GC might cause the Bible to possess. In addition, Jesus intentionally veiled spiritual truth from some people (Matthew 13:10-17), and this veiling, as an instance of the DRP, exposes the difficulty in determining the degree and nature of the clarity GC might cause the Bible to manifest. Also, since Evangelicals may understand that acquisition of spiritual truth requires an appropriate relationship to GC's Spirit (1 Corinthians 2:14), GC may be viewed by Evangelicals as having inspired the Bible in such a way as to facilitate their acquisition of spiritual truth, whereas those without the Spirit may be thoroughly confused by their inability to understand what is spiritually discerned by means of the Spirit's divine enablement. Thus, GC could so providentially arrange all human experiences, relationships, beliefs, knowledge, desires, thoughts, etc., of human history such that all those appropriately related to GC's Spirit may apprehend precisely the spiritual truth GC desires to be revealed so as to be consistent with the DRP, while all those throughout history who are predisposed to inappropriately respond to spiritual truth remain in a state of spiritual blindness. Those who love GC could find spiritual truth in the Bible, while those who hate GC could sufficiently suppress the voice of truth[1] such that their interpretation of the Bible does not lead to acquisition of greater spiritual revelation. If GC has inspired the Bible in this way, then the widespread Evangelical understanding of the value of the Bible as a legitimate source of divine revelation may be viewed as consistent with the rejection of

Biblical divine revelation by those who would not benefit from knowledge of that revelation. That is, the Biblical revelation may be sufficient to facilitate Spirit-enabled personally relevant revelation to those who would benefit from it, yet sufficiently ambiguous to confuse those who would not benefit from it. If GC exists, then we are in no position to say GC has not so inspired the Bible. Consequently, one possible explanation of Drange's evident confusion on matters pertinent to Biblical divine revelation may be that GC prevents Drange from achieving greater clarity on such matters since he would not benefit from such revelation. More importantly, given the DRP, Drange has not established that he is in a position to determine that a GC-inspired Bible would appear "perfectly clear and authoritative" and lack "appearance of merely human authorship" (premise (B)) to those who are inclined to reject an appropriate response to such revelation.

Premises (A) and (B) may be rejected for reasons discussed above. Also, premise (B) does not follow from premise (A), despite Drange's "thus" connective in premise (B). Therefore, premise (E) (p. 375:18-19) may be rejected, as it hinges on the truth of (B).

Premise (C) (p. 375:3-15) consists of a brief summary of some key points typically argued by those who reject the belief that the Bible is GC-inspired. Drange is right that "Biblical criticism is an enormous topic" (p. 379:3), and he cites some critical sources in footnotes, but he does not cite sources which favor a conservative Evangelical Christian Biblical interpretation. Drange can cite critical sources, and I could cite sources critical of the views in his sources, but "proof by citation" is not exactly compelling. A more thorough examination of these issues is needed.

As an example of the questionable quality of the scholarship referenced by Drange, consider his reference (p. 379:4-7) to the source by C. Dennis McKinsey entitled "The Encyclopedia of Biblical Errancy" (henceforth referenced as EBE).[2] In particular, consider McKinsey's analysis of the Biblical Day (EBE, pp. 226-229). Observe that McKinsey cites four Christian sources, but all of them are young-earth creationists. McKinsey failed to interact with old-earth creationist literature such as Hugh Ross, "Creation and Time"[3] or Don Stoner, "A New Look at an Old Earth: What the Creation Institutes Are Not Telling You About Genesis."[4] Both of these books were published prior to EBE's publishing date and should have been subjected to serious analysis in EBE. Needless to say, McKinsey's analysis is woefully incomplete and, thus, ought to be rejected. Surprisingly, Drange considers McKinsey's work to be "excellent".[5] Indeed, EBE is excellent….as an example of poor quality scholarship.

If one takes the position that McKinsey's Biblical Day article may actually have been written as early as 1983 (EBE, p. 9:1-2), then we may conclude that McKinsey's Biblical Day article is of value to historians, but is not relevant to the contemporary debate. More generally, we may consider McKinsey's work to be of historical interest, yet not important for settling issues relevant to the contemporary debate regarding Biblical inerrancy, since all of McKinsey's work is evidently based on articles he wrote no later than 1993 (EBE, p. 9:1-2), and since no reference dated later than 1993 appears in the bibliography (EBE, p. 505:1-2). For example, McKinsey's Biblical Day analysis is especially obsolete, given works such as David G. Hagopian, ed., "The Genesis Debate: Three Views on the Days of Creation,"[6] or Hugh Ross, "Matter of Days: Resolving A Creation Controversy,"[7] or David Snoke, "A Biblical Case for an Old Earth."[8]

Having cast a shadow of doubt on the quality of Drange's references, we now find ourselves wondering whether any of the alleged "facts about the Bible" (p. 375:3) are established by his references, or whether any of those alleged "facts" are even facts at all. Given Drange's use of poor sources, it would be prudent to restrict our analysis to the content of Drange's arguments themselves, rather than blindly accept his "proof by citation" (p. 375:24-25). Drange claims that the "facts" in premise (C) are unexpected if GC exists (p. 375:22-24), but explains neither why they would be unexpected, nor how he knows he is in a position to know what properties a GC-inspired Bible would likely possess. Drange provides no direct support of premises (C1), (C2), or (C3), but evidently assumes that his cited references establish them. Also, Drange claims he is *certain* that the original Biblical manuscripts are lost (p. 375:25-27), but certainty about such matters seems unattainable given our inability to disprove the claim that someone somewhere in an unknown location secretly possesses an original manuscript. Many ancient manuscripts exist which contain portions of what comprises the Bible, but the existence of interpolations (premise (C4)) and variant readings (premise (C5)) is not, in itself, obviously inconsistent with the hypothesis that the Bible is GC-inspired. Premise (C6) remains unsupported as well, as Drange merely asserts "the biblical canon is arbitrary" (p. 375:27-29). There may not exist a universally accepted procedure for settling disputes (premise (C7)), but the existence of a GC-inspired Bible does not entail that we should know the details of such a possibly existing procedure.

Drange then goes on to describe in some detail (and with unjustified confidence) what he thinks GC would do, if GC were to exist (p. 375:35-376:7). However, Drange does not provide justification for his beliefs, but merely asserts them. Given the DRP, and given the fact that our knowledge of the details of GC's decision procedures (assuming GC exists) is very limited, we humans are evidently in no position to claim knowledge of what particular actions GC is likely to perform, especially regarding what properties GC would likely cause the Bible to possess. Therefore, Drange has not established that "the facts in question can't be easily explained" on the hypothesis that GC exists (p. 376:7-10).

Drange claims that an errant Bible would disconfirm the existence of GC (p. 376:14-16). In response, Drange has assumed GC would not permit inerrant GC-inspired autographa (original manuscripts) to be subsequently corrupted for reasons only GC may fully understand but which may be related to the DRP. GC could arrange the formation of the human state of Biblical understanding such that GC's Spirit could facilitate divine revelation through the Bible to those who would appropriately respond, while those inclined to inappropriately respond could be abandoned by GC's Spirit to remain in the darkness of their own confused misunderstanding and misinterpretation of the Bible. GC could cause the Bible to be sufficiently clear so as to be a means by which divine revelation may be brought to those who have ears to hear, while GC could cause Bible-based claims to appear sufficiently unjustified so as to preclude divine revelation to those without ears to hear. GC could providentially arrange the development of each person's epistemic state such that the Bible is the means by which GC brings precisely the influence GC desires to exert. This position is consistent with the DRP and passages such as Matthew 13:10-17. Thus, an errant Bible is consistent with the existence of GC and is not evidence against the existence of GC (p. 376:14-16) as Niclas Berggren erroneously argues (p. 379:11-12). (Incidentally, I personally accept the Chicago Statement on Biblical Inerrancy,[9] and article X of that statement explains the distinction between the autographa and our presently available reconstructed approximation to them.)

Drange's citation of the Berggren article is misleading in that Berggren claims "it must necessarily hold that god has provided error-free translations" and "one must explain why god did not want or could see to it that the translations are also error-free" and "any such attempt to an explanation is doomed to fail while retaining the Christian concept of god."[10] The Chicago Statement on Biblical Inerrancy shows that

Berggren (and also Drange?) misconstrues a standard Evangelical conception of Biblical inerrancy. Evangelicals need not insist that all Bible translations are error-free. My explanation in the preceding paragraph meets Berggren's challenge to identify a reason why GC might permit an errant Bible and errant Bible translations, and this reason has not been shown to be inconsistent with the nature of GC. Once again, we find that Drange has cited a reference of questionable quality.

Drange attempts to establish that the Bible is self-contradictory in its doctrine of salvation (p. 376:18-29). In response, Drange evidently seeks to derive contradictions using an English language translation of the Bible, whereas a standard Evangelical conception of inerrancy applies to the autographa, not translations of reconstructed approximations to the autographa. Nevertheless, if Drange succeeds in establishing a genuine contradiction in an English Bible translation regarding a doctrine as fundamental as salvation, then Drange would indeed have disconfirmed a standard Evangelical inerrancy model, assuming a reputable translation had been used to establish the contradiction. However, Drange has not succeeded in establishing the existence of such a contradiction. For example, Luke 13:3 may be interpreted as implying that a necessary condition of the salvation of the people to whom Jesus was speaking is their repentance. John 3:16 may be interpreted as implying that belief in Jesus is a sufficient condition of one's salvation. Even if Luke 13:3 is generalized to be interpreted as implying that a necessary condition of any person's salvation (not merely the people to whom Jesus was speaking) is repentance, it does not follow that Luke 13:3 contradicts John 3:16, since, in general, a necessary condition of some event E is not necessarily identical to a sufficient condition of E. Furthermore, if one's belief in Jesus entails that one has repented, then no contradiction exists. Also, if one's repentance entails that one believes in Jesus, then no contradiction exists. Drange has not established that belief in Jesus does not entail that one has repented, and Drange has not established that repentance does not entail that one believes in Jesus. More importantly, Drange has not shown that it is incorrect to interpret Luke 13:3 as a necessary condition of salvation and John 3:16 as a sufficient condition of salvation. Therefore, Drange has failed to establish the existence of a contradiction between Luke 13:3 and John 3:16.

Drange also claims Matthew 25:31-46 is evidence that one's righteous (i.e., charitable) acts are sufficient for one's salvation, implying that repentance is not necessary for salvation, which in turn contradicts Luke 13:3 (p. 376:25-27). In response, given conditions A, B, and X, if A is a sufficient condition of X, it does not follow that B is not a necessary condition of X, since A may entail B, where B is a necessary condition of X. If A represents righteous acts, B represents repentance, and X represents salvation, then we see that although Matthew 25:31-46 may be interpreted such that A is a sufficient condition of X, this does not entail that B is not a necessary condition of X, since A may entail B, where B is a necessary condition of X. Furthermore, in none of the Biblical references Drange cites is it stated that B is not a necessary condition of X. Thus, A may be interpreted as a sufficient condition of X, where A entails B, and where B (possibly conjoined with other conditions) may be interpreted as the set of jointly necessary and sufficient conditions of X. Or, if a person J is a member of the set of all who have repented if and only if J is a member of the set of righteous people mentioned in Matthew 25:31-46, then we may interpret either A or B as a necessary and sufficient condition of X. In the context of the Chicago Statement on Biblical Inerrancy, repentance may be viewed as a necessary and sufficient condition of salvation, where other conditions such as those in other Biblical references cited by Drange (see John 5:29 and p. 379:13-18) may be viewed as either merely sufficient conditions of salvation or both necessary and sufficient conditions of salvation. In either case, no contradiction is derived, since Drange's fundamental assumption that "no mention of repentance" (p. 376:24-25) implies "it is not necessary" (p. 376:28-29) remains unjustified. To see this, consider that since Matthew 25:31-46 implies righteous people are saved, Hebrews 11:4 implies righteousness is attained by faith, James 2:17 implies living faith is necessarily accompanied by righteous acts, and Acts 26:20 implies that repentance is proved by righteous acts, it follows that the righteous people of Matthew 25:31-46 may be viewed as having repented, contradicting Drange's supposition that nothing in that passage implies repentance (p. 376:26-27). In other words, Evangelicals presuppose the whole of Scripture is a coherent divine revelation, and Drange's critique fails to account for this method of interpretation.

Drange's approach to Bible-contradiction arguments is unlikely to persuade many Evangelical Christians, if any at all, since those arguments are not grounded in the set of presuppositions Evangelicals may bring to their interpretation of the Bible. Since a standard set of presuppositions Evangelicals bring to their interpretation of the Bible entails that no Bible contradiction actually exists (as explicated in, for example, the Chicago Statement), Evangelicals may reject Bible-contradiction arguments on the grounds that they are inconsistent with the presuppositions Evangelicals bring to their interpretation of the Bible. Thus, a more potentially fruitful line of attack for Drange would be to challenge the rational basis for the Evangelical presuppositions which entail Bible contradictions don't exist, rather than attempt to argue that non-Evangelical presuppositions may be used to establish the existence of Bible contradictions.

Drange is evidently dissatisfied with the degree of clarity found in the Bible (p. 376:30-40). In response, if the Bible is GC-inspired, then we have no good reason to suppose that the degree of clarity in the Bible should be any different from what we find in the Bible. Yes, some Biblical truth may not be expressed in the most conceivably simple way, but this is not evidence against the claim that the Bible is GC-inspired. Rather, this is consistent with the DRP as exemplified in, for example, Matthew 13:10-17. Furthermore, Drange objects that GC "could have made the message perfectly clear to the readers, but failed to do so" (p. 377:14-15), yet Drange has not established why we should suppose the Bible is not perfectly consistent with GC's purposes (assuming GC exists), given the DRP, and given that Drange's degree of understanding of GC's ways is not known to be sufficient to determine whether GC has guided the formation process of the Bible in the best possible way. In addition, Drange's analogy (p. 376:41-377:15) fails to account for the fact that it is possible that some children with exceedingly clear match knowledge would burn down many houses, whereas such children with limited or confused understanding of match knowledge might burn down only one house, in which case a veiled communication of truth regarding match knowledge to such children could ultimately result in the lesser of two evil outcomes. In other words, if GC clearly reveals greater quantities of divine revelation to those inclined to act such that they are ultimately justly condemned to hell regardless of whether they ever perceive such revelation, then such revelation to such people serves the purpose of increasing their punishment in hell (assuming one's degree of punishment in hell is proportional to the quantity of revealed truth one has suppressed or rejected). Thus, GC's limitation of the degree to which hell-bound people acquire knowledge of divine revelation may be viewed as an act of love in which GC is seeking to minimize the degree to which such people suffer in their self-determined position in hell.

Drange claims GC's great desire for humanity's salvation is inconsistent with the degree to which GC is hidden in the sense that the requirements for salvation are not clearer (p. 377:16-37). In response, no inconsistency has been established. In fact, Jesus intentionally veiled truth (Matthew

13:10-17), presumably for reasons largely related to the DRP. Drange has not determined that the degree of clarity regarding the Biblical doctrine of salvation is not precisely in accordance with GC's good purposes, assuming GC exists, and Drange has not even established that he is in a position to make such a determination. Thus, Drange has scarcely begun to bridge the gap between his alleged inconsistency and an actual demonstration of that inconsistency. We may not fully understand why GC acts the way GC acts (assuming GC exists), but this hardly constitutes evidence against the existence of GC, since we are not in a position to precisely identify the decision procedures GC uses, and since we are not in a position to precisely determine how those procedures would be implemented in any particular case.

In conclusion, my critique presents good objective evidence for Drange's need to either substantially reformulate the ABD to account for my objections, or better yet, abandon it altogether. Also, contra Drange (p. 377:39-378:1), it is not the case that followers of GC must identify a moral justification of GC's ways prior to their identification of the rational basis for their belief in the existence of GC. I know GC acts, but not always why.

In chapters 5 and 6 of part 4 of IPRG, excerpts from a debate between Walter Sinnott-Armstrong and William Lane Craig are presented.[11] Craig and Sinnott-Armstrong debate a number of issues, but the excerpts focus on Sinnott-Armstrong's "Argument from Ignorance" (p. 386:3-6). In response, the Argument from Ignorance is valid, but unsound. That is, the truth of the premises would imply the conclusion of the argument, yet the falsity of the premises renders the argument inconclusive. Premise 1 (p. 386:3-4) carries with it the unstated and unjustified assumption that a principle such as the DRP does not entail that some people would not have strong evidence for the existence of God. Recall that the DRP states: God desires to maximize truth revealed to those who would choose good actions in response to that revelation, and God desires to minimize truth revealed to those who would choose bad actions in response to that revelation. Sinnott-Armstrong has not even established that he is in a position to determine what actions God would likely perform in any particular situation. Given that Sinnott-Armstrong's knowledge is surely profoundly inferior to an all-knowing God (p. 384:6), we evidently have no good reason at all to suppose he knows much at all regarding either God's decision procedures or the details of how those procedures would be implemented in any particular case. Thus, his premise 1 is not established.

Sinnott-Armstrong assumes that God has not revealed precisely the quantity of quality of evidence for God's existence to each person throughout human history in accordance with God's morally justified purposes (p. 383:6-7). However, Sinnott-Armstrong has not established that he is in a position to know how God would reveal evidence of His existence, so his claim remains unjustified. Furthermore, better evidence of God's existence could be harmful for reasons not fully understood, but which relate to the DRP (p. 383:8-9). Sinnott-Armstrong wonders why God would hide (p. 383:9, 383:14-15), but evidently fails to appreciate the fact that God's hiddenness may be due to reasons largely related to the DRP.

Sinnott-Armstrong claims "evidence does not take away any valuable kind of freedom" (p. 383:17). In response, revelation of truth can preclude one's ability to believe *falsely* (not necessarily *irrationally*, as Sinnott-Armstrong claims (p. 383:20-21), since some false beliefs may be rational) and Sinnott-Armstrong has not shown that freedom to believe falsely never has positive value. In fact, it could be good of God to not remove a person's freedom to have a false belief in atheism, if that person is inclined to inappropriately respond to that removal of freedom.

Sinnott-Armstrong speculatively assumes various consequences of a greater revelation of God (p. 383:22-28), but does not explain how he knows his assumptions are justified. "Proof by assumption" is hardly compelling, and is not an acceptable means by which the rational basis for a belief may be established. Thus, it is far from clear that God has "so little to lose and so much to gain" (p. 383:29-30) such that God's self-revelation would be greater (if God exists), given that the DRP may play a significant role in God's decision procedures, and given that we do not know that we are in a position to determine how God would likely implement those procedures. Since it is evident that God's existence does not entail that we should know a specific and detailed answer to Sinnott-Armstrong's question (p. 383:35-37), it does not follow that God's existence entails that "we would have more and better evidence than we do" (p. 383:38-39). Sinnott-Armstrong is similarly unjustified in his claim that God's existence entails that "He would make it easier for us to know Him" (p. 386:9-10).

Also, when Jesus told his followers not to hide their lamps under a bowl (Matthew 5:15-16), this command may be interpreted such that it applies to those who follow Jesus, not to Jesus (God) Himself, since Jesus (God) sometimes intentionally veiled truth (Matthew 13:10-17) for reasons presumably related to the DRP. God need not follow advice Jesus gave for His followers (p. 386:12-13).

Thus, it is evident that Sinnott-Armstrong persists in his speculation regarding how he has determined that God would act (p. 386:14-23; 387:5-8), and he fails to explain why we should believe he is in a position to make such a determination. Sure, the benefits Sinnott-Armstrong lists are conceivably possible reasons for which God might reveal stronger evidence of His existence (assuming God exists), but establishing the existence of a logically possible state of affairs in no way entails that state of affairs is likely, and he offers no justification for his assumption that God's existence would entail that we would possess better evidence of God's existence. We may, therefore, reject premise 1 (p. 386:3-4).

Sinnott-Armstrong's premise 2 (p. 386:5) succeeds if we have no good argument for God's existence. My AFTLOP and my fine-tuning arguments provide good reason to believe in the existence of a super-powerful, super-knowledgeable, effective, personal Being. Although these characteristics do not fully satisfy Sinnott-Armstrong's definition of "God" (p. 384:1-9), they are sufficient to refute any semblance of atheism.

It is possible that God's existence is necessary, in which case, in the final analysis, the claim that God exists is ultimately irrefutable. Epistemic standards which permit irrefutable beliefs are not weak (p. 381:20-23), but must permit such beliefs only if there exists a rational basis for doing so. For example, if I have a religious experience in which God enables me to know that it is God who is enabling me to know that God necessarily exists as an all-good and all-powerful being, then my irrefutable belief in God has a rational basis and, thus, is justified, even if I have no other reason to believe the experience is accurate rather than an illusion (p. 381:38-41), and even if others think there is a better explanation of my experience (p. 381:41-382:1), and even if others think my experience is distorted by emotions (p. 382:1-4), and even if some people complain that God only gives such experiences to those who seek or believe in Him (p. 382:4-6), and even if others deny the divinely-facilitated self-evident content of the miraculous revelation (p. 382:6-7; 382:15-16).

Sinnott-Armstrong evidently considers justified natural explanations of allegedly miraculous events to be grounds for rejecting the claim that the events are miraculous (p. 382:13-15). In response, since "natural explanations" are causal explanations in terms of personal action, any "natural explanations" not caused by humans may be viewed as having a nonhuman personal cause, and this critical observation of the nature of causation plays a key role in my AFTLOP (see chapter 1). Thus, "natural explanations" of allegedly miraculous events can form the raw data used to establish the existence of a being whose existence refutes atheism.

Sinnott-Armstrong claims that even if arguments grounded in recent scholarship establish that God's existence is probable, "earlier people did not have any strong evidence for the existence of God" (p. 387:14-17). Wow! Sinnott-Armstrong must be nearly omniscient! How else could he possibly know that no human in the past ever had strong evidence for the existence of God? Clearly, Sinnott-Armstrong is in no position to assert such a broad generalization regarding the epistemic state of multiplied millions of persons of centuries past. Nevertheless, Sinnott-Armstrong goes on to further assert that premise (1) is also true for these millions of persons (p. 387:17-19), yet he fails to identify his unstated and unjustified assertion that no principle such as the DRP plays a significant role in God's largely unfathomable decision procedures such that the quality and quantity of evidence of God's existence throughout human history is precisely in accordance with God's good purposes.

As an example of the weakness of Sinnott-Armstrong's attempt to shore up support for his claim that better evidence of God's existence would be beneficial, consider his hypothetical consideration of a contract killer (p. 388:1-9). He claims "this killer's potential victims would be better off it this killer believed in God" (p. 388:5-7), since the killer would not kill the set K of people, if the killer believed in God. In response, why suppose that a longer life span of the members of K is better for any of those members? Longer life spans are not necessarily better. Why suppose that the positive value of the killer's abstinence from killing the members of K would not be outweighed by the negative value of unknown possibilities? Why assume that the entire course of human history would be better if the members of K had longer life spans due to the killer's coming to believe in God's existence? Furthermore, the killer's belief in God would be of potentially significant negative value, since the killer's acquisition of justified belief in the existence of God in conjunction with the killer's refusal to love God could result in the killer's suffering a greater punishment in hell due to the killer's having suppressed and rejected a greater quantity of revelation regarding God. Additionally, we are considering different possible worlds, and since we are in no position to judge the unfathomably complex consequences of various life spans on the subsequent value of the course of human history in these different possible worlds, we are clearly unable to justify the conclusion that God should reveal Himself more clearly to the killer.

In other words, Sinnott-Armstrong's claims about how God and other people would/could/should act in some hypothetical scenario are wildly speculative and wholly unjustified. Sure, Sinnott-Armstrong evinces some principles which may play a role in God's overall decision procedures, but we have reason to suppose neither that all relevant principles have been identified, nor that all such principles are even identifiable by us humans with such limited available information. Thus, in general, Sinnott-Armstrong's musings are little different from pure fantasizing, when he concludes with naïve confidence that better evidence of God's existence would entail the existence of "more people who believe in God and love God" (p. 388:24-25), or when he concludes, in effect, that God's ways are not largely inscrutable (p. 389:1-4).

In chapter 7 of part 4 of IPRG, J.L. Schellenberg presents an atheistic argument that is based on "the reasonableness of nonbelief" (p. 390:1-401:21). In response, knowledge of premise (2) (p. 401:13) presumes we are in a position to determine that our knowledge of how God would likely act is sufficient to show that the existence of reasonable nonbelief is improbable, if God exists. Since it is not established that we are likely to be in a position to determine either God's decision procedures or the detailed results of the implementation of those procedures, we do not know that we are in a position to determine that our knowledge of how God would likely act is sufficient to show that the existence of reasonable nonblief is improbable, if God exists. Therefore, premise (2) is unsubstantiated and Schellenberg's argument is unsound.

Another way of explaining my response to Schellenberg is by considering that the set G of possibly existing perfectly loving gods may be divided into two subsets Gi and Gs, where Gi is the subset of G that consists of all possibly existing perfectly loving gods whose ways are inscrutable, where Gs is the subset of G that consists of all possibly existing perfectly loving gods whose ways are not inscrutable, and where a perfectly loving god is inscrutable if and only if no earthly human knows any details of the ways of the god other than that the god's actions are always perfectly loving and can not entail a logically impossible state of affairs. Now, premise (2) (p. 401:13) is a knowledge claim. In particular, it consists of the claim that we know that no possibly existing perfectly loving god would permit condition N if that god actually exists, where N represents the condition that reasonable nonbelief occurs. In other words, it is the claim that we know that no member of G would permit N, which entails that we know that no member of Gi would permit N, which consequently implies that we know that the existence of condition N would entail that set Gi is empty. However, it is clearly evident that no human person J possesses knowledge that the set Gi is empty, where such knowledge is acquired by means of J's knowledge of the ways of the members of Gi, since such knowledge would entail J's knowledge of particular details of the ways of each member of Gi, and since the definition of "perfectly loving inscrutable God" entails that no human can know such details. Therefore, the conclusion of Schellenberg's argument in premise (5) (p. 401:19) may be interpreted as the claim that the set Gs is empty. Even if it is granted that Gs is empty (an unjustified concession, I would argue), it does not necessarily follow that Gi is also empty. Schellenberg's argument evidently gives no reason to suppose Gi is empty, and we may thus conclude that the argument does not confirm atheism. Since an inscrutable perfectly loving God could permit condition N for reasons we do not know, our knowledge of condition N would not entail the nonexistence of an inscrutable perfectly loving God.

In other words, Schellenberg has, at most, shown that if the existence of a perfectly loving god entails that Schellenberg would know that no such god would permit N, then the existence of N entails the nonexistence of a perfectly loving god. However, Schellenberg fails to establish that the existence of a perfectly loving god entails that Schellenberg would know that no such god would permit N, as revealed by the fact that the existence of an *inscrutable* perfectly loving god is possible. We may know how knowable gods might act, but we do not know how unknowable gods might act.

The objection may be raised that the possible existence of an unknowable god, though sufficient to refute Schellenberg's atheistic argument, is nonetheless of rather limited practical value to theists. In response, although theists may use the possible existence of an unknowable inscrutable god to refute an atheistic argument such as Schellenberg's, theists may further argue that an otherwise unknowable god is, in fact, knowable after all, given the existence of sound theistic arguments presented by natural theologians, or given the existence of justified divine revelation claims. Although a thorough examination of such claims (e.g., Biblical divine revelation arguments) lies beyond the scope of the present analysis, it is sufficient to remark simply that my AFTLOP and fine-tuning arguments provide greater revelation of the ways of God, and these arguments further disconfirm Schellenberg's atheism.

Having provided a broad response to Schellenberg's general approach, I will now proceed to consider a few details of his analysis. Schellenberg's confident assertions about the ways of God are very much unjustified, given the possible existence of an inscrutable perfectly loving God. Thus, he has no good reason to so confidently assert that he knows how such a being would act (p. 390:5-6; 390:12-15). Likewise, his claim regarding God's ways (p. 391:16-18) presumes, without justification, that God would not ever delay (for reasons unknown to us) justified theistic belief until later in the lives of some human beings who are capable of personal relationship with God even prior to the time at which they actually acquire justified theistic belief. After all, if God can delay a man's restoration of sight until a time when God's work might be better displayed (John 9:1-3), then who are we to say that God would not delay Schellenberg's sight of God until some future time when God's work might be better displayed? Perhaps some people who believe their atheism is grounded in their reasonable nonbelief will subsequently convert to acceptance of theism after reading this book, and God's work might thus better be displayed for reasons we may not presently understand.

Now it should be quite clear that we may reject both P1 (p. 392:25-28) and P2 (p. 393:28-30), since they do not account for the possibility that God may have good reasons unknown to us for which He would delay (until a time later than t) S's attaining of a position to relate personally to God so that God's work might be better displayed. Again, Schellenberg presumes, without justification, that God would not hide S's sight of God until some time later than t for good reasons unknown to us (p. 393:5-9; 394:28-30).

Schellenberg considers that God would not provide exclusively inadequate evidence of God's existence to S, since S might inculpably reject belief in God's existence upon S's acquisition of the knowledge that the evidence is inadequate (p. 394:28-30). In response, it is possible that God might have good reasons unknown to us for permitting S's subsequent rejection of theistic belief. Also, it is possible that God might have good reasons unknown to us for providing more adequate evidence to S upon S's acquisition of the knowledge that the inadequate evidence was inadequate. Furthermore, it remains unclear precisely what is meant by "adequate evidence", as all our evidence may be construed as somewhat inadequate (1 Corinthians 13:12) even though sufficient for theistic belief (Romans 1:20). In addition, the degree of adequacy of evidence is person-relative, being a function of variables including those measuring one's capacity to evaluate evidence given the uniqueness of one's epistemic state. Thus, evidence adequate to justify person J's theistic belief might be inadequate to justify person K's theistic belief. Also, the evidence needed to adequately justify J's theistic belief might change as J's epistemic state evolves. It is not deceitful of God (p. 394:37-395:1) to use evidence E to justify J's theistic belief, even if J subsequently comes to perceive E as an inadequate justification of theistic belief, since God may provide more adequate evidence to J as J's analysis capacity evolves. Since we can only learn so much at one time (John 16:12), it is natural to expect our body of evidence required for justifying theistic belief to evolve as our relationship with God develops (2 Peter 3:18). So, if God causes J to know that J's theistic belief is justified no longer on the basis of evidence E1, but on the basis of evidence E2, it does not necessarily follow that J was "living out a lie" (p.

395:1-5), since J's prior justified theistic belief grounded in E1 may simply be viewed as having evolved to a new state in which E2 is now required for J's continuing in the condition of possessing justified theistic belief. Our limited knowledge should not be viewed as "living out a lie", but should be viewed as seeing darkly through a glass (1 Corinthians 13:12). Furthermore, the manner in which God facilitates the evolution of our rational basis for theistic belief may better prepare us to help others in their growth in theistic knowledge, and God may have good reasons unknown to us for permitting that growth to evolve such that propositions understood to be highly improbable are subsequently understood to be highly probable.

Schellenberg supposes (p. 394:38-40) that it is possible that a person J at time T1 could perceive that the probability P that some evidence E justifies theistic belief is sufficiently high to justify J's theistic belief at T1, whereas J at time T2 could perceive that P actually has a much lower value that does not justify J's theistic belief at T2 (T2 is some time later than T1). Schellenberg further assumes that a perfectly good God would not have permitted J at T1 to possess those inadequate grounds for theistic belief, even though J erroneously perceived at T1 that those grounds were adequate. In response, it is possible that a perfectly good God could have good reasons unknown to us for guiding us along a path that ultimately leads into all truth (John 16:13), even though that path might consist of periods during which we have some false beliefs. In fact, since it is possible that attainment of a noetic structure which consists of perfectly perceived truth might never be achieved apart from the beatific vision in the afterlife (1 Corinthians 13:12), our present possession of an imperfect noetic structure with at least one false belief may well be practically unavoidable, especially given the seemingly endless degree to which one's knowledge and understanding can expand and improve to ever better articulate one's worldview.

In conclusion, Schellenberg's argument for atheism fails, as it presumes knowledge of the ways of every possibly existing perfectly loving God, yet it fails to account for the fact that some possibly existing perfectly loving Gods are inscrutable. Since, by definition, we know very little at all about how an inscrutable God would act, it follows that we don't know that an inscrutable perfectly loving God would prevent the existence of inculpable reasonable nonbelief in persons capable of a relationship with God.

In chapter 8 of part 4 of IPRG (p. 405:1-411:13), J.L. Schellenberg responds to some objections Daniel Howard-Snyder has raised to Schellenberg's atheistic argument from reasonable nonbelief. Howard-Snyder restructured the argument (p. 406:6-15) to include the requirement that support for premise (3) (p. 406:13-14) be provided. Schellenberg responds that he need not reformulate the argument as Howard-Snyder suggests (p. 406:37-38), and he claims that his support for premise (1) (i.e., support for premise (1') without the italicized "unless" clause (p. 406:6-10)) is, incidentally, itself support for premise (3), even though such direct support need not be provided. In short, if premise (1) is true, then premise (3) is true; premise (1) is true (so Schellenberg argues); therefore, premise (3) is true (p. 408:22-24). More importantly, the preceding consideration is very much beside the point, if Schellenberg is right that Howard-Snyder's reformulation is unnecessary (p. 406:34-37).

In response, Schellenberg can support (1) only by presuming the nonexistence of an inscrutable perfectly loving God who permits the existence of inculpable reasonable nonbelief in some persons capable of a relationship with God for reasons unknown to Schellenberg. As explained in my discussion of chapter 7 of part 4 of IPRG, Schellenberg draws conclusions about the nature of the ways of every possibly existing scrutable perfectly loving God, but such conclusions are not applicable to the ways of every possibly existing inscrutable perfectly loving God since, by definition, we humans do not possess knowledge of the ways of a possibly existing *inscrutable* God. Furthermore, my AFTLOP and fine-tuning arguments provide support for the existence of a God whose ways are not entirely unknown, as these arguments reveal some details of God's ways, disconfirming Schellenberg's atheistic conclusion. In addition, the existence of justified divine revelation claims would disconfirm Schellenberg's atheistic conclusion, but an analysis of such claims lies beyond the scope of the present analysis.

The Evangelical Christian God (GC) delayed a man's physical sight until a later time (John 9:3) for the purpose of better displaying the works of God. Since we are in no position to conclude that GC would not delay a person's sight of GC for the purpose of better displaying the works of GC, no known reason for believing GC is likely to act in a particular way is sufficient to conclude that GC would not act otherwise for reasons unknown to us, given that GC's ways are, to some extent, inscrutable (see, for example, Isaiah 55:9 and Romans 11:33-34). An exception to the preceding claim, of course, would be cases in which some person J is justified in believing that GC is enabling J to know that it is GC who is enabling J to know that GC would, in fact, perform a particular detailed action, given some specified conditions. Therefore, we have no reason to suppose that Schellenberg's consideration of the nature of the ways of any possibly existing perfectly loving scrutable God also applies to GC, as GC's ways may be largely inscrutable when it comes to our attempts to determine the likelihood that GC would permit particular individuals who are capable of a relationship with GC to persist in a state of inculpable reasonable nonbelief for reasons we do not understand. GC may have good reasons for GC's degree of hiddenness in the world, and since we humans are in no position to determine otherwise, Schellenberg's atheistic argument from reasonable nonbelief crumbles.

In chapter 9 of part 4 of IPRG, J.L. Schellenberg provides two atheistic arguments from divine hiddenness. The first argument is an analogy argument (p. 414:1-423:16), and the second is a conceptual argument (p. 423:17-425:34). These arguments establish, at most, that if God's ways are not inscrutable, then God likely does not exist. In response, since God's ways may be inscrutable, we are in no position to conclude an inscrutable God does not exist, Schellenberg's arguments notwithstanding. After all, the detailed ways of an inscrutable God are, by definition, not known by us humans. Hence, we are in no position to claim divine hiddenness justifies atheism.

Schellenberg's arguments suffer from additional weaknesses related to the above consideration. For example, he claims God would provide "a quick response" (p. 416:35-37) to God's children. In response, how quick is "quick"? One second? One minute? One day? One decade? The point, here, is that unless we have good reason to expect a particular time frame, we have no reason to infer God's nonexistence from divine hiddenness, since God's response may be delayed to a better future time for reasons unknown to us. But, since God's ways may be inscrutable, we have no reason to suppose that we should know why God (assuming God exists) would enable us to know why God's hiddenness is as it is. Thus, we have no reason to suppose divine hiddenness justifies atheism.

Schellenberg states that "it is hard to see" why God would delay revelation of God's existence in some cases (p. 420:37-41). In response, Schellenberg should not expect to see why God would delay such revelation (assuming God exists), since God's ways may be hidden for inscrutable good reasons.

Schellenberg also cites the infinite resourcefulness of God as evidence that God has "literally an *infinite number* of ways" of achieving a relationship with people (p. 421:4-12). In response, since Schellenberg has not even established that an actually infinite quantity can exist, it is far from clear that an actually infinite number of possible actions would be available as live options to God. Furthermore, given the set S of possible actions available as live options to God, we have no reason to suppose each member of S is equally valuable. Indeed, it appears likely that not all members of S would be equally valuable. Furthermore, if God performs the action that corresponds to the most valuable member of S (or an action that corresponds to the subset of S whose members possess a value that exceeds some critical threshold unknown to us), our position in which we possess such limited human knowledge evidently renders us incapable of determining what specific action God is likely to perform. This fact does not contradict the theistic doctrine of the greatness of God (p. 421:9-10), but only serves to emphasize that we are not in a position to determine the size of the space of metaphysically possible worlds, given God's attributes and our limited understanding. The conjunction of all God's attributes may explain God's self-imposed constraints on divine action in ways we do not understand such that God has morally sufficient reasons for all instances of divine hiddenness. Furthermore, the number of possible actions available to God as live options may be small for reasons we do not know. Hence, we are not in a position to identify when God "could help it" (p. 417:21-37). Thus, we may answer Schellenberg's question (p. 421:38-422:1) by noting that it is possible that God has good reasons unknown to us for permitting some seekers to persist in doubt and nonbelief for a temporal period of unknown length, and our inability to confidently estimate the probability of this possibility establishes that the analogy argument fails.

To the degree that we are confident that a loving mother would not have unknown reasons for remaining hidden, absence of evidence of a loving mother would constitute evidence of absence of a loving mother. The God/mother analogy breaks down, however, when we consider that our knowledge of the ways of a loving mother is not reasonably supposed to be analogous to our knowledge of the ways of a loving God, since loving mothers do not possess the relevant attributes which entail that God (and not a loving mother) is likely to possess unfathomably extensive knowledge of relevant considerations unknown to us. Therefore, in the context of our discussion of divine hiddenness, absence of evidence of the existence of God is not evidence of absence of the existence of God.

Although my theistic defense against the atheistic argument from divine hiddenness need not consist of the elucidation of detailed reasons for which God might possibly remain hidden in specific circumstances, it may be useful to do so, as such reasons will help to more clearly illustrate our inability to assess the probability of their actuality. A first example, as mentioned earlier, is that God may remain hidden from person J for a temporal period T of unknown length for good reasons unknown to J. In general, we are in no position to determine the best length of T for J. Since we have no way of knowing (apart from divine revelation) the best length of T for J, we have no way of knowing whether any person sensing divine hiddenness has simply not yet reached the end of that person's period of sensing divine hiddenness.

As a second example, consider that the Evangelical Christian God (GC) might remain hidden from the set Q of sincere seekers who, upon perceiving GC's existence, might develop a relationship with GC that is later ultimately abandoned. It could be good of GC to remain hidden from the members of Q, since those members could suffer a lesser punishment in hell than if they knew GC in greater measure, but subsequently abandoned GC at a later time (in this connection recall Hebrews 6:4-6; Hebrews 10:26-31). This example presumes that one's punishment in hell is somehow proportional to the measure of revelation the unredeemed have rejected (Luke 12:47-48). Since we are not in a position to determine whether any particular individual perceiving divine hiddenness is a member of Q, we are not in a position to determine that an individual's perception of divine hiddenness is evidence against the existence of GC.

The objection may be raised that it is unjust to punish person J, where J does not know that J's actions are deserving of punishment. In response, it is not unjust to so punish J, if J is at fault for being in that state of lack of knowledge. Given the potential darkening effect of sin upon one's thinking (Romans 1:21), J's sinful actions and proclivities may be such that GC permits J to enter a state in which J's moral perceptions lead J to live such that J views J's actions as justified, yet the fact that they are not justified ultimately leads to J's death (Proverbs 14:12). Thus, contra Schellenberg, at least some seekers who "seem in fact to be quite blameless in the relevant respects" (p. 419:24-26) may be responsible for having entered the state of delusion in which they perceive they are blameless, yet they actually are not. J's immediate belief B in the hiddenness of GC might be involuntary (p. 419:29-32), but since it does not follow that the conditions which contribute to the formation of J's sense of divine hiddenness are unrelated to J's actions, J may nevertheless be responsible for J's belief B, even if GC exists. GC's permitting J to enter this state of delusion may, further, be viewed as justified, since it serves to minimize J's punishment in J's self-determined destiny in hell (Luke 12:48).

GC loves even those who reject him, and GC's efforts to minimize the punishment of those determined to enter everlasting punishment may be viewed as loving. Contrary to the views of some critics, a state of everlasting punishment is, itself, not only a consequence of divine justice, but also a manifestation GC's love, since sin deserves punishment, and since those who are in a self-determined state of eternal damnation may be so thoroughly obsessed with the anguish of the ongoing punishment that they are not capable of further increasing their measure of punishment by sinning further. Falling into the hands of an angry God is, indeed, a dreadful thing, but even GC's administration of justice, with its horrifying consequences, may be viewed as consonant with perfect love.

As a third example, GC sometimes intentionally veils revelation of truth (Matthew 13:10-17) for reasons which may sometimes include those that relate to the better display of the work of GC (John 9:1-3). Since GC's ways are largely inscrutable (Isaiah 55:8-9; Romans 11:33-34), we are evidently not in a position to determine whether GC has morally sufficient reasons unknown to us for which GC permits the observed degree of divine hiddenness in the world such that GC acts so as to maximize the value of the possible world GC chooses to actualize. Thus, divine hiddenness is not evidence against the existence of GC, since knowledge of such reasons would surely be beyond our ken.

The objection may be raised that my general form of argumentation might be used to establish that since we have no evidence of the absence of the existence of the divine Great Pumpkin, we are not justified in disbelieving in the Great Pumpkin. In response, other arguments for the existence of God (not the Great Pumpkin) may be used to establish God's existence (see, for example, my AFTLOP and fine-tuning arguments presented earlier). Also, arguments for the existence of GC may justify a more detailed claim to understand greater details of the ways of God, but such arguments lie beyond the scope of the present analysis. Hence, our belief in the existence of God need not be grounded in a fallacious argument from ignorance, but may be rationally grounded in positive evidence for the existence of God, where the positive evidence includes consideration of the fact that although we are ignorant of the ways of a largely inscrutable God, we nonetheless possess evidence sufficient to justify belief in God's existence. <u>I know God acts, but not always why</u>. The Evangelical may further assert: I know more of GC's ways than those who accept only natural theology, but I do not always know the detailed morally sufficient reasons for which GC acts in a particular way.

Schellenberg claims that those who consider theism and atheism to be approximately equally probable should certainly favor atheism upon consideration of the problem of divine hiddenness (p. 422:27-30). In response, this claim might possibly work for those who favor atheism with respect to fully scrutable gods, but since inscrutable gods should not be expected to enable us to understand reasons for divine hiddenness, the problem of divine hiddenness does not justify atheism with respect to gods whose ways are at least partially inscrutable. Thus, the "problem" of divine hiddenness is not a problem at all, since the theist may have justifying reasons for believing God has morally sufficient reasons for divine hiddenness, and since the atheist can not know good reasons for disbelieving in the actualization of the possible ways of a possibly existing inscrutable God, as the definition of "inscrutable God" entails that the ways of an inscrutable God are not known.

Schellenberg considers that a theist might lose theistic belief upon consideration of the nature of divine hiddenness (p. 422:30-37). In response, this possibility is unlikely, unless the conversion away from theism occurs in a person J who believes the conjunction of God's divine attributes and J's relatively inferior human knowledge entails that J knows that God's ways are not inscrutable with respect to the degree of divine hiddenness in the world. However, this entailment is unlikekly to be espoused by many theists, and is unjustified, as my analysis has shown.

The failures of the analogy argument are, in many respects, relevant to the failures of the conceptual argument as well (p. 423:17-425:34). The fundamental weakness is related to Schellenberg's failure to adequately account for the possibility that God's ways may be largely inscrutable with respect to the nature of divine hiddenness in the world.

For example, God may have reasons unknown to us which establish that it is consistent with his nature that evidence sufficient to form belief in God's existence may be unavailable to some persons who are both capable of relationship with God and not likely to inappropriately respond to that evidence (p. 423:25-30). Thus, it is simply not known that "God would necessarily seek personal relationship" with all nonresisters such that evidence sufficient for belief in God's existence would be brought to their conscious awareness (p. 423:30-424:13). God may have good reasons unknown to us which establish that no person who is presently a nonresister should be presently provided with conscious awareness of evidence sufficient for belief in God's existence, and it is not the case that a nonresister's possibility of engaging in a loving relationship with God entails that such evidence must be presently available to nonresisters. Perhaps God will make such evidence available to nonresisters at some better future time unknown to us.

Also, evidence sufficient to justify belief in God's existence might be available to (but not yet discovered by) nonresisters. Since nonresisters are, by definition, nonseekers (p. 423:33-424:1) and since we are in no position to determine whether God has good reasons unknown to us for permitting all nonseekers to persist (for a temporal period of unknown length) in their state of not seeking, then God may be justified in presently preventing nonresisters from acquiring conscious knowledge of evidence of God's existence. For example, there could exist some nonresisters whose epistemic state is such that they would have formed a relationship with God if they had read this book, but since they have not yet read this book, they have not yet actualized the possibility of forming a relationship with God. A book may be available to me in the library, but if I don't seek it, then I may well not acquire that book-relevant knowledge, and God may have good reasons for preventing me from acquiring that knowledge until some better future time. Hence, evidence sufficient for belief in God's existence may be available to all nonresisters, and all nonresisters may not acquire conscious awareness of that availability until some good future time.

In conclusion, a person can know God exists, yet not always know the morally sufficient reasons for all God's actions, and knowledge of such reasons is not a necessary precondition of either the knowledge of the existence of God or knowledge of a limited revelation of God's ways. I know God acts, but not always why.

NOTES

1. By the way, my favorite song right now is "*The Voice of Truth*". Artist: Casting Crowns. Label: Reunion. Relase date: October 2003. ASIN:B0000CDL6V.

2. McKinsey, C. Dennis (1995). *The Encyclopedia of Biblical Errancy*. Amherst, NY: Prometheus Books.

3. Ross, Hugh (1994). *Creation and Time*. Colorado Springs, CO: Navpress.

4. Stoner, Don (1992). *A New Look at an Old Earth: What the Creation Institutes Are Not Telling You About Genesis*. Paramount, CA: Schroeder Publishing.

5. Drange, Theodore (1998). *Nonbelief & Evil: Two Arguments for the Nonexistence of God*. Amherst, NY: Prometheus Books, p. 362, Note 3.

6. Hagopian, David G., ed. (2000). *The Genesis Debate: Three Views on the Days of Creation*. McLean, VA: Global Publishing Services.

7. Ross, Hugh (2004). *Matter of days: Resolving A Creation Controversy*. Colorado Springs, CO: Navpress.

8. Snoke, David (2006). *A Biblical Case for an Old Earth*. Grand Rapids, MI: Baker Books.

9. Youngblood, Ronald, ed. (1984). *Evangelicals and Inerrancy*. Nashville, TN: Thomas Nelson Publishers, pp. 230-239.

10. This may be verified by accessing the 1996 article which may be found online at http://www.infidels.org/library/modern/niclas_berggren/funda.html, section 2.2, paragraph 3.

11. For the full debate, see Craig, William Lane and Sinnott-Armstrong, Walter (2004). *God? A Debate Between a Christian and an Atheist*. Oxford: Oxford University Press.

In the appendix of IPRG, an atheistic essay by Paul Thiry D'Holbach entitled "The Ideas of the Divinity" is provided (p. 427:1-432:41). The essay may be of historical interest to those seeking understanding of atheistic thought, but does not contain a serious attempt to thoroughly justify its atheistic perspective. Rather, ideas likely to be espoused by atheists are uncritically assumed and accepted. Since the tactic of resorting to unanswered questioning is frequently employed, the essay falls considerably short of an actual demonstration that its theme is established. Nevertheless, it is informative to see how a mind unenlightened by the light of theistic revelation may be inclined to muse.

In conclusion, it is plainly evident that a new edition of IPRG is needed, as its first edition now stands thoroughly criticized and in need of substantial revision. It is also my hope that the following corrections will be made in a future edition of IPRG:

(P. 142:37-38)   Replace "A huge range of values are…" with "A huge range of values is…"

(P. 166:26-27)   Note the exclusion of Kwon's "Appendix 1" from IPRG, or include it in IPRG.

(P. 205:13-15)   Replace "treated" with "created".

(P. 213:32-33)   Replace "al" with "at".

(P. 376:26-27)   Replace "tht" with "that".

(P. 417:25-28)   Replace "actors" with "factors".

Finally, I welcome your feedback and encourage you to visit www.atheismisfalse.com for author contact details.

CHAPTER 7

Richard Dawkins And His Atheism Delusion

I now examine the atheistic argument presented by Richard Dawkins in his book "The God Delusion", published by Houghton Mifflin Company in 2006, ISBN: 978-0-618-68000-9. I urge you to purchase a copy of "The God Delusion" so that you may fully understand the context of the critical remarks below.

His argument is focused in chapter 4 (p. 111:1-159:5), and contains "the central argument" of the book (p. 157:26-28). First, though, the Thomas Jefferson quotation (p. 111:1-4) deserves a quick response. Jefferson's quotation implies scientific advancement is the enemy of the justification of religious thought. However, as emphasized in my Introduction, scientific advancement is the source of the raw data which form the foundation upon which my theistic arguments are built, and scientific progress is in the direction of increasingly confirming the theistic hypothesis.

Dawkins summarizes his argument for atheism in six points (p. 157:29-158:30). Point (3) is grounded in the assumption that theistic design hypotheses do not adequately deal with the problem of explaining who designed the designer (p. 158:1-8). In response, it is not generally required that "Person J knows Y causes Z" only if J knows the cause of Y. Rather, J could know Y causes Z, yet not know much at all about the nature of Y. Physicists may postulate and subsequently observe that some particle P exists under some specified conditions C, yet not know much at all regarding the nature of P except that P exists under conditions C. Likewise, it is theoretically possible that some theists could know God designed the universe, yet not know much else regarding the nature of God.

We have no justification for the requirement R that proper identification of "J knows Y causes Z" entails J knows the cause of Y. Indeed, such a requirement would lead to the demand for knowledge of an infinite regress. This may be seen as follows. R implies that "J knows Y causes Z" only if "J knows cause X is the cause of Y", which, in turn, implies that "J knows X causes Y" only if "J knows cause W is the cause of X", which, in turn, implies that "J knows W causes X" only if "J knows cause V is the cause of W", etc. Thus, R entails that a cause can be identified only if an infinite sequence of prior causes is also known. However, since an infinite sequence of prior causes can not be known by humans, and since causes are known to be identified by humans, it follows that we may reject R, and with it, the unjustified requirement Dawkins demands when insisting that identification of a theistic designer necessarily requires identification of the cause of the design of the designer.

An infinite regress is something Dawkins would presumably seek to avoid. Thus, Dawkins must explain how to justify upholding R, with its implausible presumption that we possess knowledge of an infinite regress in every case in which we properly identify a cause. Or, if Dawkins wishes to avoid the regress, he must either abandon R or identify causal sequences as having originated in the uncaused free action of a person. However, if Dawkins abandons R, then he also abandons the requirement that theists identify who designed the designer, and if Dawkins grounds causal sequences ultimately in the free uncaused originating action of persons, then the door is opened wide to theistic design. In either case, the force of the atheistic argument Dawkins presents is fully defused.

The objection might be raised that Dawkins has another way out of this dilemma, since he could simply assert that all physical events are either uncaused or caused by (possibly unknown) prior physical events. In response, this option is unwarranted and it flies in the face of the nature of causation as detailed in my AFTLOP (see chapter 1 for details), and is further disconfirmed by my fine-tuning arguments (see chapter 2 for details). Thus, it is evident that Dawkins ought to either reformulate his atheistic argument to account for the issues raised in my critique, or better yet, abandon it altogether and convert to theism.

Point (3) is also grounded in the assumption that the theistic design hypothesis is objectionable in that it is, itself, highly improbable (p. 158:1-8). In response, the theistic hypothesis is presented as an alternative to a natural explanation given purely in terms of physical laws and processes. As such, the theistic design hypothesis is, of course, an improbable natural explanation, since it is not a natural explanation at all! It is misleading, if not dishonest, to object that theistic design is naturalistically improbable, when theists need not be committed to the supposition that it is not. Theistic design is a personal causal explanation, and such explanations need not be described in purely naturalistic physical terms. Dawkins evidently assumes that God, as designer of the universe, would, Himself, need to be described in terms of some kind of "crane" explanation in which physical laws cause all physical events, including those events alleged by theists to have been divinely designed (p. 158:9-30). Herein lies the <u>Dawkins Fallacy</u>: all persons (including any possibly existing God), as well as all personal actions, must be explained in terms of physical laws. In response, Dawkins is seen to embrace naturalistic presuppositions which lead him to erroneously assume that God (if God exists) must be a natural physical event explainable in terms of laws of physics. Clearly, this assumption is unjustified, as it simply begs the question in favor of naturalism. It is possible that there could exist a God who is not explained or explainable in terms of any physical law, and Dawkins clings to unwarranted materialistic naturalism when unjustifiably rejecting this possibility.

Furthermore, Dawkins fails to adequately respond to a standard theistic perspective, namely, that God is a nonphysical person who causes physical events to form patterns we identify as physical laws, yet God is not, Himself, subject to those laws. Thus, the "problem of who designed the designer" (p. 158:1-3) is seen to be a pseudoproblem, since theism is not committed to the claim that God is, Himself, designed, and since unwarranted materialistic assumptions do not rationally obligate theists to accept that claim. Theists may assert that God is uncaused and timeless prior to creation,[1] and Dawkins is evidently unaware of this view or the rational basis for it. The theistic hypothesis, more generally, is strongly confirmed by my AFTLOP and fine-tuning arguments (see chapter 1 and chapter 2), refuting the assumption by Dawkins that the theistic design hypothesis is, itself, statistically improbable (p. 158:4-5).

Having now responded to the general argument form presented by Dawkins, I shall now comment on some additional related issues. First, I can not help but mention that theistic design arguments need not be characterized as arguments from improbability (p. 113:1), for if theistic design was known to be improbable, then it would be wise for us all to reject arguments in its favor, and there would be little more to discuss. Of course, Dawkins has something rather different in mind, namely, that theistic design arguments seek to ground the inference to theistic design in the improbability of natural explanations that are in terms of laws of physics. The point, here, is that theistic design arguments are somewhat better characterized as *arguments from the improbability of natural explanations*.

In "The Ultimate Boeing 747" (p. 113:1-114:31) Dawkins expresses a confused claim regarding probabilities (p. 114:9-11). Presumably what Dawkins has in mind is that the probability that an object X is personally designed is less than or equal to the probability that X has an impersonal natural cause in terms of physical laws. Needless to say, this claim is far from self-evident and in need of support. Also, given the preference Dawkins shares for impersonal natural causes (p. 158:24-30), Dawkins would evidently prefer rejection of explanations in terms of personal design, at least with respect to objects not humanly designed. In response, as detailed in my AFTLOP (see chapter 1 for details), we have good reasons to reject the claim that impersonal causes exist, and we have good reasons to accept the claim that explanations in terms of laws of physics are generally caused by God. Dawkins, however, apparently assumes physical laws constitute impersonal causes, yet fails to account for the results of my analysis in the AFTLOP which entail that physical laws are not causes, but are descriptions of physical event patterns, where the events are caused by a person. Dawkins offers no support for the contention that physical laws actually cause the events they describe. As shall be seen, a fundamental weakness in the case presented by Dawkins is the erroneous assumption that if object X is described in terms of a physical law, then X is caused by that law. By definition, laws are descriptive. The bizarre contention that a description of X can also be the cause of X is especially in need of defense, and Dawkins fails to provide such a fundamental defense of his view that physical laws (e.g., Darwinian natural selection laws or evolutionary multiverse hypotheses) actually cause the physical events they describe. Thus, even if Dawkins and others eventually discovered their much sought after "crane" (p. 158:24-30), the task of eliminating the existence of a designer of that crane would not be consequently accomplished, and on this point the atheistic argument presented by Dawkins crumbles to dust.

So, even if Dawkins had achieved the goal of establishing his claim that natural selection "explains the whole of life" (p. 116:5-9), it would not follow that his explanation in terms of natural selection would be a *causal* explanation. The situation for Dawkins is even worse, though, since he has not even demonstrated that natural selection explains the whole of life. Even if we grant every example of explanation he provides in terms of natural selection, it does not follow that "the whole of life" is consequently rightly assumed to be explained in terms of natural selection, especially when we have considerable evidence to the contrary (see chapter 1 and chapter 2 for details). From "Darwinian natural selection explains the physical evolution of some instances of biological complexity" it does not follow that "all instances of biological complexity are explained in terms of Darwinian natural selection". The evidently fallacious nature of this inference is of even greater "stunning simplicity" than the natural selection of which Dawkins speaks (p. 117:8-11).

Dawkins again assumes, without justification, that his natural selection explanations are causal in the sense that they describe how a thing can *make* a thing (p. 117:15-17), as his Daniel Dennett quotation illustrates that he takes natural selection to be a counterexample to the claim that it must be the case that to *make* a lesser thing, a big fancy smart thing must do the *making* (italics mine). Also, Dawkins claims that natural selection is causal in the sense that the effects of natural selection are "brought about" (p. 140:6-7) through natural selection. In addition, Dawkins claims that natural selection is causal in the sense that it is "capable of *generating* complexity out of simplicity" (p. 150:36-151:2, italics mine). In response, unless Dawkins (or Dennett) provides a reason for supposing that natural selection explanations are themselves causal (rather than merely descriptive of events caused by a person), these claims may be properly viewed as merely begging the question in favor of naturalistic explanations. Dawkins would do well to accept the position advocated by atheist David Mills, which is that it is "absurd" to suppose that physical laws "cause the outcome of the observed phenomena."[2] Strangely, Dawkins has written that the work of David Mills is "admirable",[3] yet Dawkins does not even show understanding of the fundamental fact that physical laws are, by definition, descriptive (not causal).

So indeed, my critique of natural selection is consciousness-raising, as it raises us to a point of conscious awareness of the fundamental unjustified naturalistic assumption that physical laws are both descriptive and causal. It should now be evident, however, that physical laws are, by definition, descriptive, and the supposition that those laws are also causal is in need of justification, but sadly, Dawkins provides none. Thus, even if we did grant Dawkins the great power he attributes to natural selection (p. 117:31-33), there remains unexplained the source of that power. From whence the power?

Some designed complex objects are known to be caused to be designed by persons. No complex object is known to be *caused* by natural selection. Even if we make the unnecessary concession to Dawkins that natural selection describes the evolution of every example of a complex physical object he provides, it does not follow that natural selection causes the evolution of those complex objects. Powerful descriptions are not necessarily powerful causes. It is insufficient to assert that natural selection is a workable solution of "stunning elegance and power" (p. 121:21-22). Rather, Dawkins must persuade us that natural selection is a workable solution of stunning elegance and *causal* power, else we may respond to Dawkins: Who caused natural selection? Natural selection can not have caused itself, as self-causation is, in general, highly implausible. So again, we may ask: Who caused natural selection? Dawkins might respond that natural selection is grounded in some more fundamental physical law. But then, in turn, we may ask: Who caused the more fundamental law? Dawkins might answer that all physical laws are a necessary consequence of continuously existing matter in a region of spacetime. But then, we may ask: Who causes matter to continue to exist? Dawkins might respond that matter exists as a consequence of some presently unknown Theory Of Everything. But then, we may ask: Who caused the Theory Of Everything? In other words, far from solving the fundamental problem of identifying the causal origin of the biological world (or the physical world, in general), natural selection merely leads us to inquire regarding the origin of that world in which natural selection supposedly generates biological complexity. Needless to say, atheism is not at all established by appeals to natural selection.

Thus, far from shattering the illusion of design (p. 118:9-11), the causal powers Dawkins unjustifiably attributes to his natural selection descriptions should teach us to be suspicious of any kind of naturalistic causal hypothesis espoused by any atheistic scientists, especially Dawkins. If he wishes to step up to the plate and justify his naturalistic assumptions, then I am all ears! Until then, his explication of example after example of Darwinian evolution by natural selection is little more than an exercise in "proof by assertion", and he would do well to respond to his own complaint that "repetition of example after example gets us nowhere" (p. 121:7-8). He can assert that natural selection is causal until the cows come home, but if Dawkins seriously expects good thinkers to convert to his position (p. 116:21-23), he must provide us with good thinking. "Proof by assertion" is not good thinking, especially when I have mounted considerable evidence contradicting that assertion (see chapter 1 and chapter 2 for details).

I am not personally inclined to embrace so-called "theistic evolution", wherein Darwinian evolutionary explanations in terms of natural selection are taken to be physical laws which describe physical event patterns caused by God. Nevertheless, theistic evolution is of greater explanatory value than the Dawkins interpretation, as theistic evolution identifies a cause of the obtaining of the descriptive natural selection law, whereas on the Dawkins interpretation, natural selection is assumed (without justification) to be both descriptive and causal. Dawkins thoroughly fails to adequately represent theistic evolution (which, recall, I do not accept), as he erroneously assumes "God wouldn't need to do anything at all!" (p. 118:27-28). In response, on theistic evolution, God does much indeed, as God is the cause of the continuing existence of physical entities which continue to evolve in accordance with natural selection laws God continually causes to obtain. Atkins's construal of theistic evolution as a scenario in which God is a *deus otiosus* (p. 118:31-34) erroneously assumes that theistic evolution entails that physical laws are originated, but not sustained in existence, by God. Surprisingly, Dawkins apparently accepts Atkins's incorrect interpretation of theistic evolution, and his cursory one-paragraph treatment (p. 118:23-119:2), relying as it does on a misinterpretation of theistic evolution and a lack of appreciation of its explanatory value, strongly suggests Dawkins is not fairly representing or responding to those whose views are opposed to his own.[4]

Dawkins clearly explains that he believes that naturalistically improbable biological events should not be viewed as having been caused either by chance or design (p. 121:14), but should rather be viewed as having been caused either by chance, design, or natural selection, where natural selection is taken to be the best alternative (p. 121:14-22). In response, if natural selection (as Dawkins understands it) is probably the correct explanation of naturalistically improbable biological events, then those events are not really properly understood as naturalistically improbable, since natural selection would render those events naturalistically probable. More importantly, the Dawkins interpretation of natural selection as a causal (rather than merely descriptive) explanation remains unjustified, and so does not solve the problem of the causal origin of biological complexity. Also, even if natural selection is understood as the descriptive (and not causal) explanation of the evolutionary origin of biological complexity, the door remains open to theistic design, as God may be understood as the sustaining cause of the continuing existence of the physical world which continues to exist and evolve in accordance with natural selection laws. Furthermore, Dawkins has not even shown that natural selection is the best descriptive explanation of the origin of biological complexity, as the inference is fallacious from "some measure of complexity in biological forms is explained in terms of natural selection" to "the whole of life is explained in terms of natural selection". In addition, Dawkins favors natural selection explanations over theistic design explanations, in part, due to the erroneous assumption (as explained earlier) that theistic design is improbable due to its requirement that we accept the improbable claim that the theistic designer was designed. Theistic design, properly understood, need not entail that the designer is designed, and Dawkins is repeatedly attacking a straw man in reiterating the supposition that if God is the designer of biological complexity, then God must, Himself, be designed. If Dawkins assumes that any possibly existing theistic designer must be designed due to acceptance of the naturalistic assumption that all designers must be explained in terms of physical laws, then he is seen to simply be begging the question in favor of atheistic naturalism. To make his case, Dawkins must either respond to theistic arguments that the theistic designer is not designed, or he must explain why all designers must be explained in naturalistic terms. Dawkins has not made his case.

Dawkins clearly uses natural selection explanations to show the means by which biological complexity could conceivably gradually accumulate over time (p. 121:23-125:18), and creationists who fail to understand the "Mount Improbable" parable should pay close attention (p. 121:37-122:12). Nevertheless, it is not sufficient to explain how an eye or wing could conceivably gradually evolve (p. 124:21-24), since demonstration of conceivable possibility is a far cry from demonstrating that the possibility is actualized. Also, creationists need not be understood as always assuming that "biological adaptation is a question of the jackpot or nothing" (p. 122:25-27), as creationists might argue that individual steps in the gradualist explanations are naturalistically improbable. More importantly, creationists may emphasize that Darwinian gradualism natural selection explanations, if taken to disconfirm theistic design, suffer from the many difficulties outlined in the previous paragraph. In addition, my AFTLOP and fine-tuning arguments strongly confirm theistic design.

As I mentioned earlier, the so-called "argument from improbability" is somewhat better understood as an argument from the improbability of natural explanations. So, if no natural explanation of some event E is likely, then E is likely explained in terms of a non-natural (supernatural) explanation. Thus, a creationist might argue that "the improbability of all presently known natural explanations of E" entails "E is probably best understood in terms of a supernatural explanation." The problem with this inference, however, is that it fails to account for the possibility of future discoveries. After all, a present gap in understanding of natural explanations of events such as E might eventually be filled, in the future, with new understanding of natural explanations of events such as E. Hence the problem of gaps (p. 125:19-134:27).

The problem of gaps in present understanding is, in general, an epistemological problem. One conceivable solution to the problem is to simply deny knowledge of any given proposition X by claiming that principle S entails X is unknown, where S is the claim that we are unable to estimate the probability that $P(X|N) \approx P(X|F)$, where N represents the conjunction of all propositions known now, and where F represents the conjunction of all propositions known at some time in the future. The problem with this skeptical denial of knowledge is that it is self-refuting, for if X represents "Principle S is now known", then present acceptance of S requires present rejection of X, which, in turn, requires present rejection of S. Thus, principle S can not be presently known, nor could it ever be known. Also, knowledge must not be denied on the grounds that future discoveries may render unlikely what is presently known to be likely. It follows that if it is presently known that natural explanations of event E are likely to be improbable, then this fact may not be claimed to be unknown on the grounds that future discoveries may be such that natural explanations of E are likely to be probable.

So, if present understanding entails that a knowledge gap is unlikely to be filled by a natural explanation, then the possibility of a future discovery of a natural explanation of the gap does not justify rejection of the claim that the gap is unlikely to be filled by a natural explanation. However, gaps do sometimes get filled, contrary to expectations, and understanding must be modified accordingly. The real challenge for the creationist, though, is establishing that a gap is unlikely to be filled by a natural explanation. Dawkins is right to object that a gap in knowledge of a natural explanation does not necessarily entail the gap probably has no natural explanation. In addition, human knowledge is increasing rapidly, and many knowledge gaps are being filled with natural explanations as scientific discovery advances.

How, then, can a creationist respond to the allegation that theists unjustifiably fill current scientific knowledge gaps with ignorant appeal to God (p. 133:33-134:1)? One approach may be called the Argument From Miracles. (An event E is miraculous if and only if E is known to be caused by God such that no known law of physics explains E). In this approach, we could identify a set G of gaps, where G is the subset of all gaps such that each member of G would likely not presently be a gap, if it had a natural explanation. This approach, unlike the gap theology to which Dawkins objects, could conceivably generate results that could form the raw data upon which a justified inference to divine action could be grounded, since the inference would be based not merely on the present existence of a gap, but also on the improbability of a future filling of that gap purely in terms of physical laws. The difficulty in this approach is that it is not always clear how to assess the probability that sufficient research exists to justify the conclusion that a natural explanation is unlikely. How can we know what we don't know? There may sometimes be cases in which we achieve confidence regarding the possibility of the existence of some particular category of presently unknown natural explanations in terms of physical laws, but sometimes we may be unable to estimate the likelihood of such possibilities. Even in cases in which such possibilities are difficult to estimate, particularly recalcitrant gaps that appear to almost forcibly resist explanation in natural terms might be better explained in the context of miraculous divine activity, but the specification of the detailed criteria for proper identification of such activity would require careful attention to detail, as well as consideration of the broader religious-historical context of the putative miraculous event.

Creation/evolution debates may often get mired in the sometimes sticky details of how, precisely, to structure a sound Argument From Miracles, as described above. Further compounding the problem is the difficulty associated with attaining the required expertise sufficient to evaluate detailed arguments that some or another entity is (or is not) likely to ever be explained in terms of physical laws. (Incidentally, I submit that my fine-tuning arguments in chapter 2 meet the challenge of establishing that we are justified in believing that a specific category of physical events is unlikely to possess a natural explanation purely in terms of physical laws).

Fortunately for the theist (and unfortunately for the atheist), there is an alternative to the Argument From Miracles approach mentioned above, and this alternative recasts the entire debate into a completely different light. Theists may point out that my AFTLOP establishes that physical laws generally describe God-caused events (see chapter 1 for details). The advancement of scientific discovery only serves to increase our knowledge of the nature of God's activity in the world, and consequently, we find that theists need not say "just give up, and appeal to God" (p. 132:30-31), but they may say "God did it, so let's seek a physical law that describes it!" Atheists, on the other hand, must be forced to say "don't seek an explanation in terms of physical laws, lest we discover even more evidence of God's action in the world!" (recall Romans 1:20-21). Theists may rejoice in the discovery of new physical laws, as such discovery provides greater insight into the nature of God's creative activity. Also, many events not presently explained in terms of physical laws are likely to be so explained in the future, and this provides further evidence of divine action. God is not hiding in scientific knowledge gaps, but is declaring His handiwork in every new scientific discovery, regardless of whether natural selection explanations appear compelling (again, recall I am skeptical regarding the adequacy of natural selection explanations, but this is beside the point).

Thus, the debate regarding whether some scientific knowledge gap is likely to be filled in the future is very much beside the point that *physical laws declare God's action.* Hence, it is incorrect to pit Darwinism against design (p. 134:13-17), since Darwinian evolution via natural selection, even if true (and I have my reservations), would be an example of a physical law designed by God.

Go ahead, dear atheists, and seek out new laws of physics. Fill scientific knowledge gaps to your heart's content! For in so doing, you shall only serve to increase the evidence for the existence of God! (Again, see chapter 1 for details).

Dawkins presumes to know how God would design the world (p. 134:13-17), assuming God exists. Also, he claims to know that natural selection is cruel and wasteful (p. 134:24-25). In response, if an omniscient, omnipotent, omnibenevolent God exists, then we are doubtfully in a position to identify the decision procedures God is likely to employ, and, consequently, we do not know (apart from divine revelation) what action God is likely to perform in any particular case. Dawkins has not established that God's existence would entail that Dawkins would know how God would likely design the world. Also, since it is possible that there exists a God whose ways are inscrutable regarding the degree to which God permits some people to sense (perhaps erroneously) that natural selection (assuming it is a physical law) is cruel and wasteful, it does not follow that the description Dawkins gives of a cruel and wasteful natural selection law constitutes evidence against such a God. Furthermore, on some versions of atheism, cruelty (evil) does not even objectively exist as a moral property, and since Dawkins appears to favor the view that objective morality does not generally exist (p. 232), then it is incorrect to label natural selection as objectively cruel.

As mentioned in my Introduction, the "God-of-the-gaps" problem should be seen to be no problem at all for the theist, and scientific discovery turns out to be an increasingly difficult problem for the atheist. Problems for atheism only increase, however, when we turn to my fine-tuning arguments (see chapter 2 for details). In my fine-tuning arguments, I establish not merely that there exists no natural explanation of various anthropic coincidences in terms of physical laws, but also that the probability of a natural explanation of those coincidences is very minute. Thus, I infer a non-natural (supernatural) causal explanation of those coincidences not merely from a presently existing scientific knowledge gap, but from the high improbability of that gap being filled with a natural explanation. My fine-tuning arguments are, therefore, seen to be immune to the objections Dawkins raises against gap theology, as my arguments are grounded not in ignorance, but in scientifically established knowledge of the limitations of natural explanations.[5]

If Dawkins chooses to hold out for the possibility that a presently unknown (and presently known to be likely nonexistent) natural explanation of the anthropic coincidences that I discuss in my fine-tuning arguments might be discovered in the future, then Dawkins is seen to simply reject what is scientifically established. If Dawkins must reject what is scientifically established so as to hold on to his atheism, then perhaps it is time for him to come out of the closet and acknowledge the anti-realist nature of his atheism. Given that Dawkins is genuinely interested in discovering "important truths about the real world" (p. 133:18-20), I eagerly await his conversion to theism and his acceptance of divine design. Even if, for some reason unknown to me, Dawkins persists in his rejection of science in favor of atheism, theists are nevertheless warranted in their belief in theistic design, as that belief is confirmed by my AFTLOP and fine-tuning arguments, and is grounded in the results of modern science. In addition, theistic belief is further confirmed by the failure of attempts to justify atheism.

Dawkins discusses the anthropic principle is his discussion of the problem of the origin of life-friendly conditions on earth and the problem of the origin of life on earth (p. 134:28-141:18). His interpretation of the principle is that present human existence as a living, eukaryotic and conscious biological life-form on a life-friendly planet entails that our planet must be a life-friendly planet on which living, eukaryotic and conscious biological life-forms exist due to some natural explanation (p. 136:23-25; p. 140:37-141:1). The idea is that either a natural explanation N of the origin of life on our life-friendly planet exists or it does not, but since the nonexistence of N entails our nonexistence on Earth, it follows that our existence on Earth entails the existence of N. In short, there *must* be a natural explanation of the problem of the origin of life on our life-friendly Earth….otherwise we wouldn't be here to ponder the problem. In response, this understanding of the anthropic principle clearly begs the question in favor of naturalism in that it presumes the existence of a naturalistic explanation of the origin of life on our life-friendly Earth, and, by default, it presumes the nonexistence of a non-natural (supernatural) explanation. Thus, the interpretation of the anthropic principle provided by Dawkins does not solve the problem of our biological origin in a life-friendly place (p. 136:32-35), but merely grounds the presumption of a naturalistic explanation of that origin in unjustified naturalistic presuppositions.

Clearly, if we are interested in settling the debate, we must not embrace a principle that simply begs the question. The anthropic principle may, thus, be restated in neutral terms: present human existence as a living, eukaryotic and conscious biological life-form on a life-friendly planet entails that our planet must be a life-friendly planet on which living, eukaryotic and conscious biological life-forms exist due to some *causal* explanation. With my revision to the principle, it no longer begs the question in favor of naturalism, but simply contains the fundamental assumption that there exists a causal explanation of the origin of human life on life-friendly Earth. Perhaps the explanation is natural. Perhaps the explanation is not natural. My neutralized version of the anthropic principle presupposes neither possibility. Also, so long as we have reason to suppose physical events are caused, the fundamental assumption in my neutralized principle is justified, and my AFTLOP (see chapter 1) provides justification for that supposition. Note that my revised version of the anthropic principle need not be taken as an alternative to theistic design, but leaves open the possibility of either a natural or supernatural explanation of the origin of all life on Earth. Thus, if we desire to embrace an anthropic principle that does not beg the question in favor of naturalism, then we must not pit theistic design against the anthropic principle, as Dawkins does (p. 136:35-37).

Dawkins wonders why theists are excited about the anthropic principle (p. 136:26-37). My excitement is due to the fact that the principle draws attention to unsolved scientific problems, where the improbability of naturalistic solutions to those problems confirms theism, as detailed in my fine-tuning arguments (see chapter 2 for details). Sure, our existence on Earth entails, minimally, that "the origin of life only had to happen once" (p. 135:4-5), but it does not entail that it had to happen due to natural causes. Furthermore, the improbability of a natural cause confirms theistic design. So, the anthropic principle, though expressed in different forms by different authors, nonetheless draws attention to the insufficiency of natural explanations, thereby contributing to the rational basis for belief in the existence of God. Atheists are, thus, forced to embrace an anthropic principle that presupposes naturalistic causes in their faulty attempt to justify atheistic science, whereas theists find theistic science further justified by the inadequacy of natural explanations of conditions in the context of a neutral anthropic principle.

Dawkins, perhaps recognizing the implausibility of his naturalistic version of the anthropic principle, seeks to beef up that principle with what he calls "the 'billions of planets' anthropic principle" (p. 141:3-4), which may be stated as follows: given the set S of existing planets, S has billions of members, and Earth is necessarily a member of the subset of S whose members consists of evolution-friendly planets (p. 141:14-17). Setting aside the question of whether biological evolutionary explanations are plausible, this principle blatantly begs the question in favor of a naturalistic explanation of the origin of evolution-friendly conditions on Earth, as it assumes that it is plausible that at least one such planet should exist due to natural causes. The reference to the existence of large numbers of planets does not diminish the force of my objection here.

Furthermore, the appeal to "billions of planets" does not help Dawkins solve the problem of the origin of life on a life-friendly planet unless the probability of a naturalistic explanation of that origin is sufficiently high. Hugh Ross illustrates this problem in his rough estimate of the probability of a naturalistic explanation of some parameters necessary for the support of carbon-based life on a planet in our universe.[6] Ross estimates that the probability of the naturalistic origin of life-friendly conditions on a planet such as Earth, even given the existence of 10^{22} planets, is infinitesimal. Dawkins, evidently ignorant of calculations such as this, states that "it is likely that there is intelligent life elsewhere" (p. 138:36-38). Remarkably, Dawkins even seriously considers that natural explanations are sufficient to suppose there are "billions of planets that have developed life at the level of bacteria" (p. 140:31-33). Clearly, Dawkins owes us an explanation of why he believes the Ross calculation is incorrect, and pending such explanation, his claim remains unjustified that the problem of the origin of life on a life-friendly planet is a scientific knowledge gap that can be "easily filled by statistically informed science" (p. 139:8-11). Thus, the "magic of large numbers" to which Dawkins appeals (p. 137:33-34) does not confirm atheism, and he would do well to discern the theistic implications of his magic. (Also, the reader is referred to my critique earlier this chapter for a refutation of the "Ultimate 747" objection Dawkins again references in his attempt to deny the plausibility of theistic design (p. 139:8-11; 141:6-10)).

Dawkins also discusses the anthropic principle in the context of cosmology (p. 141:19-151:5), and his interpretation of the principle in this context is as follows: our biological existence in a life-friendly universe entails that physical laws (or conditions) must exist which are capable of producing our biological existence in a life-friendly universe (p. 141:20-21; 144:11-14; 145:33-35). In response, observe that this anthropic principle presumes (without justification) that physical laws or conditions possess productive causal power. This is a standard naturalistic presupposition, and in need of justification. My AFTLOP (see chapter 1), however, solidly refutes this presupposition by revealing the rational basis for the belief that only persons possess causal power.

In addition, the cosmological anthropic principle embraced by Dawkins presupposes that our existence in a life-friendly universe entails the existence of a natural explanation of our existence. Needless to say, this is simply an example of begging the question in favor of a naturalistic explanation of our existence in a life-friendly universe. Dawkins accepts a principle which entails non-natural (supernatural) explanations can not be true. Once again, Dawkins is seen to ground rejection of theistic design explanations, in part, in the unjustified acceptance of a principle that presupposes the nonexistence of theistic design explanations.

If Dawkins is seriously interested in resolving the creation debate at the cosmological level, then he should not rely on a question-begging principle to make his case. Rather, he should embrace a neutralized version of his cosmological principle which may be stated as follows: our biological existence in a life-friendly universe entails that a causal explanation exists which identifies the cause of our biological existence in a life-friendly universe. Note that my neutral cosmological principle simply consists of the fundamental assumption that our physical existence entails the existence of a cause of our physical existence, and that cause is, at the outset, neither presumed to be a naturalistic cause, nor presumed to be a non-naturalistic cause. To the extent that we are justified in supposing that physical events are caused, my fundamental assumption here is warranted, and my AFTLOP (see chapter 1) explores the reasons which establish that this assumption is warranted.

Dawkins introduces his cosmological anthropic principle as a way of solving the problem of the naturalistic origin of the apparent fine-tuning of various fundamental physical constants. He reasons that even if it is necessary that these constants must be exquisitely fine-tuned as a prerequisite for the naturalistic origin of any kind of physical life in a universe, our physical existence in our universe entails that those constants must be so fine-tuned, else we would not exist to ponder the problem of their causal origin. In response, setting aside the objections already raised above, this reasoning is unsatisfying in that it fails to identify the causal origin of the fine-tuned constants. Sure, if we grant that a natural explanation of our existence must exist (an unnecessary concession, I might add), and if we grant that fine-tuned physical constants are a necessary component of any natural explanation of our existence, then of course it follows that our existence entails the existence of those fine-tuned constants. However, it does not also follow that we have identified the cause of the existence of those fine-tuned constants. Thus, the anthropic cosmological principle provided by Dawkins fails to accomplish its intended purpose of identifying the causal origin of the fine-tuned constants.

Dawkins is sensitive to this problem (p. 145:1-2), and recognizing his desire, as an atheist, to seek naturalistic solutions, he briefly explores possible naturalistic solutions in terms of oscillating universe theory, a Theory Of Everything, and multiverse theory. Dawkins acknowledges that oscillating universe theory is disconfirmed and not accepted, and he also concedes that there exists no known Theory Of Everything that can explain all physical laws as the logically necessary consequence of matter existing in spacetime.

There remains multiverse theory as a possible naturalistic explanation of the existence of the constants seemingly fine-tuned for life in a universe. Simply put, multiverse theory entails that our universe is but one of a multitude of universes which comprises a multiverse in which each universe possesses different physical conditions resulting from different values of fundamental physical constants. Given some version of a multiverse theory, it should be no surprise that some subset (presumably a small subset) of the universes in the multiverse should possess life-friendly conditions that include "fine-tuned" fundamental constants.

In response, even if multiverse theory is true, that theory is a description of a physical law caused by a person (see chapter 1), and so leaves open wide the door to theistic design of the multiverse. In other words, Dawkins mistakenly supposes that a multiverse law is a causal explanation, rather than understands that multiverse law is a description of person-caused physical events.

Also, multiverse theory appears untestable in that the spacetime manifolds of no two distinct universes can overlap. Thus, direct observation of any universe other than our own is evidently not possible. The number of universes known to be physically observed is one.

Thus we are faced with two broad alternatives: theistic design of our (and any other) universe, or a naturalistic multiverse explanation. Which alternative is simpler? Belief in a potential infinity of unobservable universes grounded in untestable theory? Or belief in a God-caused universe (or multiverse, if it exists) grounded in established science?

These questions may be answered by first emphasizing that we may agree that we should "always prefer the simplest hypothesis that fits the facts" (p. 147:25-27). However, the critical fact Dawkins fails to consider is that physical events are caused only by persons (see chapter 1). Thus, naturalistic multiverse theory is inferior to theistic multiverse theory, since only the latter identifies a cause of the physical events of the multiverse, whereas the former rejects the known nature of causation by rejecting its origin in personal free action. Thus, theistic design of the multiverse better accounts for the facts and is consequently a better explanation than naturalistic multiverse theory.

If, on the other hand, only our universe exists, then presently available naturalistic explanations would appear wholly incapable of accounting for the values of various fundamental physical constants. However, theists must exercise caution here, lest they erroneously infer divine action from the mere fact that life-permitting physical constants happen to lie within the very narrow life-permitting ranges. Recall that nonexistence of a presently known natural explanation does not entail that no natural explanation will ever be known. Also, the extreme narrowness of the life-permitting range of various physical constants does not entail the improbability of the existence of a natural explanation of the fact that those constants lie within that range. Indeed, unless a naturalistic basis is established from which we may infer the range of values that those constants could naturalistically assume, we are not able to assess the probability of a naturalistic explanation of the fact that the constants lie within the critical life-permitting ranges. Without a naturalistic probability function which gives the naturalistic probability that a fundamental constant would assume any particular value, we are unable to identify the space of possible naturalistically-attainable values. Consequently, given this probability space objection, it is not known that some of the seemingly fine-tuned fundamental constants are unlikely to assume values within life-permitting ranges for reasons related to presently unknown natural explanations.

This is not the end of fine-tuning arguments for theists, however, as my fine-tuning arguments in chapter 2 are grounded in consideration of physical conditions, where the probability of any natural explanation of those conditions is estimable. Also, theists need not completely abandon fine-tuning arguments grounded in the observation that fundamental physical constants are observed to possess values that lie within extremely narrow life-permitting ranges, as those constants may be understood as rather curious "fingerprint of God" properties of physical events which are known to be God-caused for reasons explained in my AFTLOP (see chapter 1 for details).

Dawkins objects to a theistic causal explanation of a naturalistically improbable effect E on the grounds that a theistic cause of E is less probable than the naturalistic improbability of E (p. 144:5-11; 147:2-10; 147:18-22; 149:16-29; 151:3-5; 153:29-31). Dawkins frequently raises objections along these lines, and it appears to be the central reason he rejects theistic explanations. However, this objection is basically a restatement of the "Who designed God?" objection to theistic causal explanations, and I have already responded to this objection in my critique, above, of the "Ultimate Boeing 747 gambit" argument presented by Dawkins. To briefly restate my response, recall that theistic explanations are causal and naturalistic explanations are merely descriptive. Theistic explanations identify the cause of E, whereas naturalistic descriptive explanations merely identify a physical law that describes how events of type E relate to other types of physical events. Hence, theistic explanations have greater explanatory power. Theistic explanations are confirmed by my AFTLOP and fine-tuning arguments (see chapter 1 and 2 for details), and naturalistic explanations, if taken to be both descriptive and causal, presuppose an unjustified interpretation of the nature of causation. Also, since we may, in general, identify a cause of E, yet not know much about the nature of the cause of E, justification for the belief that a cause of E is known does not require extensive knowledge of the nature of the cause of E. Thus, belief that God is the cause of E is not justified only if much is also known about the nature of God. Also, the improbability of a natural explanation of a theistic design explanation is no evidence against the theistic explanation, since theistic explanations are not natural explanations, and since theists need not accept that justified theistic explanations should be naturalistically probable. Therefore, naturalistically improbable theistic explanations may, nevertheless, be probable theistic explanations.

Dawkins objects that the theistic hypothesis is not simple that postulates a God who sustains the existence of the physical entities of the universe in accordance with physical laws (p. 149:16-19). In response, this theistic hypothesis is justified, as shown in my AFTLOP (chapter 1). Sure, the AFTLOP entails that God's knowledge is astoundingly greater than that of man, and the full explication of such knowledge is hardly capable of being expressed in any simple proposition, but that is beside the point. The personal nature of physical causation grounds the inference to divine sustenance of the physical world, and although the complex (non-simple) nature of God's knowledge is an interesting corollary to this inference, it is hardly evidence against it. Indeed, complex knowledge and immensely great power are not only not disconfirming of the theistic hypothesis, but are very much a consequence of the rational basis for that hypothesis. So, it is pure confusion to object that the established rational basis for the existence of a supremely knowledgeable and powerful God may be challenged on the grounds that the hypothesis entails the existence of a non-simple being, the full comprehension of whose nature is likely far beyond our ken. Rather, the supernatural nature of the God who sustains our universe would reasonably be expected to be unfathomably great, not naturalistically simple, as Dawkins wrongly seems to require. Yes, we may prefer the simplest explanation that best fits the facts, but that explanation may well turn out to be quite complex.

Furthermore, what alternative causal explanation does Dawkins wish to provide for the sustained existence of the universe and all of its constituent parts? An answer in terms of physical laws will not do, since physical laws are descriptive, not causal. So again, what causal explanation does Dawkins wish to provide? An answer in terms of simple fundamental particles will not do (p. 147:29-32), for then we may ask: from whence the particles?

Dawkins could respond that fundamental particles ultimately find their causal origin in the first physical cause which must have been simple, where that first cause can not have been the complex theistic personal designer of the world who possesses immensely great knowledge and power (p. 155:1-28), since the theistic hypothesis is neither simple nor an explanation (p. 155:23-27). In response, why must the first cause be simple? Dawkins simply assumes the first cause must be simple, but evidently provides no reason for this assumption, nor does he rigorously flesh out a more precise definition of the inherently ambiguous term "simple". Rather, he merely assumes that the first cause must have been "the simple basis for a self-bootstrapping crane" (p. 155:8-10), yet provides no justification for this assumption. Furthermore, why does Dawkins assume the theistic hypothesis is not an explanation? Clearly, the theistic hypothesis is a causal explanation. Unless Dawkins can clearly explain his definition of "explanation", and unless he can subsequently demonstrate that the theistic hypothesis does not satisfy that definition, his claim that theistic creation/design is not even an explanation is truly bizarre and wholly unjustified.

Dawkins also claims that if theistic design is true, then the designer must be the end product of some process (p. 156:6-11). He also claims that if God exists, then God's mind and powers must be derived from something constructed (p. 154:34-38). In response, these are unjustified presuppositions. Clearly, the set S of possibly existing theistic designers is large, and not all members of S possess the same properties, and not all members of S would be the end product of some process such as Darwinism in another universe, and not all members of S would possess a mind and powers derived from something constructed. It is possible that the mind and powers of a possibly existing God always exist and are not derived from something constructed, yet Dawkins arbitrarily supposes this is not the case. It is possible that God exists timelessly prior to creation, in which case God is not possibly the end product of any process. Dawkins is rather obviously unaware of this view or the rational basis for it.[7] It is not sufficient for Dawkins to write off the possibility of God's timeless existence prior to creation with a naïve passing comment in which he makes the bald, unwarranted assertion that God most certainly has not always existed (p. 156:4-6).

Theists need not be committed to the claim that their reasons for believing in the existence of God must be immune to rational argument (p. 154:12-15). Clearly, my case for theism in this book is subject to verification through rational analysis. Also, there is a somewhat veiled suggestion that "rational argument" is synonymous with "scientific knowing" (p. 154:15-19), and theists need not accept this suggestion, since personal, *objective* experience of God may be viewed as a component of one's rational basis for belief in God, even if that experience consists of events which are not properly the object of investigation by the physical sciences due either to the fact that the events are nonphysical, or due to the fact that such events are not capable of empirical scientific verification, given present limitations on human scientific methodology. For example, if God causes person J to perceive that it is God who is causing J to perceive that some proposition X is likely, then J's mental perception of the likelihood of X would presumably be accompanied by some corresponding physical brain state S, where God's action is a contributing cause of S. In this case, S is, of course, subject to scientific analysis as Dawkins argues (p. 154:26-31), but only in the limited sense that humans presently have only a limited means of measuring such brain activity. Also, present limitations on human interpretation of brain activity, as well as present limitations on human understanding of brain-mind relationships, are such that direct scientific physical analysis of S may be unlikely to provide empirical confirmation of the hypothesis that God causes J to perceive that God is causing J to perceive that X. (Note that my general point here remains, even if we make the unnecessary concession that the brain and the mind are identical.) Thus, objective experience of God, though possibly technically subject to scientific physical analysis to some degree, is such that the experience may be unlikely to rest heavily (if at all) on such analysis when it is included as a component of a theist's rational basis for belief in the existence of God. This should not be surprising, given that God is spirit (John 4:24).

Observe, further, that it is indeed true that not all categories of knowledge must be grounded in empirical physical scientific confirmation as a prerequisite for constituting a component of one's rationally established knowledge. To help drive home this point, consider, for example, that our perception of abstract entities (e.g., mathematical truths) is a perception of an abstract realm that is not subject to direct scientific physical observation. Nevertheless, we are surely justified in our claim to possess a rational basis for such knowledge. Likewise, God could cause nonphysical events which facilitate human perception of spiritual truth, where the content of that truth could be rationally established as known by a human, yet the divine means of communication of that content may be wholly unverifiable by methods in the physical sciences, since that means of communication may be wholly nonphysical. This position is quite evidently not a self-preserving defining of theism into an "epistemological Safe Zone" immune to rational argument (p. 154:12-15), as religious experience is, itself, subject to appropriate methods of rational analysis.

Dawkins claims that entities such as a universe or a rainforest must be explained in terms of a "crane", not a "skyhook" (p. 155:30-32). Even if we grant Dawkins this unnecessary concession, we may ask: from whence the crane? The answer can not be "some physical process such as natural selection", since that physical process *is* the crane, and a physical process can not come from itself. So again we may ask: from whence the crane?

Dawkins claims that the rational minds of many Christians know that the virgin birth and resurrection are absurd, and he implies that many such Christians would prefer not to be asked about the rational basis for such beliefs (p. 157:9-12). In response, the fact that some Christians may not be prepared to give good reasons that provide a rational basis for their beliefs does not entail the nonexistence of such reasons. Furthermore, many Christian thinkers have argued that the virgin birth and resurrection are miraculous components of a conservative Evangelical worldview, and they have claimed there exists a rational basis for acceptance of that worldview. In addition, those who think an event such as the resurrection is absurd are arguably not even Christians (1 Corinthians 15:14, Romans 10:9-10), so it is misleading of Dawkins to label such skeptics as "Christians".

Dawkins presents his Ultimate 747 gambit as a serious argument. Indeed, it is serious....seriously unsound, that is. I have thoroughly sliced and diced it to pieces, and its clearly evident status as unsound leads me to suspect that Dawkins has not genuinely made an effort to seek an informed conservative theological response, despite his claims to the contrary (p. 157:15-20). Dennett's acceptance of the gambit as "unrebuttable" (p. 157:20-22) only serves to diminish our confidence in Dennett's philosophical abilities as well.

The theistic "skyhook" explanation does not postpone the solution to the problem of physical origins, as the free action of a person may be viewed as the uncaused originating cause of physical events, and specifically, God's free action may be viewed as the uncaused originating cause of physical events not caused by other persons. Since humans did not cause physical origins, a non-human person (God) may be identified as the personal cause of physical origins. The "skyhook" explanation is, therefore, not a self-defeating hypothesis (p. 158:25-30), since free actions are uncaused and, consequently, do not demand a regress to a causal explanation of such action. On the other hand, the "crane" explanatory approach espoused by Dawkins is, itself, a regressive postponement of the solution to the problem of physical origins, since we may ask: from whence the crane?

Dawkins is happy to claim that science "explains complex things in terms of the interactions of simpler things" (p. 147:27-29), yet he is strangely quiet regarding the causal origin of either those simpler things or the physical laws which describe them. Discerning theists, however, may recognize God as the sustaining cause of the continuing existence of the physical entities God causes to change in accordance with physical laws (see chapter 1), where those laws are, themselves, the basis upon which divine design may be inferred (see chapter 2).

Given the above considerations, as well as the content of this entire book, theism is eminently more plausible, and is not embarrassing (p. 157:4-5). Also, Dawkins, in his failed attempt to justify atheism, only serves to exemplify the intellectual bankruptcy of atheism insofar as this leading proponent's failure to justify it disconfirms that version of it.

I wish to formally announce my invitation to Richard Dawkins to publish in physical print (not in changeable online articles) a response to my critique. I am sure I could learn much from him, and I am confident that a charitable dialogue could benefit us both in our search for truth.

To my fellow theists: let us make an effort to reach Richard Dawkins and those of his philosophical stripe. Rather than forward to them publications of dubious quality (p. 119:6-25), let us confront them with better literature. Our efforts shall not be in vain, for given a sufficient number of copies of this book sent to their desks, atheists such as Dawkins would doubtfully fail to respond, thereby forcing recognition that Dawkins-style atheism is a delusion.

NOTES

1. Craig, William Lane (2001). *Time and Eternity: Exploring God's Relationship to Time.* Wheaton, IL: Crossway Books.

2. Mills, David (2006). Atheist Universe. Berkeley, CA: Ulysses Press, p. 70.

3. Ibid., front cover. See also Dawkins, Richard (2006). *The God Delusion.* Boston: Houghton Mifflin Company, p. 44.

4. Two noteworthy authors sympathetic to some form of compatibility between creation and evolution include: Ruse, Michael (2000). *Can a Darwinian be a Christian? The Relationship Between Science and Religion.* Cambridge: Cambridge University Press; and also Collins, Francis S. (2007). *The Language of God: A Scientist Presents Evidence for Belief.* New York: Free Press.

5. In this connection, it is worth noting that the limitations of Darwinian explanations of the origin of biological complexity are now also being examined. See Behe, Michael (2007). The *Edge of Evolution: The Search for the Limits of Darwinism.* New York: Free Press.

6. Ross, Hugh (2001). *Creator and the Cosmos: How the Greatest Scientific Discoveries of the Century Reveal God.* Colorado Springs, CO: Navpress, 3rd edition, pp. 195-198.

7. Craig (2001).

CONCLUSION

The purpose of this study has been to participate in the project of answering critical questions about God by presenting new arguments for the existence of God, and by refuting contemporary arguments for atheism. I submit that my analysis has shown that good reasons exist for believing in the existence of God, where "God" is here defined as the person who is the creator-sustainer-designer of the physical world, and who possesses immensely greater power and knowledge than that of man. Atheism is false, and the reader is welcomed to examine the arguments in the atheism books listed in the Bibliography to verify that my position, somewhat novel as it may be in its detailed formulation, stands firm and unchallenged by any atheistic argument found in those referenced sources. Please also visit www.atheismisfalse.com for author contact details, as I appreciate any feedback you may wish to provide.

Having established the existence of God, we may desire to inquire as to whether additional divine revelation is available by which we may acquire further knowledge of God's ways. My AFTLOP and fine-tuning arguments (see chapters 1 and 2) may be understood as a perception of a form of divine revelation in which the nature of God's causal activity in the physical world is revealed. If, in addition to this natural theology, God has provided special revelation through, say, one of the world's great religions, then this revelation may help us determine the answers to such fundamental questions as: what do God's moral laws require of me? Will I give account of my life to God on a future day of judgment? Does heaven (or hell) exist? Can I form a proper relationship with a God of immeasurably great love and justice?

The conservative Evangelical Christian worldview contains answers to these and many other questions. Although a full-blown explication and defense of this worldview lies beyond the scope of the present analysis, I have reason to believe this view of the world is true and deserving of your serious consideration and acceptance. The book written by J. P. Moreland and William Lane Craig entitled "Philosophical Foundations for a Christian Worldview," published in 2003 by InterVarsity Press, along with Stuart C. Hackett's "The Reconstruction of the Christian Revelation Claim: A Philosophical and Critical Apologetic," published in 1984 by Baker Book House, together provide an example of how theists might proceed to elucidate more of the rational basis for the belief that God exists and has inspired the Biblical Scriptures such that they may be viewed as a source of divine revelation by which we may acquire enhanced insight into the nature and purposes of the supremely loving God who commands us to repent and receive, by grace through faith, the free gift of eternally joyous and abundant life that is available to us through our personal identification with the life, death, and resurrection of Jesus Christ whose atoning sacrifice for our sins is alone sufficient to secure for us forgiveness and reconciliation unto God, and sufficient to bring us into the company of the redeemed who attain the fullest possible measure of human fulfillment in their love of God and others expressed through service and obedience to the gospel by which we are saved from the wrath to come. Since the Christian Gospel is true, loving God is our central focus as we fully integrate the Christian worldview into our personal lives. Loving others is also a central focus as we defend and promote the Christian worldview in the marketplace of ideas, with special emphasis on global evangelization and discipleship.

So, I ask: is the Lord of the physical world the Lord of your personal life?

I commend to you the book by Ray Comfort and Kirk Cameron, "The Way of the Master," published in 2006 by Bridge-Logos, in which the gospel of the Lord Jesus Christ is presented in very simple language.

I ask once more: is the Master of the universe the Master of your life?

BIBLIOGRAPHY

BOOKS ARGUING FOR ATHEISM

Angeles, Peter A. (1986). *The Problem of God: A Short Introduction*. Buffalo, NY: Prometheus Books.

Angeles, Peter A. (1997). *Critiques of God: Making the Case Against Belief in God*. Amherst, NY: Prometheus Books.

Baggini, Julian (2003). *Atheism: A Very Short Introduction*. Oxford: Oxford University Press.

Barker, Dan (1992). *Losing Faith in Faith: From Preacher to Atheist*. Madison, WI: Freedom From Religion Foundation.

Carrier, Richard (2005). *Sense and Goodness Without God: A Defense of Metaphysical Naturalism*. Bloomington, IN: AuthorHouse.

Dawkins, Richard (2006). *The God Delusion*. Boston: Houghton Mifflin Company.

Drange, Theodore (1998). Non*belief & Evil: Two Arguments for the Nonexistence of God*. Amherst, NY: Prometheus Books.

Edis, Taner (2002). *The Ghost in the Universe: God in Light of Modern Science*. Amherst, NY: Prometheus Books.

Eller, David (2004). *Natural Atheism*. Cranford, NJ: American Atheist Press.

Everitt, Nicholas (2004). *The Non-existence of God*. New York: Routledge.

Flew, Antony (2005). *God and Philosophy*. Amherst, NY: Prometheus Books.

Gale, Richard (1993). *On the Nature and Existence of God*. Cambridge: Cambridge University Press.

Johnson, B. C. (1983). *Atheist Debater's Handbook*. Amherst, NY: Prometheus Books.

Joshi, S. T. (2003). *God's Defenders: What They Believe and Why They Are Wrong*. Amherst, NY: Prometheus Books.

Krueger, Douglas (1998). *What is Atheism?* Amherst, NY: Prometheus Books.

Le Poidevin, Robin (1996). *Arguing for Atheism: An Introduction to the Philosophy of Religion*. New York: Routledge.

Mackie, J. L. (1982). *The Miracle of Theism: Arguments For and Against the Existence of God*. Oxford: Oxford University Press.

Martin, Michael (1990). *Atheism: A Philosophical Justification*. Philadelphia: Temple University Press.

Martin, Michael and Monnier, Ricki, eds. (2003). *The Impossibility of God*. Amherst, NY: Prometheus Books.

Martin, Michael and Monnier, Ricki, eds. (2006). *The Improbability of God*. Amherst, NY: Prometheus Books.

Martin, Michael, ed. (2007). *The Cambridge Companion to Atheism*. Cambridge: Cambridge University Press.

Matson, Wallace (1965). *The Existence of God*. Ithaca, NY: Cornell University Press.

Mills, David (2006). *Atheist Universe*. Berkeley, CA: Ulysses Press.

Narciso, Dianna (2005). *Like Rolling Uphill: Realizing the Honesty of Atheism*. Coral Springs, FL: Llumina Press.

Nielsen, Kai (2001). *Naturalism and Religion*. Amherst, NY: Prometheus Books.

Nielsen, Kai (2005). *Atheism and Philosophy*. Amherst, NY: Prometheus Books.

O'Hair, Madalyn Murray, 2nd rev. ed. (1991). *Why I Am An Atheist*. Austin, TX: American Atheist Press.

Oppy, Graham (2006). *Arguing About Gods*. Cambridge: Cambridge University Press.

Pigliucci, Massimo (2000). *Tales of the Rational: Skeptical Essays About Nature and Science*. Smyrna, GA: Freethought Press.

Schellenberg, J. L. (2006). *Divine Hiddenness and Human Reason*. Ithaca, NY: Cornell University Press.

Schellenberg, J. L. (2007). *Wisdom to Doubt*. Ithaca, NY: Cornell University Press.

Scriven, Michael (1966). *Primary Philosophy*. New York: McGraw-Hill Book Company.

Shermer, Michael (2003). *How We Believe: Science, Skepticism, and the Search for God*. New York: Owl Books.

Smith, George (1989). *Atheism: The Case Against God*. Buffalo, NY: Prometheus Books.

Sobel, Jordan Howard (2003). *Logic and Theism: Arguments For and Against Beliefs in God*. Cambridge: Cambridge University Press.

Stenger, Victor (2003). *Has Science Found God? The Latest Results in the Search for Purpose in the Universe*. Amherst, NY: Prometheus Books.

Stenger, Victor (2007). *God: The Failed Hypothesis: How Science Shows That God Does Not Exist*. Amherst, NY: Prometheus Books.

Tremblay, Francois (2003). *Handbook of Atheistic Apologetics*. Morrisville, NC: Lulu Press.

Tremblay, Francois (2004). *Short Handbook of Atheistic Apologetics*. Morrisville, NC: Lulu Press.

White, Hugh (2002). *What's Real? God is not: A Realistic View on Belief in Gods and Religions*. Bloomington, IN: 1stBooks Library.

Young, Matt (2001). *No Sense of Obligation: Science and Religion in an Impersonal Universe*. Bloomington, IN: 1stBooks Library.

OTHER WORKS CITED OR RECOMMENDED

Alston, William P. (1993). *Perceiving God: The Epistemology of Religious Experience*. Ithaca, NY: Cornell University Press.

Beckwith, Francis J., Mosser, Carl, and Owen, Paul eds. (2002). *The New Mormon Challenge: Responding to the Latest Defenses of a Fast-Growing Movement*. Grand Rapids, MI: Zondervan.

Behe, Michael (2007). *The Edge of Evolution: The Search for the Limits of Darwinism*. New York: Free Press.

Blanchard, John (1995). *Whatever Happened to Hell?* Wheaton, IL: Crossway Books.

Collins, Francis S. (2007). *The Language of God: A Scientist Presents Evidence for Belief*. New York: Free Press.

Comfort, Ray and Cameron, Kirk (2006). *The Way of the Master*. Orlando, FL: Bridge-Logos.

Craig, William Lane (1994). *Reasonable Faith: Christian Truth and Apologetics*. Wheaton, IL: Crossway Books.

Craig, William Lane (2001). *Time and Eternity: Exploring God's Relationship to Time*. Wheaton, IL: Crossway Books.

Craig, William Lane and Moreland, J. P. (2003). *Philosophical Foundations for a Christian Worldview*. Downers Grove, IL: InterVarsity Press.

Craig, William Lane and Sinnott-Armstrong, Walter (2004). *God? A Debate Between a Christian and an Atheist*. Oxford: Oxford University Press.

Dockery, David S., Mathews, Kenneth A., and Sloan, Robert B. eds. (1994). *Foundations for Biblical Interpretation*. Nashville, TN: Broadman & Holman Publishers.

Elwell, Walter A., ed. (1989). *Evangelical Commentary on the Bible*. Grand Rapids, MI: Baker Book House.

Futuyma, Douglas J. (1995). *Science on Trial: The Case for Evolution*. Sunderland, MA: Sinauer Associates, Inc.

Geisler, Norman L. and MacKenzie, Ralph E. (1995). *Roman Catholics and Evangelicals: Agreements and Differences*. Grand Rapids, MI: Baker Books.

Geisler, Norman L. and Hoffman, Paul K. (2006). *Why I Am A Christian*. Grand Rapids, MI: Baker Book House.

Geivett, R. Douglas and Habermas, Gary R. (1997). *In Defense of Miracles: A Comprehensive Case for God's Action in History*. Downers Grove, IL: InterVarsity Press.

Hackett, Stuart C. (1984). *Reconstruction of the Christian Revelation Claim: A Philosophical and Critical Apologetic*. Grand Rapids, MI: Baker Book House.

Hagopian, David G., ed. (2000). *The Genesis Debate: Three Views on the Days of Creation*. McLean, VA: Global Publishing Services.

Kafatos, Minas C. and Henry, Richard B. C., eds. (1985). *The Crab Nebula and Related Supernova Remnants*. Cambridge: Cambridge University Press.

Kaiser, Walter C., Davids, Peter H., Bruce, F. F., and Brauch, Manfred T. (1996). *Hard Sayings of the Bible*. Downers Grove, IL: InterVarsity Press.

McGrath, P. J. (1987). *Atheism or Agnosticism*. Analysis, v. 47, pp. 54-57.

McKinsey, C. Dennis (1995). *Encyclopedia of Biblical Errancy*. Amherst, NY: Prometheus Books.

Moreland, J. P. and Rae, Scott B. (2000). *Body & Soul: Human Nature & the Crisis in Ethics*. Downers Grove, IL: InterVarsity Press.

Moss, Claude Beaufort (2005). *The Christian Faith: An Introduction to Dogmatic Theology*. Eugene, OR: Wipf & Stock Publishers.

Murphy, Ed (2003). *The Handbook For Spiritual Warfare*. Nashville, TN: Thomas Nelson Publishers.

Osborne, Grant R. (1991). *The Hermeneutical Spiral: A Comprehensive Introduction to Biblical Interpretation*. Downers Grove, IL: InterVarsity Press.

Packer, J. I. (1993). *Knowing God*. Downers Grove, IL: InterVarsity Press.

Payne, J. Barton (1980). *Encyclopedia of Biblical Prophecy*. Grand Rapids, MI: Baker Books.

Perakh, Mark (2004). *Unintelligent Design*. Amherst, NY: Prometheus Books.

Plantinga, Alvin (1999). *Warranted Christian Belief*. Oxford: Oxford University Press.

Ross, Hugh (1994). *Creation and Time*. Colorado Springs, CO: Navpress.

Ross, Hugh (2001). *The Genesis Question: Scientific Advances and the Accuracy of Genesis*. Colorado Springs, CO: Navpress.

Ross, Hugh (2001). *Creator and the Cosmos: How the Greatest Scientific Discoveries of the Century Reveal God*. Colorado Springs, CO: Navpress, 3rd edition.

Ross, Hugh (2004). *Matter of Days: Resolving A Creation Controversy*. Colorado Springs, CO: Navpress.

Ross, Hugh (2004). *Origins of Life: Biblical and Evolutionary Models Face Off*. Colorado Springs, CO: Navpress.

Ross, Hugh (2006). *Creation as Science: A Testable Model Approach to End the Creation/Evolution Wars*. Colorado Springs, CO: Navpress.

Rundle, Bede (2006). *Why There is Something Rather Than Nothing*. Oxford: Oxford University Press.

Ruse, Michael (2000). *Can a Darwinian be a Christian? The Relationship Between Science and Religion*. Cambridge: Cambridge University Press.

Ruse, Michael (2006). *Darwinism and Its Discontents*. Cambridge: Cambridge University Press.

Russell, Robert John, ed. (1993). *Quantum Cosmology and the Laws of Nature: Scientific Perspectives on Divine Action*. Vatican City State: Vatican Observatory Publications and Berkeley, CA: The Center for Theology and the Natural Sciences.

Scott, Eugenie C. (2004). *Evolution vs. Creationism: An Introduction*. Berkeley, CA: University of California Press.

Shanks, Niall (2006). *God, the Devil, and Darwin: A Critique of Intelligent Design Theory*. Oxford: Oxford University Press.

Snoke, David (2006). *A Biblical Case for an Old Earth*. Grand Rapids, MI: Baker Books.

Stein, Gordon (1990). *God Pro and Con: A Bibliography of Atheism*. New York: Garland Publishing, Inc.

Stenger, Victor (2006). *The Comprehensible Cosmos: Where Do the Laws of Physics Come From?* Amherst, NY: Prometheus Books.

Stoner, Don (1992). *A New Look at an Old Earth: What the Creation Institutes Are Not Telling You About Genesis*. Paramount, CA: Schroeder Publishing.

Tegmark, Max (1998). *Is "the Theory of Everything" Merely the Ultimate Ensemble Theory?* Annals of Physics, v. 270, pp. 1-51.

Walvoord, John F. (1999). *Every Prophecy of the Bible*. Colorado Springs, CO: Chariot Victor Publishing.

Wiese, Bill (2006). *23 Minutes in Hell*. Lake Mary, FL: Charisma House.

Wilkins, Michael J. and Moreland, J. P., eds. (1994). *Jesus Under Fire: Modern Scholarship Reinvents the Historical Jesus*. Grand Rapids, MI: Zondervan.

Willard, Dallas (2006). *The Great Omission: Reclaiming Jesus's Essential Teachings on Discipleship*. New York: HarperOne.

Wright, N. T. (2003). *The Resurrection of the Son of God*. Minneapolis, MN: Augsburg Fortress Publishers.

Young, Matt and Edis, Taner, eds. (2004). *Why Intelligent Design Fails: A Scientific Critique of the New Creationism*. Piscataway, NJ: Rutgers University Press.

Youngblood, Ronald, ed. (1984). *Evangelicals and Inerrancy*. Nashville, TN: Thomas Nelson Publishers.

Lightning Source UK Ltd.
Milton Keynes UK
UKOW050657191111

182340UK00001B/105/A